The Saga of Hen-Thorir

Original Text, Translations, and Word Lists

Translated by
Matthew Leigh Embleton

Copyright ©2025 Matthew Leigh Embleton. All rights reserved.

The Saga of Hen-Thorir

The Saga of Hen-Thorir (*Old Norse*)	4
Word List *(Old Norse to English)*	69
Word List *(English to Old Norse)*	93
The Saga of Hen-Thorir (*Old Icelandic*)	112
Word List *(Old Icelandic to English)*	175
Word List *(English to Old Icelandic)*	199
A Word Comparison of Old Norse and Old Icelandic Words	218

Cover: Old Norse text over an outline of Iceland. Author's design.

The original Old Norse and Old Icelandic texts are in the public domain.
These translations ©2022 Matthew Leigh Embleton
©2025 Matthew Leigh Embleton (This Edition)

Acknowledgments

I have long been fascinated by languages and history, and I am very grateful to the special people in my life who have supported and encouraged me in my work. Thank you for believing in me. You know who you are.

Introduction

Old Norse is a North Germanic language spoken by inhabitants of Scandinavia from about the 7th to the 15th centuries. Old Icelandic is a variety of Old West Norse that emerged during the Norse settlement of Iceland in the second half of the 9th century. The rich tradition of Icelandic literature survived by oral tradition over several centuries before being written down in the 13th Century. The Saga of Hen-Thorir (*Hænsa-Þóris saga*) is one of the many Sags of Icelanders or *Íslendingasögur*. The word '*saga*' (plural: '*sǫgur*' or '*sögur*') translates as 'what is said', an 'utterance', an 'oral account', or a 'notification'.

This book contains:
- The Saga of Hen-Thorir (*Hænsa-Þóris saga*) (Old Norse Version)
- An Old Norse to English Word List
- An English to Old Norse Word List
- The Saga of Hen-Thorir (*Hænsa-Þóris saga*) (Old Icelandic Version)
- An Old Icelandic to English Word List
- An English to Old Icelandic Word List
- A Word Comparison of Old Norse and Old Icelandic words

The texts are presented in their original form, with a literal word-for-word line-by-line translation, and a Modern English translation, all side-by-side. In this way, it is possible to see and feel how the worked and how it has evolved. This book is designed to be of use and interest to anyone with a passion for the Old Norse or Old Icelandic language, Norse history, or languages and history in general.

The Saga of Hen-Thorir (Old Norse)

The Saga of Hen-Thorir (*Old Norse*)

Old Norse	Literal	English
1	**1**	**1**
Oddr hét maðr Önundarson breiðskeggs, Úlfarssonar, Úlfssonar á Fitjum, Skeggjasonar, Þórissonar hlammanda.	Odd named man son-of-Onund Broad-Beard, son-of-Ulf, son-of-Ulf of Fitiar, Skeggja's-sons, son-of-Thori The-Stamper.	There was a man named Odd, the son of Onund Broad-Beard, son of Ulf, son of Ulf of Fitjar, Skeggja's sons, son of Thori the Stamper.
Hann bjó á Breiðabólstað í Reykjardal í Borgarfirði.	He lived of Breidabolstad in Reykjardal in Borgafjord.	He lived at Breidabolstad in Reykjardal in Borgafjord.
Hann átti þá konu, er Jórunn hét.	He had then a-wife, was Jorun named.	He had a wife then who was named Jorun.
Hon var vitr kona ok vel látin.	She was wise woman and well spoken-of.	She was a wise woman and well spoken of.
Þau áttu fjögur börn, sonu tvá vel mannaða ok dætr tvær.	They had four children, sons two well manly and daughters two.	They had four children, two sons who were manly, and two daughters.
Annarr sonr þeira hét Þóroddr, en annarr Þorvaldr.	One sons theirs named Thorodd, and another Thorvald.	One son of theirs was named Thorodd, and another Thorvald.
Þuríðr hét dóttir Odds, en önnur Jófríðr.	Thurid named daughter Odd's, and the-other Jofrid.	Odd's daughter was named Thurid, and the other Jofrid.
Hann var kallaðr Tungu-Oddr.	He was called Tungu-Odd.	He was called Tungu Odd.
Engi var hann kallaðr jafnaðarmaðr.	Not was he called an-even-man.	He was not called a fair man.
Torfi hét maðr ok var Valbrandsson, Valþjófssonar, Örlygssonar frá Esjubergi.	Torfi named a-man and was son-of-Valbrand, son-of-Valthjof, son-of-Orlyg from Esyuberg.	There was a man named Torfi, the son of Valbrand, son of Valthjof, son of Orlyg from Esyuberg.
Hann átti Þuríði Tungu-Oddsdóttur.	He had Thurid Daughter-of-Tungu-Odd.	He married Thurid, the daughter of Tungu Odd.
Þau bjuggu á öðrum Breiðabólstað.	They dwelt of other Breidabolstad.	They lived at another farm in Breidabolstad.

The Saga of Hen-Thorir (Old Norse)

Old Norse	Literal	English
Arngrímr hét maðr Helgasonar, Högnasonar, er út kom með Hrómundi.	Arngrim named man son-of-Helgi, son-of-Hogni, was out came with Hromund.	There was a man named Arngrim, the son of Helfi, son of Hogni, who came out (to Iceland) with Hromund.
Hann bjó í Norðrtungu.	He lived in North-Tongue.	He lived at North Tongue.
Hann var kallaðr Arngrímr goði.	He was called Arngrim the-chieftain.	He was called Arngrim the chieftain priest.
Helgi hét sonr hans.	Helgi named son his.	He had a son named Helgi.
Blund-Ketill hét maðr, sonr Geirs ins auðga ór Geirshlíð, Ketilssonar blunds, er Blundsvatn er við kennt.	Blund-Ketill named man, son Geir's the wealthy from Geir's-Slope, son-of-Ketil Blund, was Blundsvatn was with known.	There was a man named Blund-Ketill, the son of Geir the wealthy, from Geir's Slope, the son of Ketil Blund, for which Blundsvatn is known.
Hann bjó í Örnólfsdal.	He lived in Ornolfsdal.	He lived in Ornolfsdal.
Þat var nökkuru ofar en nú stendr bærinn.	That was somewhat above and now are-standing the-farm.	That was a little way above where the farm now stands.
Var þar margt bæja upp í frá.	Was there many homes up in from.	There were many homes above there.
Hersteinn hét sonr hans.	Herstein named son his.	His son was named Herstein.
Blund-Ketill var manna auðgastr ok bezt at sér í fornum sið.	Blund-Ketill was a-man wealthy and the-best of him in the-older traditions.	Blund-Ketill was a wealthy man and kept the best of the old traditions.
Hann átti þrjá tigu leigulanda.	He had three ten tenant-farms.	He had thirty tenant farms.
Hann var inn vinsælasti maðr í heraðinu.	He was in most-popular man in the-district.	He was the most popular man in the district.
Þorkell trefill hét maðr.	Thorkel Trefill named man.	There was a man named Thorkel Trefill.
Hann var Rauða-Bjarnarson.	He was son-of-Rauda-Bjarni.	He was the son of Rauda Bjarni.
Hann bjó í Svignaskarði fyrir útan Norðrá.	He lived in Svignaskard before beyond North-River.	He lived in Svignaskard by the North River.

The Saga of Hen-Thorir (Old Norse)

Old Norse	Literal	English
Helgi var bróðir Þorkels, er bjó í Hvammi í Norðrárdal.	Helgi was brother Thorkel's, was lived in Hvamm in North-River-Valley.	Thorkel's brother was Helgi, who lived at Hvamm in the North River Valley.
Annarr var Gunnvaldr, faðir Þorkels, er átti Helgu, dóttur Þorgeirs á Víðimýri.	Another was Gunnvald, father Thorkel's, was had Helgi, daughter Thorgeir of Vidimyr.	Another was Gunnvald, Thorkel's father, who married Helga, daughter of Thorgeir at Vidmyr.
Þorkell trefill var vitr maðr ok vel vinsæll, stórauðigr at fé.	Thorkel Trefill was wise man and well popular, rich in wealth.	Thorkel Trefil was a wise man and very popular, and rich in wealth.
Þórir hét maðr.	Thorir named man.	There was a man named Thorir.
Hann var snauðr at fé ok eigi mjök vinsæll af alþýðu manna.	He was poor in wealth and not much popular of-the-people a-man.	He was poor in wealth, and had not much in the way of friends of the people.
Hann lagði þat í vanða sinn, at hann fór með sumarkaup sitt heraða í milli ok seldi þat í öðru, er hann keypti í öðru, ok græddist honum brátt fé af kaupum sínum.	He became that in custom his, that he for with summer-market the districts in among and selling that in another, was he bought in another, and gained him soon wealth of trading his.	He made it his custom to travel to the summer markets in among the districts selling what he bought from one in another, and he soon gained wealth from his trading.
Ok eitt sinn, er Þórir fór sunnan um heiði, hafði hann með sér hæns í för norðr um land ok seldi þau með öðrum kaupskap, ok því var hann kallaðr Hænsa-Þórir.	And once his, was Thorir for the-south about the-heath, had he with him hens in journey north about the-land and selling they with other goods, and therefore was he called Hen-Thorir.	And once when Thorir travelled south about the heath he had hens with him on his journey north about the land, and then sold them with other goods, and he was therefore called Hen-Thorir.
Nú græðir Þórir svá mikit, at hann kaupir sér land, er at Vatni heitir upp frá Norðrtungu,	Now accumulated Thorir so much, that he bought him the-land, was at Vatn (Water) was-named up from North-Tongue,	Now Thorir accumulated so much that he bought himself land that was named Vatn, up from North Tongue.
ok fá vetr hafði hann búit, áðr hann gerðist svá mikill auðmaðr, at hann átti undir vel hverjum manni stórfé.	and a-few winters had he dwelled, before he became so much wealthy-man, that he had under well everyone people great-fee.	And when he had dwelled there a few winters he became such a wealthy man that he had many people that owed him great wealth.

The Saga of Hen-Thorir (Old Norse)

Old Norse	Literal	English
En þó at honum græddist fé mikit, þá heldust þó óvinsældir hans, því at varla var til ópokkasælli maðr en Hænsa-Þórir var.	And though that him gained wealth much, then rather though unpopularity his, therefore that rarely was to disliked man and Hen-Thorir was.	But though he gathered much wealth, his unpopularity rather remained, because rarely was a man so disliked than Hen Thorir was.

2

Old Norse	Literal	English
Einn dag gerir Þórir heiman ferð sína ok ríðr í Norðrtungu ok hitti Arngrím goða ok bauð honum barnfóstr.	One day did Thorir from-home travel his and rode in North-Tongue and met Arngrim the-chieftain and invited him foster-child.	One day Thorir travelled from his home and rode to North Tongue and met Arngrim the chieftain priest and offered to foster one of his children.
"Vil ek taka við Helga, syni þínum, ok geyma sem ek kann, en ek vil hafa vináttu þína í mót ok fylgi til þess, at ek ná réttu af mönnum".	"Will I take with Helgi, son yours, and keep as I know, and I wish to-have friendship yours in towards and following to this, that I near rights of men".	"I will take your son Helgi and keep him as well as I know, but I wish to have your friendship going forward and your following so that I can get my rights from people".
Arngrímr svarar:	Arngrim answered:	Arngrim answered:
"Svá lízt mér sem lítill höfuðburðr muni mér at þessu barnfóstri".	"So appears to-me as little head-bearing would to-me of this child-fostering".	"So it appears to me that little shall I bear my head for this child-fostering".
Þórir svarar:	Thorir answered:	Thorir answered:
"Ek vil gefa sveininum hálft fé mitt, heldr en ek ná eigi barnfóstrinu, en þú skalt rétta hluta minn ok vera skyldr til, við hvern sem ek á um".	"I wish to-give the-boy half-of wealth mine, rather and I near not child-fostering, and you shall rights lot mine and being should to, with each as I of about".	I wish to give the boy hald of my wealth, rather than foster him, but you shall help me with my rights, with each that I am about to deal with".
Arngrímr svarar:	Arngrim answered:	Arngrim answered:
"Þat ætla ek mála sannast at neita eigi því, er svá vel er boðit".	"That intend I the-matter surely to refuse not because, is so well as offered".	"I intend not to refuse the matter because it is so well offered".
Fór þá Helgi heim með Þóri, ok heitir þar nú síðan bærinn at Helgavatni.	Travelled then Helgi home with Thori, and named there now since the-farm that Helgivatn.	Helgi then travelled home with Thori and there has since been named Helgivatn.

The Saga of Hen-Thorir (Old Norse)

Old Norse	Literal	English
Arngrímr veitti Þóri umsjá, ok þykkir þegar ódæla við hann, ok náir hann nú réttu máli af hverjum manni.	Arngrim gave Thori protection, and seemed from-there uneasy with him, and brought he now rights the-matter of everyone people.	Arngrim gave Thori protection and he seemed from then on uneasy, and he now brought rights in the matters of each man.
Græðist honum nú stórmikit fé ok gerist inn mesti auðmaðr.	Gathered he now great wealth and became in most wealthy-man.	He now gathered great wealth and became the most wealthy man.
Helzt honum enn óvinsældin.	Held him in unpopularity.	His unpopularity held.
Þat var eitt sumar, at skip kom af hafi í Borgarfjörð, ok lögðu þeir eigi inn í ósinn, en lögðu útarliga á höfnina.	It was once summer, that a-ship came of harbour in Borgarfjord, and laid there not in at inlet, and laid out-lying of the-harbour.	It was one summer that a ship came to the harbour in Borgafjord, and did not lay in an inlet but outside the harbour.
Örn hét stýrimaðr.	Orn named the-steersman.	The steersman was named Orn.
Hann var vinsæll maðr ok inn bezti kaupdrengr.	He was popular man and in best merchant.	He was a popular man and the best merchant.
Oddr frétti skipkvámuna.	Odd heard the-ship-arrival.	Odd heard of the ship's arrival.
Hann var vanr í fyrra lagi í kaupstefnur at koma ok leggja lag á varning manna, því at hann hafði heraðsstjórn.	He was used-to in before laying in trading-post that come and grant lay of wares a-man, therefore that he had district-administration.	He was accustomed to come to the trading post and have grant of the wares of people because he was the administrator of the district.
Þótti engum dælt fyrr at kaupa en vissi, hvat hann vildi at gera.	Thought none dealt before that purchase and to-know, what he wished that be-done.	No one thought to deal or purchase until they knew what he wished to be done.
Nú hittir hann kaupmenn ok fréttir eftir, hversu þeir ætla sína ferð eða hve skjótar sölur þeir vildu hafa, ok sagði þann vanða, at hann legði lag á varning manna.	Now met he trading-men and news after, how-so there suppose his travelled or how soon sell there wished to-have, and said then custom, that he leave lay of wares a-man.	Now he met the trading men and asked them their business, and how soon they wished to sell their goods, saying that it was his custom to grant wares to people.
Örn svarar:	Orn answered:	Orn answered:

The Saga of Hen-Thorir (Old Norse)

Old Norse	Literal	English
"Sjálfir ætlum vér at ráða várri eigu fyrir þér, því þú átt engan pening með várum varnaði, ok muntu ráða at sinni eigi meira en þú mælir".	"Ourselves intend we that rule provisions our-own before you, therefore you own none money with our keeping, and should-you rule that yours not more and you speak".	"We intend to decide upon our provisions ourselves without you, because you have no money with us to rule, and you shall rule over no more than the words you speak.
Oddr svarar:	Odd answered:	Odd answered:
"Þat grunar mik, at þat gegni þér verr en mér, ok svá skal vera.	"That suspect me, that that suits you worse than me, and so shall being.	"I suspect that it will suit you worse than me, but so it shall be.
Er því at lýsa, at vér bönnum öllum mönnum kaup við yðr at eiga ok svá flutningar allar, svá at ek skal fé af þeim taka, sem yðr veita nökkura björg,	Is therefore that proclaim, that we-are banning all men buying with you that own and so moving all, so that I shall wealth of them take, as you grant any help,	I therefore proclaim that we are banning all men from buying from you, and so I shall take fines from any who help you.
en ek veit, at þér flytizt eigi ór höfninni fyrir misgöngin".	and I know, that you move not out-from the-port before tide-change".	Then I know that you cannot move out from the port until the tide changes".
Örn svarar:	Orn answered:	Orn answered:
"Ráða máttu ummælum þínum,	"Rule as-might about-the-matter yours,	"Decide as you might about your matter.
en eigi látum vér kúgast at heldr".	and not allow we to-be-oppressed that either".	We will not allow ourselves to be oppressed either.
Oddr ríðr nú heim, en Austmenn liggja þar í höfninni, ok gefr þeim eigi í brottu.	Odd rode now home, and The-Easterners remained there in the-port, and gave they not in away.	Odd now rode home and the Norwegians remained there in the port and could not get away.

3

Annan dag eftir reið Hersteinn Blund-Ketillsson út á Nes.	Next day after rode Herstein son-of-Blund-Ketill out of The-Headland.	The next day after Herstein son of Blund-Ketill rode out to the headland.
Hann fann Austmenn, er hann reið útan.	He found The-Easterners, was he rode out.	As he rode out he found the Norwegians.
Kannast hann við stýrimann ok varð vel at skapi.	Knew he with the-steersman and became well that mood.	He knew the steersman and became good in his mood.

The Saga of Hen-Thorir (Old Norse)

Old Norse	Literal	English
Örn sagði Hersteini, hversu mikinn ójafnað Oddr bauð þeim,	Orn said Herstein, how-so greatly un-equally Odd invited them,	Orn told Herstein how unequally Odd had dealt with them,
"ok þykkjumst vér eigi vita, hversu vér skulum með fara váru máli".	"and we-think we not knowing, how-so we shall with go our the-matter".	"and we think that we do not know how we shall go forward with the matter".
Þeir talast við um daginn, ok at kveldi ríðr Hersteinn heim ok segir föður sínum frá farmönnum ok hvar nú er komit þeira máli.	There talked with about the-day, and that evening rode Herstein home and said father his from travelling-men and where now was come they the-matter.	They talked together about the day and towards the evening Herstein rode home and told his father about the travelling men and where they had come to this matter.
Blund-Ketill svarar:	Blund-Ketill answered:	Blund-Ketill answered:
"Við kennumst ek mann þenna at þinni frásögn, at því, at ek var með föður hans, þá ek var barn, ok hefi ek eigi nýtra dreng fundit en hans föður, ok er þat illa, at hans kosti er þröngt,	"With knowing I man this that you from-said, that therefore, that I was with father his, then I was child, and have I not more-helpful fellow found than his father, and was that ill, that his cost was presses,	"I know this man from what you have said, and I was with his father when I was a child, and I have not found a more helpful fellow than his father, and it is bad that this pressing matter is costly.
ok þat mundi faðir hans ætla, at ek mynda nökkut líta á hans mál, ef hann þyrfti þess við.	and that would father his suppose, that I would something company of his matter, if he needs this with.	And his father would intend that I should accompany him in this matter if he needs it.
Ok nú á morgin snemma skaltu ríða út í Höfn ok bjóða honum hingat með svá marga menn sem hann vill,	And now of morning early shall-you ride out in The-harbour and invite him here with so many men as he wills,	And now early in the morning you shall ride out to the harbour and invite him here with as many men as he wishes.
en ef hann vill annat heldr, þá skal flytja hann, hvert er hann vill, suðr eða norðr, ok skal ek leggja á allan hug, sem ek hefi föng á, honum við at hjálpa".	and if he will another rather, then shall carry he, which was he will, south or north, and shall I grant of all mind, as I have got of, him with that help".	But if he wishes rather another way, then shall we carry him as he wishes, north or south, and I shall grant to him all my mind to help him".
Hersteinn kvað þat gott ráð ok drengiligt.	Herstein spoke that good decision and manly.	Herstein said that it was a good and manly decision.
"Er þó er meiri ván, at þar fyrir hafim vér óvingan annarrra".	"Was though was more expected, that there before have we difficulty others".	"It is though more expected that before this we shall have difficulty wih others".

The Saga of Hen-Thorir (Old Norse)

Old Norse	Literal	English
Blund-Ketill svarar:	Blund-Ketill answered:	Blund-Ketill answered:
"Þar sem vér berum eigi verra mál til en Oddr, þá kann vera, at oss falli þat létt".	"There as we bear not worse matter to and Odd, then know being, that us falls that light".	"Since we don't have a worse case than Oddr, it may be that we take it easy".
Nú líðr nóttin.	Now passed the-night.	Now the night passed.
En þegar um morgininn snemma lætr Blund-Ketill safna hrossum ór haga, ok er þá búin ferð, ok rekr Hersteinn hundrað hrossa í móti kaupmönnum, ok þurfti einkis á bú at biðja.	And from-there about morning early had Blund-Ketill gathered horses from pasture, and was then ready to-travel, and drove Herstein a-hundred horses to meet the-trading-men, and needed nothing of preprations to ask-for.	then from there about early morning Blund-Ketill had gathered horses from pasture and was then ready to travel, and Herstein drove a hundred horses to meet the trading men, and they needed nothing in the way of provisions to ask for.
Hann kemr út þangat ok sagði Erni tillag föður síns.	He came out from-there and told Orn proposal father his.	He came out from there and told Orn about his father's proposal.
Örn kvaðst gjarna þenna kost þiggja vilja, en kvaðst þó hyggja, at þeir feðgar myndi fá óvináttu annarra manna fyrir þetta.	Orn spoke gladly this choose accept willed, then said though think, that they father-and-son would get un-friendship other men from that.	Orn said that he would gladly wish to accept, then said though that father and son would bet enmity from other men for that.
Hersteinn kvað þá eigi verða farit at því.	Herstein spoke then not become going-away that therefore.	Herstein said that they would not become put off because of it.
Örn mælti:	Orn spoke:	Orn spoke:
"Þá skulu hásetar mínir flytja sik í önnur heruð, ok er þó ærit í ábyrgð, þó at vér sém eigi allir í einu heraði".	"Then shall sailors mine carry themselves in the-other districts, and is though necessity in risk, though that we see not all in one district".	"Then shall my sailors carry themselves to other districts, and there is a need to avoid the risk that we are not all seen together in one district".
Hersteinn flytr nú Örn heim með sér ok varning hans ok skilst eigi fyrr við en allir kaupmenn eru í brottu ok búit um skip ok öllu til skila komit.	Herstein brought now Orn home with him and wares his and parted not before with and all trading-men they-were in away and prepared about a-ship and all to return come.	Herstein now brought Orn home with him and his wares, and did not part until all the traders were away from there, and the ship laid up, and everything prepared to return.
Blund-Ketill tekr æfar vel við Erni.	Blund-Ketill took great well with Orn.	Blund-Ketill received Orn well.

The Saga of Hen-Thorir (Old Norse)

Old Norse	Literal	English
Sat hann þar í góðum fagnaði.	Sat he there in good celebration.	He stayed there in good celebration.
Kómu nú tíðendi þessi fyrir Odd, hvat Blund-Ketill hefir ráðs tekit, ok tala menn nú um, at hann hafi sýnt sik í mótgangi við hann.	Came now the-news this before Odd, what Blund-Ketill had plan taken, and told men now about, that he harbour seemed himself in meeting-going with he.	Now this news came to Odd, what Blund-Ketill had planned, and people were now saying that he had shown himself in opposition to him.
Oddr svarar:	Odd answered:	Odd answered:
"Kalla má þat svá, en þar er sá maðr, er bæði er vinsæll ok kappsamr.	"Call may that so, and there was seen man, was both was popular and zealous.	"You can call it that, but there is a man who is both popular and ambitious.
Þó vil ek um sinn vera láta".	Though wish I about his being allowed".	However, for the time being I want to be alone".
Ok var nú enn kyrrt.	And was now in peace.	And for now things were peaceful.

4

Sumar þetta var lítill grasvöxtr ok eigi góðr, fyrir því at lítt þorrnaði, ok varð alllítil heybjörg manna.	Summer that was little hay-crop and not good, before because that little dried, and became all-little haystacks people.	That summer there was little grass growth and not a good one, because it did not dry out much, and there was very little hay.
Blund-Ketill fór um haustit til landseta sinna ok segir, at hann vill heyleigur hafa á öllum löndum sínum:	Blund-Ketill for about autumn to tenants his and said, that he will hay-allowance to-have of all the-lands his:	Blund-Ketill went to his lands in the autumn and said that he wants to have a hay lease on all his lands:
"Eigum vér margt fé ganganda, en hey fást lítil.	"Own we many wealth going, and hay getting little.	"We have a lot of cattle, but we've got little hay.
Ek vil ok ráða fyrir, hversu miklu slátrat er í haust á hverju búi allra minna landseta, ok mun þá vel hlýða".	I will also decide for, how great slaughter is in autumn for each farm all my tenants, and should then well obeyed".	I also want to decide how much slaughter there is this autumn on every farm of all my landholders, and I will instruct them".
Nú líðr sumar, ok kemr vetr ok er snemma nauðamikill norðr um Hlíðina, en viðrbúningr lítill.	Now passed summer, and came winter and was early need-much north about The-Slope, and with-laid little.	Now the summer was over, and winter was coming, and there was an early need north of Hlíðin, but there was little preparation.

The Saga of Hen-Thorir (Old Norse)

Old Norse	Literal	English
Fellr mönnum þungt.	Fell men difficulty.	Men fell into difficulty.
Ferr svá fram um jól.	Went so from about yule.	And so it went until about until Yule.
Ok er þorri kemr, þá ekr hart at mönnum, ok eru margir þá upptefldir.	And was drought came, then drives roughly that men, and they-were many then uprooted.	And when the drought came, it drove people hard, and many were then uprooted.
Ok at kveldi eins dags kemr landseti Blund-Ketills ok segir sik vera í heyþroti ok krefr órlausna.	And that evening one day came a-tenant Blund-Ketill and said him being in hay-need and needed solution.	And in the evening one day, a tenant of Blund-Ketill's came and said that he was in trouble and demanded a solution.
Bóndi svarar:	The-farmer answered:	The farmer answered:
"Hverju gegnir þat?	"How goes that?	"How is this?
Ek þóttumst svá til ætla at hausti, at ek hugða, at vel myndi hlýða".	I thought so to suppose that autumn, that I thought, that well would obeyed".	I thought so that I supposed the autumn would be well observed".
Sjá svarar, at færra var slátrat en hann sagði.	See answers, that fewer were slaughtered than he said.	He answered that he had slaughtered fewer that he said.
Blund-Ketill sagði:	Blund-Ketill said:	Blund-Ketill said:
"Vit skulum eiga kaup saman.	"With shall own deal together.	"We shall have a deal together.
Ek mun leysa þik ór vandræði þessu um sinn, en þú seg þetta engum manni, því at ek vil eigi venja menn upp á mik, allra helzt síðan þér hafið þó eigi haft mín tillög".	I shall redeem you out-of trouble this about yours, and you say this none people, because that I wish not accustomed men up of me, all rather than you have though not had my suggestions".	I shall help you out of this trouble of yours, but say nothing of this to people because I do not wish to be accustomed to men approaching me, especially since you have not done as I suggested".
Sá fór heim ok sagði sínum vin, at Blund-Ketill sé afbragð annarrra manna í öllum viðskiptum, ok kvað hann sik ór vandræði leyst hafa.	So went home and told his friend, that Blund-Ketill being outstanding others a-man in all dealings, and spoke he his about trouble release had.	So he went home and told his friend that Blund-Ketill was an outstanding man for all his dealings, and about how he had released him from his troubles.
En sá sagði sínum vin, ok verðr þat svá víst um allt heraðit.	Then so said-to his friend, and became it so known about all the-district.	Then he told his friend, and so it became known about the whole district.

The Saga of Hen-Thorir (Old Norse)

Old Norse	Literal	English
Líðr stund, ok kemr Gói.	Passed awhile, and came Gói (month, February).	A while passed and then came the month of Gói (February).
Þá koma tveir landsetar hans ok segja sik í heyþroti.	Then came two tenants his and said to-him of hay-need.	Then two tenants of his came and said to him that they had need of hay.
Blund-Ketill svarar:	Blund-Ketill answered:	Blund-Ketill answered:
"Illa hafið þér gert, at þér hafið af brugðit mínum ráðum, því at þat er þann veg, þó at vér hafim hey mikil, þá höfum vér ok fé því fleira.	"Ill have you done, that you have of broken my instructions, therefore that that was then the-way, though that we have hay much, then have we and cattle therefore more.	"You have done wrong, that you have rejected my advice, because it is this way, although we have a lot of hay, we also have more cattle.
Nú ef ek miðla yðr, þá hefi ek ekki til míns fjár.	Now if I share to-you, then have I not to my cattle.	Now if I share it with you, then I will have none for my own cattle.
Er nú hér um at kjósa".	Is now here about to choose".	This is now the choice here".
Þeir ala á málit ok tjá vesöld sína,	They bore about the-matter and expressed misery theirs,	They continued expressing their misery in this matter.
en honum þótti hörmuligt at heyra á þeira veinan ok lét reka heim fjóra tigu hrossa ok hundrað ok lét drepa fjóra tigu hrossa, þau er verst váru, en gaf landsetum sínum þat fóðr, sem hrossunum var ætlat áðr.	and he thought tragic that heard of their wailing and had driven home four tens horses and a-hundred and had killed four ten horses, they which the-worst were, and gave the-tenants his that fodder, as the-horses were intended before.	Then he thought it tragic to hear their wailing, and had forty horses and a hundred driven home, slaughtered the forty that were the worst, and gave his tenants the fodder that was intended for those horses.
Fara þeir heim fegnir.	Went they home celebrating.	They went home celebrating.
Vetrinn gerist því verri sem meir leið á, ok verðr örkola fyrir mörgum.	Winter became therefore worse as more passed of, and became a-burn-out before many.	The winter became worse the more it passed, and hopes turned to ashed for many.

5

Nú kemr einmánuðr, ok koma tveir landsetar Blund-Ketills.	Now came one-month, and come two tenants Blund-Ketill.	Now the next month came in, and two of Blund-Ketill's tenants came.

14

The Saga of Hen-Thorir (Old Norse)

Old Norse	Literal	English
Þeir áttu sér hóti helzt nökkurs kosti í fémunum, en þó váru þeir nú í heyþroti ok biðja hann órlausnar.	There had him a-good-deal rather some cost in goods, and though wares there now in hay-need and invited he a-solution.	They had themselves a good deal of benefit of goods and wares, but they were now in need of hay, and they asked for a solution.
Hann svarar þá ok kvaðst eigi til hafa, enda lézt hann eigi vilja drepa fleira fé.	He answered then and spoke not to to-have, end let he not wish killed more cattle.	He then answered and said he didn't have any, since he didn't want to kill any more cattle.
Þeir fréttu, ef hann viti nökkura þá menn, er hey hefðu til sölu.	They asked, if he knew someone then men, was hay had to sell.	They asked if he knew any men who had hay for sale.
Hann kveðst eigi víst vita.	He said not knowing certainly.	He said that he did not know for certain.
Þeir sækja fast eftir ok segja nú, at fé þeira muni deyja, ef þeir fá enga hjálp af honum.	They sought fast after and said now, that cattle theirs would die, if they got none help of him.	They pressed hard and now said that their cattle will die if they don't get help from him.
Hann sagði þat af sjálfdáðum orðit, "en sagt er mér, at Hænsa-Þórir muni hafa hey til sölu".	He said that of self-judgement words, "but told am I, that Hen-Thorir should have hay to sell".	He said they had done it of their own judgement, "but I am told that Hen-Thorir should have hay to sell".
Þeir svara:	There answered:	They answered:
"Af honum munum vér eigi fá, nema þú farir með oss, ok mun hann þá þegar selja, ef þú gengr í vörzlu fyrir oss um kaupin".	"Of him should we not a-few, unless you travel with us, and should he then from-there sell, if you going in vouch before us about the-purchase".	"We will not get anything from him unless you go with us, and he will sell immediately if you take care of the purchase for us".
Hann svarar:	He answered:	He answered:
"Þat má ek gera at fara með yðr, en þat er sannligt, at þeir seli, sem til hafa".	"That may I be-done that go with you, and it is right, that they sell, who to have".	"I can do that and go with you, for it is right that those who have it should sell it".
Þeir fara snemma um morgininn, ok var á norðan strykr sá ok heldr kaldr.	They travelled early about morning, and was over the-north windy so and rather cold.	They left early in the morning, and it was windy over the north and rather cold.

The Saga of Hen-Thorir (Old Norse)

Old Norse	Literal	English
Þórir bóndi var úti staddr í þat mund, sér mennina fara at garði, gengr inn síðan ok rekr aftr hurð ok lætr fyrir loku, ferr til dagverðar.	Thorir the-farmer was outside standing at the time, saw men travelling to the-farmyard, went in then and drove after the-door and had before locked, went to breakfast.	Farmer Thorir was outside at the time, saw the men coming to the garden, then went inside and pushed the door back and closed it, going to breakfast.
Nú er drepit á dyrr.	Now was knock of the-door.	Now there was a knock on the door.
Sveinninn Helgi tekr til orða:	The-boy Helgi took to words:	The boy Helgi spoke:
"Gakktu út, fóstri, því at menn munu vilja hitta þik".	"Go-you out, foster, because that men would wish to-meet you".	"Go out, foster, because people will wish to meet you".
Þórir kvaðst mundu matast fyrst, en sveinninn hleypr undan borðum ok gengr til hurðar ok heilsar þeim vel, er komnir váru.	Thorir spoke would eat first, and the-boy ran from the-table and went to the-doors and greeted them well, who arrived were.	Thorir said that they would eat first, but the boy ran from the tables and went to the door and greeted those who had arrived.
Blund-Ketill spurði, hvárt Þórir væri heima.	Blund-Ketill asked, whether Thorir was home.	Blund-Ketill asked whether Thorir was home.
Hann sagði svá væri.	He said so was.	He said it was so.
"Bið þú hann útgöngu",	"Ask you he to-come-out",	"Ask him to come out",
sagði hann.	said he.	he said.
Sveinninn gerði svá ok sagði, at Blund-Ketill var kominn úti ok vildi hitta hann.	The-boy went so and said, that Blund-Ketill was come outside and wished to-meet he.	The boy did so and said that Blund-Ketill had come out and wanted to see him.
Þórir svaraði:	Thorir answered:	Thorir answered:
"Af hverju mun Blund-Ketill draga nasarnar?	"Of each should Blund-Ketill dragging his-nose?	"Of what should Blund-Ketill be so nosy about?
Kynligt, ef hann ferr at góðu.	Wonder, if he goes that good.	It would be a wonder if he is up to any good.
Ekki erendi á ek við hann".	Not errand of I with he".	I have no errand with him".
Sveinninn ferr ok sagði þeim, at Þórir vildi eigi út ganga.	The-boy went and said them, that Thorir wished not out to-go.	The boy went and told them that Thorir did not wish to go out.

The Saga of Hen-Thorir (Old Norse)

Old Norse	Literal	English
"Já",	"Yes",	"Yes",
sagði Blund-Ketill, "þá skulum vér inn ganga".	said Blund-Ketill, "then shall we in to-go".	said Blund-Ketill, "then we shall come in".
Þeir ganga til stofu, ok var þeim heilsat, en Þórir þagði.	There to-go to the-main-room, and was them greeted, and Thorir silent.	They went into the main room and were greeted, but Thorir was silent.
"Svá er varit",	"So was the-situation",	"So this is the situation",
sagði Blund-Ketill, "at vér viljum kaupa hey at þér, Þórir".	said Blund-Ketill, "that we wish-to purchase hay that you, Thorir".	said Blund-Ketill, "that we wish to buy hay from you, Thorir".
Þórir svarar:	Thorir answered:	Thorir answered:
"Eigi er mér þitt fé betra en mitt".	"Not was to-me your wealth better and mine".	"I don't think your wealth is better than mine".
Blund-Ketill mælti:	Blund-Ketill spoke:	Blund-Ketill spoke:
"Ýmisst veitir þat".	"Or provide that".	"It provides various things".
Þórir svarar:	Thorir answered:	Thorir answered:
"Hví ertu í heyþroti, auðigr maðr?"	"Why are-you in hay-need, wealthy-man man?"	"Why are you in need of hay, wealthy man?"
Blund-Ketill segir:	Blund-Ketill said:	Blund-Ketill said:
"Eigi em ek greiðliga í heyþroti, ok fala ek fyrir landseta mína, er þurfa þykkjast órlausna.	"Not am I quite in hay-need, and bargain I before tenants mine, was need to-see solution.	"I am not in need of may myself, but I bargain for my tenants that need a solution.
Vilda ek gjarna fá þeim, ef til væri".	Will I gladly get them, if to were".	I would gladly get them some if it were possible".
"Þat muntu eiga allra heimilast at veita öðrum þitt, en eigi mitt".	"That should-you own all right to give others yours, but not mine".	"That should you have all right to give others what is yours, but not what is mine".
Blund-Ketill svarar:	Blund-Ketill answered:	Blund-Ketill answered:
"Eigi skulum vér gjafar at biðja.	"Not shall we gifts to ask-for.	"We are not asking for gifts.

The Saga of Hen-Thorir (Old Norse)

Old Norse	Literal	English
Láttu Odd ok Arngrím gera verð fyrir þína hönd, en þar á ofan vil ek gefa þér gjafar".	Let Odd and Arngrim make the-price for your hand, and there of above wish I to-give you gifts".	Let Odd and Arngrim make the price on your hand, and thereabove I wish to give you gifts".
Þórir kvaðst eigi hey hafa til at selja,	Thorir said not hay have to that sell,	Thorir said that he did not have hay to sell.
"enda vil ek eigi selja".	"end wish I not sell".	"and I do not wish to sell".
Þá gengr Blund-Ketill út ok þeir félagar ok sveinninn með þeim.	Then going Blund-Ketill out and there followers and the-boy with them.	Then Blund-Ketill went outside with his followers, and the boy went with them.
Þá tekr Blund-Ketill til orða:	Then took Blund-Ketill to words:	Then Blund-Ketill took to words:
"Hvárt er heldr, at fóstri þinn hefir engi hey til sölu, eða vill hann eigi selja?"	"Which is-it rather, that foster yours has not hay to sell, or wishes he not sell?"	"Which is it? That your foster father does not have hay to sell, or does not wish to sell?"
Sveinninn svarar:	The-boy answered:	The boy answered:
"Hefir hann víst, ef hann vill".	"Had he certainly, if he wishes".	"He certainly has, if he wishes".
Blund-Ketill mælti:	Blund-Ketill spoke:	Blund-Ketill spoke:
"Fylgðu oss þangat til, sem heyin eru".	"Follow us there to, where haystacks they-are".	"Lead us to where the haystacks are".
Hann gerir svá.	He did so.	He did so.
Nú gerir Blund-Ketill til fjár Þóris ok hugðist svá at, þó at algjafta væri til alþingis, at þó myndi af ganga fimm stakkar.	Now did Blund-Ketill to cattle Thori's and thought so that, though that hay-feed was to the-assembly, that though would of to-go five stacks.	Now Blund-Ketill to Thorir's cattle, and thought that he had enough hay to feed until the next assembly, and that left five stacks.
Ok eftir þat ganga þeir inn.	And after that to-go there in.	And after that they went in.
Blund-Ketill mælti:	Blund-Ketill spoke:	Blund-Ketill spoke:
"Svá hyggst mér um heykost þinn, at góðr fengr mun af ganga, þó at fé þínu öllu sé inni gefit til alþingis, ok vil ek þat kaupa".	"So seems to-me about hay-supply yours, that good getting should of go, though to cattle yours all as in given until the-assembly, and wish I that to-buy".	"So it seems to me that your hay supply will be good for all your cattle until the assembly, and the remainder I wish to buy".

The Saga of Hen-Thorir (Old Norse)

Old Norse	Literal	English
Þórir svarar:	Thorir answered:	Thorir answered:
"Hvat skal ek þá hafa annan vetr, ef þá er slíkr vetr eða verri?"	"What shall I then have next winter, if then was such winters or worse?"	"Then what shall I have for another winter, if it is such a winter as this one or worse?"
Blund-Ketill svarar:	Blund-Ketill answered:	Blund-Ketill answered:
"Gera mun ek þér þann kost at fá þér jafnmikinn kost í heyjum í sumar ok þó at engu verri ok færa í garða þína".	"Be-done should I you then choose that a-few you equally-great choose in hay in summer and though that nothing worse and brought in farmyard yours".	"I will give you the opportunity to get an equal amount of hay this summer, and if nothing worse, also move it to your gardens".
Þórir svarar:	Thorir answered:	Thorir answered:
"Ef þér hafið nú yðr eigi heybjörg, hvat munuð þér þá heldr hafa í sumar?	"If you have now yours not haystacks, what shall you then rather to-have in summer?	"If you don't have a haystack now, what will you have this summer?
En veit ek, at sá er ríkismunr okkarr, at þú munt taka mega hey af mér, ef þú vill".	And know I, that seen was powerful ours, that you might take be-able-to hay of to-me, if you will".	But I know that that is our state different, that you will take a lot of hay from me if you want".
Blund-Ketill svarar:	Blund-Ketill answered:	Blund-Ketill answered:
"Eigi er þann veg upp at taka.	"Not was then the-way up that take.	"That's not the way to go.
Þat veiztu, at silfr gengr í allar skuldir hér á landi, ok gef ek þér þat við".	That know-you, that silver going in all debts here of the-land, and give I you that with".	You know that silver goes into all debts in this country, and I'll give you that".
Þórir svarar:	Thorir answered:	Thorir answered:
"Eigi vil ek silfr þitt".	"Not wish I silver yours".	"I don't want your silver".
"Þá tak þú þvílíka vöru, sem þeir gera til handa þér, Oddr ok Arngrímr".	"Then take you as-you-like goods, as they make to hand to-you, Odd and Arngrim".	"Then you take the goods they make for you, Oddr and Arngrímr".
"Fátt er hér verkmanna",	"Few are here work-men",	"There are few workers here",
segir Þórir, "en ek nenni lítt ferðum, ok vil ek eigi vasast í slíku".	said Thorir, "and I bother little travel, and wish I not entangle-with as such".	said Thorir, "but I don't want to travel, and I don't want to get stuck in such a thing".

The Saga of Hen-Thorir (Old Norse)

Old Norse	Literal	English
Blund-Ketill svarar:	Blund-Ketill answered:	Blund-Ketill answered:
"Þá skal ek láta færa þér heim".	"Then shall I have brought to-your home".	"Then I shall have it brought to your home".
Þórir mælti:	Thorir spoke:	Thorir spoke:
"Eigi hefi ek húsakost til þess, at örvænt sé, at eigi spillist".	"Not have I house-choice to this, that surely being, that not get-spoiled".	"I do not have the house room for it, so it is sure to be spoilt".
Blund-Ketill svarar:	Blund-Ketill answered:	Blund-Ketill answered:
"Ek skal fá til húðir ok búa um, svá at vel sé".	"I shall a-few to hides and prepare about, so that well being".	"I'll get hides and prepare around, so that it will be good".
Þórir svarar:	Thorir answered:	Thorir answered:
"Eigi vil ek spark annarrra manna í húsum mínum".	"Not wish I trampling other a-man in house my".	"I don't want other people trampling in my house".
Blund-Ketill svarar:	Blund-Ketill answered:	Blund-Ketill answered:
"Þá skal vera hjá oss í vetr, ok mun ek varðveita".	"Then shall being by us in winter, and should I safeguard".	"Then it will stay with us this winter, and I will preserve it".
"Veit ek gjálgrun þína",	"Know I idle-talk yours",	"I know your idle alk",
segir Þórir, "ok vil ek engu kaupa við þik".	said Thorir, "and wish I nothing purchase with you".	said Thorir, "and I don't want to buy anything from you".
Blund-Ketill mælti:	Blund-Ketill spoke:	Blund-Ketill spoke:
"Þá mun fara verr, ok munum vér allt at einu hafa heyit, þó at þú bannir, en leggja verð í staðinn ok njóta þess, at vér erum fleiri".	"Then should go worse, and should we all that one to-have hay, though that you banned, and grant the-worth in there and enjoy this, that we are more".	"Then it will go worse, because we mean to have the hay all the same, even though you forbid it, and take advantage of the fact that we are more in number".
Þá þagnar Þórir ok gerir eigi gott í skapi.	Then silent Thorir and did not good in mood.	Then Thorir was silent and not in a good mood.
Blund-Ketill lætr taka reip ok binda heyit.	Blund-Ketill had take ropes and bound the-hay.	Blund-Ketill had the ropes taken and bound the hay.

The Saga of Hen-Thorir (Old Norse)

Old Norse	Literal	English
Eftir þat hefja þeir upp klyfjar ok bera í brott heyit, en ætla vel til alls fjár.	After that heaved they up the-load and carried to away the-hay, and intended well to all cattle.	After that they heaved up the load and carried away the hay, then made provision for all the cattle.

6

Old Norse	Literal	English
Nú skal segja frá, hvat Þórir hafðist at.	Now shall say from, what Thorir had to.	Now shall be told what Thorir did.
Hann býr heiman ferð sína ok Helgi, fóstri hans, með honum.	He farm home travelled-from his and Helgi, foster his, with him.	He travelled home to his farm, and Helgi, his foster-son with him.
Þeir ríða í Norðrtungu, ok var þar tekit við þeim afar vel.	They rode to North-Tongue, and were there received with them great well.	They rode to North-Tongue and were received well there.
Spurði Arngrímr tíðenda.	Asked Arngrim tidings.	Arngrim asked for the news.
Þórir svarar:	Thorir answered:	Thorir answered:
"Ekki hefi ek nú nýligra spurt en ránit".	"Not have I now newer learned and the-robbery".	"I have not learned of anything newer than the robbery".
"Hvat var ránit?"	"What was robbery?"	"What robbery was this?"
sagði Arngrímr.	said Arngrim.	said Arngrim.
Þórir svarar:	Thorir answered:	Thorir answered:
"Blund-Ketill hefir rænt mik öllum heyjum, svá at eigi ætlak forkast eftir nautum í köldu veðri".	"Blund-Ketill has robbed me all hay, so that not suppose fodder after cattle in cold weather".	"Blund-Ketill has robbed me of all my hay, so I cannot count on any fodder for the cattle in cold weather".
"Er svá Helgi?"	"Was so Helgi?"	"Is that so Helgi?"
segir Arngrímr.	said Arngrim.	said Arngrim.
"Engu gegnir þat",	"Nothing goes that",	"That is not how it went",
segir Helgi, "fór Blund-Ketill vel með sínu máli".	said Helgi, "went Blund-Ketill well with his the-matter".	said Helgi, "Blund-Ketill behaved well in the matter".
Sagði Helgi þá, hversu farit hafði með þeim.	Said Helgi then, how-so went had with them.	Helgi said how it had gone.

The Saga of Hen-Thorir (Old Norse)

Old Norse	Literal	English
Þá sagði Arngrímr:	Then said Arngrim:	Then Arngrim said:
"Þat var líkara.	"That was likely.	"That sounds more likely.
Betr er þat hey komit, at hann hefir, en hitt, er fúnar fyrir þér".	Better is it hay comes, that he has, than find, it rots before you".	It is better use for the hay that he has it, than find it rots before you".
Þórir svarar:	Thorir answered:	Thorir answered:
"Illu heilli bauð ek þér barnfóstr.	"Ill fairly offered I to-you child-foster.	"It is unfortunate that I offered to foster you.
Skal oss aldri þat illbýli gert, at oss sé hér tilgangr at heldr ok at várr hlutr sé réttr, ok eru slíkt firn mikil".	Shall we never that ill-harm done, to us being here point to rather and to out lot is right, and they-are such abomination great".	May we never be harmed that we have a purpose here and that our part is right and such things are a great abomination".
Arngrímr svarar:	Arngrim answered:	Arngrim answered:
"Þat var þegar ófyrirsynju, því at ek ætla þar vándum manni at duga, sem þú ert".	"It was already unexpected, because that I suppose there trouble man to be-helping, as you are".	"It was already unexpected because I suppose there will be trouble for such poor help as yours".
Þórir svarar:	Thorir answered:	Thorir answered:
"Eigi em ek orðsjúkr maðr, en illa uni ek, at þú launar svá mína gerð eða þat, þó at menn ræna mik, því at eigi er þetta síðr frá þér tekit",	"Not am I word-sickened man, but ill win I, that you are-repaid so mine made or that, then as men steal me, because that not is that side from to-you taken",	"I am not a man of words, but I hate how you repay me for my actions or that, even though people rob me, because is this not also taken away from you".
ok skilðust við svá búit.	and separated with so prepared.	And on that they parted.
Ríðr Þórir á braut ok koma á Breiðabólstað, ok heilsar Oddr honum vel ok spyrr tíðenda.	Rode Thorir to away and came to Breidabolstad, and greeted Odd him well and asked the-news.	Thorir rode away and came to Breidabolstad and greeted Odd well and asked what news there was.
"Ekki hefi ek nýligra frétt en ránit".	"Not have I newer news than the-robbery".	"I have not any news newer than the robbery".
"Hvat ráni var þat?"	"What robbery was that?"	"What robbery was that?"

The Saga of Hen-Thorir (Old Norse)

Old Norse	Literal	English
sagði Oddr.	said Odd.	said Odd.
Þórir svarar:	Thorir answered:	Thorir answered:
"Blund-Ketill tók hey mín öll, svá at ek em nú með öllu óbirgr.	"Blund-Ketill took hay mine all, so that I am now with all un-stocked.	"Blund-Ketill took all my hay so that I am now out of stock.
Vildi ek gjarna hafa þína ásjá, en þetta mál kemr ok til þín, þar sem þú ert forráðsmaðr heraðsins, at rétta þat, sem rangt er gert, ok máttu þat áminnast, at hann gerðist þinn fjandmaðr".	Wished I gladly to-have yours assistance, and that matter came and to yours, there as you are manager district, that rights that, as wrong was done, and as-might that remember, that he became your fiend-man".	I would gladly wish to have your assistance in this matterm and it concerns you too, as you are the head of the district, to right that which is wrong, and you may remember that he has become your enemy".
Oddr spurði:	Odd asked:	Odd asked:
"Er svá, Helgi?"	"Is-that so, Helgi?"	"Is that so Helgi?"
Hann sagði, at Þórir affærði stórmjök, greinir nú allt, hversu fór.	He said, that Thorir taken-away a-great-much, article now all, how-so for.	He said that Thorir had taken away a great deal, and now told him how so it went.
Oddr svarar:	Odd answered:	Odd answered:
"Eigi vil ek mér af skipta.	"Not wish I to-me of this-exchange.	"I do not wish to have any part of this exchange.
Mynda ek svá hafa gert, ef ek þyrfta".	Should I so have done, if I needed".	I should have done the same, had I the need".
Þórir svarar:	Thorir answered:	Thorir answered:
"Satt er þat, er mælt er, at spyrja er bezt til váligra þegna, ok án er illt um gengi, nema heiman hafi".	"Truly said that, is said is, that to-learn is best to woeful thanes, and without is ill about going, except from-home having".	"It's true is what is said, it is best to learn of bad things from woeful people, and bad things do not go about unless they are from home".
Ríðr Þórir í brott við svá búit ok Helgi með honum ok ferr heim ok unir illa við.	Rode Thorir to away with so settled and Helgi with him and travelling home and satisfied ill with.	This this, Thorir rode away with Helgi, and travelled home unsatisfied with the situation.

The Saga of Hen-Thorir (Old Norse)

Old Norse	Literal	English
# 7	# 7	# 7
Þorvaldr, sonr Tungu-Odds, hafði út komit um sumarit fyrir norðan land, ok þar vistaðist hann um vetrinn.	Thorvald, son-of Tungu-odd's, had out came about summer for the-north lands, and there guested he about the-winter.	Thorvald son of Tungu had travelled abroad in the summer to the north lnds, and was a guest there about the winter.
Hann fór norðan, er leið at sumri, á fund föður síns ok gisti um nótt í Norðrtungu í góðum beina.	He travelled north, as passed the summer, to meet father his and guest about the-night in North-Tongue in good assistance.	He travelled north when summer had passed and met his father, and guested for the night in North Tongue with a good welcome.
Sá maðr var þar fyrir á gistingu, er Víðfari hét.	So a-man was there before in guesting was Vidfari named.	There was a man already there as a guest named Vidfari.
Hann var reikunarmaðr,	He was a-roaming-man,	He was a roaming man.
hljóp hann á milli landshorna.	ran he of among lands-corners.	He ran among the corners of the land.
Hann var frændi Þóris náinn ok ápekkr honum í skapsmunum.	He was a-kinsman Thori's near and similar him in disposition.	He was a kinsman of Thori's and near to him in disposition.
Þetta sama kveld tekr Víðfari föt sín ok stökkr á brott ok léttir eigi fyrr en hann kemr til Þóris.	That same evening took Vidfari bed-clothing his and heels to away and remained not before that he came to Thori's.	That same evening, Vídfari took his bed clothes and took to his heels away, and did not stop until he came to Thori's.
Hann tekr við honum báðum höndum:	He took with him both hands:	He received him well with both hands.
"Veit ek ok, at nökkut gott mun mér leiða af þinni Kvámu".	"Knew I also, that some good would to-me lead of your Coming".	"I know that some good comes my way when you do".
Hann svarar:	He answered:	He answered:
"Gerast mætti þat, því at nú er Þorvaldr Oddsson kominn í Norðrtungu ok er þar nú á gistingu".	"Be may it, because that now is Thorvald Oddson come to North-Tongue and is there now a guest".	"It may be, for Thorvald Oddson has come to North Tontue and is a guest there now".
Þórir svarar:	Thorir answered:	Thorir answered:

The Saga of Hen-Thorir (Old Norse)

Old Norse	Literal	English
"Þat vissi ek at sjá, at mér myndi nökkut gott at höndum koma, því at mér varð allgott við, er ek sá þik".	"That knew I that see, that to-me would some good of hands came, because that to-me became all-good with, that I saw you".	"I knew to see that something good would happen to me, because I felt good when I saw you".
Nú líðr nóttin af hendi, ok þegar um morgininn ríðr Þórir ok þeir fóstrar í Norðrtungu.	Now passed the-night of hand, and from-there about morning rode Thorir and their foster in North-Tongue.	Now the night in hand passed, and from there early in the morning Thorir and his foster rode to North Tongue.
Er þar fjölði manna kominn, ok var sveininum gefit seturúm, en Þórir reikar á gólfinu.	Was there many people come, and was the-boy given a-seat, while Thorir wandered about the-floor.	There were many people who had come there and the boy was found a seat, while Thorir paced around the floor.
Þat getr Þorvaldr at líta, er hann sitr á pallinum ok þeir Arngrímr ok töluðu sín á milli.	It may Thorvald to company, when he sat on the-seat and there Arngrim also talked him in among.	Thorvaldr could see that when he was sitting on the bench that he and Arngrím were talking to each other.
"Hverr er sjá maðr, er reikar um gólfit?"	"Who is see man, that wanders about the-floor?"	"Who is that man I see that wanders around the floor?"
segir Þorvaldr.	said Thorvald.	said Thorvald.
Arngrímr svarar:	Arngrim answered:	Arngrim answered:
"Hann er barnfóstri minn".	"He was child-fostering mine".	"He is my son's foster-father",
"Já",	"Yes",	"Yes",
segir Þorvaldr, "hví skal honum eigi rúm gefast?"	said Thorvald, "why shall him not room be-given?"	said Thorvald, "why shall he not be given room?"
Arngrímr kvað hann eigi varða.	Arngrim spoke he not a-concern.	Arngrim spokr that it was not a concern for him.
"Eigi skal svá vera",	"Not shall so being",	"It shall not be so",
sagði Þorvaldr ok lætr kalla hann til sín ok gefr honum rúm at sitja hjá sér,	said Thorvald and had called he to his and gave him room to sit beside him,	said Thorvald, and had him called to him and gave him room to sit beside him.
spyrjast síðan almæltra tíðenda.	asked then all-matters tidings.	He then asked him what was the news.
Hann svarar Þórir:	He answered Thorir:	He answered Thorir:

The Saga of Hen-Thorir (Old Norse)

Old Norse	Literal	English
"Raun var þetta, er Blund-Ketill rænti mik".	"Torment was that, when Blund-Ketill robbed me".	"It was a torment when Blund-Ketill robbed me".
Þorvaldr spurði:	Thorvald asked:	Thorvald asked:
"Er sætzt á?"	"Is seen about?"	"Has this been seen about?"
"Fjarri ferr um þat",	"Far went about it",	"Far from it",
segir Þórir.	said Thorir.	said Thorir.
"Hví gegnir þat, Arngrímr",	"Why goes that, Arngrim",	"How goes it Arngrim",
sagði Þorvaldr, "at þér höfðingjar látið þá skömm fram fara?"	said Thorvald, "that you chieftains let then shame from go?"	said Thorvald, "that you chieftains let such shameful things go on?"
Arngrímr svarar:	Arngrim answered:	Arngrim answered:
"Lýgr hann mestan hlut frá, ok er alllítit til haft".	"Lies he mostly part from, and is all-little to have".	"Most of what he says is lies, and there is little to it".
"Var þat þó satt at hann hafði heyit?"	"Was it though true that he had the-hay?"	"Was it though true that he took the hay?"
segir Þorvaldr.	said Thorvald.	said Thorvald.
"Hafði hann víst",	"Had he known",	"He certainly had",
segir Arngrímr.	said Arngrim.	said Arngrim.
"Bærr er hverr at ráða sínu",	"Dwelling is who to rule his",	"Everyone rules his dwelling",
sagði Þorvaldr, "ok kemr honum fyrir lítit vinfengi við þik, ef hann skal þó undir fótum troðinn".	said Thorvald, "and came him for little friendship with you, if he shall then under feet trodden".	said Thorvald "and he gains little benefit from being your friend if he shall then be trodden underfoot".
Þórir mælti:	Thorir spoke:	Thorir spoke:
"Allvel lízt mér á þik, Þorvaldr, ok svá segir mér hugr um, at þú munir nökkut leiðrétta mitt mál".	"All-well behold me to you, Thorvald, and so said my thoughts about, that you would some have-right mine matter".	"All right, I like you, Thorvaldr, and so my heart tells me that you will correct my case somewhat".
Þorvaldr mælti:	Thorvald spoke:	Thorvald spoke:

The Saga of Hen-Thorir (Old Norse)

Old Norse	Literal	English
"Ek hefi lítit traust undir mér".	"I have little trust under me".	"I have little confidence in myself".
Þórir mælti:	Thorir spoke:	Thorir spoke:
"Ek vil gefa þér fé mitt hálft til þess, at þú réttir málit ok hafir annathvárt sekðir eða sjálfdæmi, svá at óvinir mínir siti eigi yfir mínu".	"I will give you wealth mine half-of to this, that you right the-matter and have either-way penalty or self-judgement, so that enemies mine sit not over mine".	"I want to give you half of my money so that you do the right thing and have some guilt or self-control, so that my enemies do not sit over me".
Arngrímr mælti:	Arngrim spoke:	Arngrim spoke:
"Ger eigi þetta, Þorvaldr, því at eigi er góðum dreng at duga, þar sem hann er, en þú átt við þann um, er bæði er vitr ok vel at sér ok at öllu vinsæll".	"Do not that, Thorvald, because that not is good fellow that helping, there as he as, but you have with then about, is both is wise and well that his and to all befriended".	"Don't do this, Thorvald, because a good boy is not enough where he is, but you are talking about the one who is both wise and well-behaved and generally popular".
"Sé ek",	"See I",	"I see",
segir Þorvaldr, *"at þér leikr öfund á, ef ek tek við fé hans, ok anntu mér þess eigi".*	said Thorvald, "that to-you like envy about, if I take with wealth his, and care to-me this not".	said Thorvaldr, "that you will be jealous if I take his money, and I don't care".
Þórir mælti:	Thorir said:	Thorir said:
"Svá er at at hyggja, Þorvaldr, at fé mitt mun reynast frítt, ok aðrir menn vitu, at mér er eigi fé goldit víða fyrir mitt eigin".	"So is it that considered, Thorvald, that wealth mine will turn-out free, and other men know, that to-me is not wealth paid with before mine own".	"It's a good thing to think, Thorvaldr, that my money will turn out to be free, and other people know that I don't have much money for my own".
Arngrímr mælti:	Arngrim spoke:	Arngrim said:
"Letja vil ek þik enn, Þorvaldr, at þú takir við máli þessu, en þú munt gera sem þér líkar.	"Discourage wish I you in, Thorvald, that you take with the-matter this, and you might be-done as you like.	"I still want to discourage you, Thorvald, to accept this matter, but you will do what you like.
Uggir mik, at mikit hljótist af".	Dread me, that much to-get of".	I sense that there is much dread in it".
Þorvaldr svarar:	Thorvald answered:	Thorvald answered:

The Saga of Hen-Thorir (Old Norse)

Old Norse	Literal	English
"Eigi mun ek neita fjárviðtökunni".	"Not should I refuse wealth-with-betokened".	"I will not refuse the receipt of funds".
Nú handsalar Þórir honum fé sitt hálft ok þar með málit á hendr Blund-Katli.	Now hands-over Thorir to-him wealth his half-of and there with the-matter in hand Blund-Ketill.	Now Thorir paid him half of his money, and with that the matter of Blund-Ketill is in his hands.
Arngrímr mælti þá enn:	Arngrim spoke then but:	Arngrim then spoke:
"Hversu ætlar þú með at fara máli þessu, Þorvaldr?"	"How-so intend you with to go the-matter this, Thorvald?"	"How do you intend to fo on with the matter, Thorvald?"
"Ek mun fara fyrst á fund föður míns ok hyggja þaðan at ráðum".	"I should go first of meet father my and think from-there that instructions".	"I shall travel first to meet my father and consider counsel from there".
Þórir mælti:	Thorir spoke:	Thorir spoke:
"Eigi hugnar mér þat,	"Not to-mind to-me that,	"I do not have a mind for that".
vil ek eigi hinkr.	will I not hang-back.	I wll not hang back.
Hefi ek mikit til unnit, ok vil ek þegar á morgin láta fara ok stefna Blund-Katli".	Have I much to win, and will I from-there in the-morning have sent and direct Blund-Ketill".	I have achieved a lot, and I want to leave already in the morning and summon for Blund-Ketill".
Þorvaldr svarar:	Thorvald answered:	Thorvald answered:
"Þetta mun vera reyndar, at þú munt vera engi gæfumaðr ok illt mun af þér hljótast.	"That will being seen, that you would being not lucky-man and ill will of you to-get.	"It will be seen that you are not a lucky man, and you will get ill will.
En svá mun nú vera verða".	But so will now being become".	But so will it now be what it is to become".
Ok binda þeir Þórir at hittast í ákveðnum stað um morgininn.	And bound they Thorir to meet in meeting place about morning.	And he and Thorir agreed to meet at a meeting place in the morning.

8   8   8

Þegar snemma um morgininn ríðr Þorvaldr ok Arngrímr með honum með þrjá tigu manna.	From-there soon about morning rode Thorvald and Arngrim with him with three tens people.	From there early in the morning Thorvald and Arngrim rode with thirty people.

The Saga of Hen-Thorir (Old Norse)

Old Norse	Literal	English
Hitta þeir Þóri, ok var hann við þriðja mann.	To-meet there Thori, and was he with third man.	They met Thorir who was one of three men.
Þar var Helgi Arngrímsson ok Víðfari frændi Þóris.	There was Helgi son-of-Arngrim and Vidfari a-kinsman Thori.	Helgi son of Arngrim and Thorir's kinsman Vidfari.
Þorvaldr mælti:	Thorvald spoke:	Thorvald spoke:
"Hví ertu svá fámennr, Þórir?"	"Why are-you so few-men, Thorir?"	"Why are you so few men, Thorir?"
Hann svarar:	He answered:	He answered:
"Ek vissa, at þik myndi eigi lið skorta".	"I knew, that you should not company be-short-of".	"I knew you would not be short of company".
Þeir ríða nú upp eftir Hlíðinni.	There ride now up after The-slope.	They now rode up ober The Slope.
Mannferðin var sén af bæjunum, ok hleypir hverr af sínum bæ.	Men-travelling was seen from the-towns, and ran who of his dwelling.	Men travelling were seen from the towns and everyone ran from their dwelling.
Þykkist sá bezt hafa, er fyrst kemr til Blund-Ketills, ok er þar margt manna fyrir.	Thought saw best have, who first came to Blund-Ketill, and that there many people before.	He thought it best who first came to Blund-Ketill before with the news of many people.
Þeir Þorvaldr ríða at garði ok stíga þar af hestum sínum ok ganga heim at bænum.	There Thorvald rode to yard and leapt there of horses his and to-go house that-the-farm.	Thorvald and his men rode up to the yard and leapt off their horses and walked to the house of the farm.
Þegar Blund-Ketill sér þetta, gengr hann móti þeim ok býðr þeim þar at þiggja allan greiða.	From-there Blund-Ketill saw that, went he to-meet them and bids them there to receive all assistance.	As soon as Blund-Ketill saw that, he went to meet them, and invited them to take with his hospitality.
Þorvaldr mælti:	Thorvald spoke:	Thorvald spoke:
"Annat er erendi hingat en eta mat.	"Other is errand here than eating food.	"Our errand is other than eating food.
Ek vil vita, hverju þú vilt svara fyrir mál þat, er þú tókt upp hey Þóris".	I will know, how you will answer for matter that, is you took up hay Thori".	I wish to know how you will answer for the matter of taking Thori's hay".
Blund-Ketill svarar:	Blund-Ketill answered:	Blund-Ketill answered:

The Saga of Hen-Thorir (Old Norse)

Old Norse	Literal	English
"Slíku þér sem honum.	"Such you as him.	"The same to you as to him.
Ger einn fyrir svá mikit sem þér líkar, ok þó skal ek gefa þér gjafar ofan á, því betri ok meiri sem þú ert meira verðr en Þórir, ok svá mikinn skal ek þinn sóma gera, at þat sé allra manna mál, at þú sér vel sæmðr af".	Make one for so much as to-you like, and though shall I give to-you gifts above about, accordingly better and greater as you are more worth than Thorir, and so much shall I your honour do, to that see all people matter, to you are well honoured of".	Make one as much as you like, and I shall give you gifts on top of that, accordingly better and greater they are in worth than Thorir, and so much shall I do your honour that all the people will see in this matter that you are well honoured".
Þorvaldr þagnar ok þótti vel boðit.	Thorvald silenced and thought well offered.	Thorvald was silent, and thought it was a good offer.
Þórir svarar þá:	Thorir answered then:	Then Thorir answered.
"Eigi er þetta at þiggja, ok þarf eigi at hugsa um þat.	"Not are that to accept, and need not to consider about that.	"That is not acceptable, and there is no need to consider it.
Löngu átta ek þenna kost, ok kalla ek mér lið eigi veitt, þó at slíkt sé, ok til lítils kom mér at gefa þér fé mitt".	Long had I then choice, and call I to-me company not given, though to such being, and to little come to-me to give to-you wealth mine".	For a long time I had this advantage, and I call myself a company not granted, even though such a thing is and to little it came to me to give you my money".
Þá mælti Þorvaldr:	Then spoke Thorvald:	Then Thorvald spoke:
"Hvat viltu þá gera fyrir lögmálsstaðinn?"	"What will-you then do for law-matter-standing?"	"What do you wish to do for the legal standing of this matter?"
Blund-Ketill mælti:	Blund-Ketill spoke:	Blund-Ketill spoke:
"Eigi annat en þú gerir ok einn skapir, slíkt er þú vill".	"Not other but you do and one mind, such that you will".	"None other than you as you are minded to do, and make it such however you want".
Þá svarar Þorvaldr:	Then answered Thorvald:	Then Thorvald Answered:
"Svá lízt mér sem engi sé annarr á gerr en at stefna".	"So seems to-me as nothing being other-than to do but to agreement".	"So it seems to me that there is nothing else to do but to the agreement".
Hann stefnir þá Blund-Katli um rán ok nefnir sér vátta ok hefir þau orð ok umkvæði, sem hann fekk frekust haft.	He summoned then Blund-Ketill about robbery and named his witnesses and had them word and about-speaking, as he got most-often have.	He then summoned Blund-Ketil for the robbery and named his witnesses, and had the most frequent words and phrases he could find.

The Saga of Hen-Thorir (Old Norse)

Old Norse	Literal	English
Nú snýr Blund-Ketill heim at húsum ok mætir Austmanninum Erni, er hann gekk at varnaði sínum.	Now turned Blund-Ketill home that house and met The-Eastern-Men Orn, was he went that keeping his.	Now Blund-Ketill returned home and met Erni the Easterner, as he went to his defense.
Örn spurði:	Orn asked:	Orn asked:
"Ertu sárr, bóndi, er þú ert svá rauðr sem blóð?"	"Are-you wounded, the-farmer, that you are so red as blood?"	"Are you hurt, farmer, are you as red as blood?"
Hann svarar:	He answered:	He answered:
"Eigi em ek sárr, en eigi er þetta betra.	"Not am I wounded, but not is that better.	"I am not hurt, but this is not better.
Þau orð eru töluð við mik, sem aldri hafa áðr töluð verit,	They words they-were told with me, as never have before told been,	Words are spoken to me that have never been spoken before,
ek em kallaðr þjófr ok ránsmaðr".	I am called thief and robber-man".	I am called a thief and a robber".
Örn tekr boga sinn ok lætr koma ör á streng ok kemr þá út í því er þeir stigu á bak.	Orn took bow his and had came an-arrow on the-string and came then out as because were they stepping out back.	Orn took his bow and put an arrow on the string and brought them when they stepped back outside.
Hann skaut, ok varð maðr fyrir ok lætr sígast niðr af hestinum, ok var þat Helgi, sonr Arngríms goða.	He shot, and became man for and had sank down of horse, and was that Helgi, son Arngrim the-chieftain.	He shot and a man was hit by it and he sank from the horse, and it was Helgi son of Arngrím the chieftain.
Þeir hlaupa at honum.	They ran at him.	They ran at him.
Þórir otar sér fram milli manna ok hratt mönnum frá sér ok biðr gefa sér rúm,	Thorir pushed his from among people and quickly men from his and bid to-give his room,	Thorir pushed forward between them, and people quickly moved away from him to give him room.
"því at mér mun mest umhugat".	"because to to-me should most about-concern".	"For this is of the most concern to me.
Hann laut at Helga niðr, ok var hann þá dauðr.	He leant to Helgi down, and was he then dead.	He leant down to Helgi and then he was dead.
Þórir mælti:	Thorir spoke:	Thorir spoke:

The Saga of Hen-Thorir (Old Norse)

Old Norse	Literal	English
"Er lítill máttrinn, fóstri minn?"	"Is little power, foster mine?"	"Do you have so little power, my foster-son?"
Þórir réttist þá frá honum ok mælti:	Thorir straightened-up then from him and spoke:	Thor then straightened up from him and spoke:
"Talaði sveinninn við mik.	"Said the-boy with me.	"The boy spoke with me.
Sagði hann tysvar it sama, þetta hérna:	Spoke he twice then the-same, that here:	He spoke the same thing twice, and it was this:"
"Brenni, brenni	"Burn, burn	"Burn, burn
Blund-Ketill inni".	Blund-Ketill in".	Blund-Ketill in".
Arngrímr svarar þá:	Arngrim answered then:	Then Arngrim answered:
"Nú fór sem mik varði, at oft hlýtr illt af illum, ok grunaði mik, at mikit illt myndi af þér hljótast, Þórir, ok eigi veit ek, hvat sveinninn hefir sagt, þó at þú fleiprir eitthvert,	"Now goes as me expected, to often must ill of evil, and mistrust me, to much ill should of you to-get, Thorir, and not know I, what the-boy had told, though that you babble something,	"Now it occurred to me that evil often comes from evil, and I suspected that a lot of evil would come from you, Thorir, and I don't know what the boy had said, even though you're babbling something.
en þó er eigi ólíkligt, at slíkt verði gert.	but though is not unlike, to such became done.	but it is not unlikely that such a thing will be done.
Hófst þetta mál illa.	Began that matter ill.	The matter began badly.
Kann ok vera, at svá lúkist".	Know and being, that so end".	And I know it will end so".
Þórir svarar:	Thorir answered:	Thorir answered:
"Eiga þykkir mér þú nökkut nauðsynligra en ávíta mik".	"Not thought I you some need-like but to-rebuke me".	"I did not think you would have some need to rebuke me".
Þeir Arngrímr ríða nú brott undir skógarnef eitt ok stíga af hestum ok eru nú þar, til þess at náttar.	There Arngrim ride now away under woods-outskirts once and leapt of horses and they-were now there, to this that nightfall.	Arngrim and his men now rode away along the outskirts of the woods, and leapt off their horses, and there they were until nightfall.
En Blund-Ketill þakkar mönnum vel sitt liðsinni ok bað hvern mann ríða heimleiðis sem bezt gegndi.	But Blund-Ketill thanked men well his assistance and bid each man ride home-ways as best might.	But Blund-Ketill thanked the men well for their assistance and bid each man to ride homeward best he might.

The Saga of Hen-Thorir (Old Norse)

Old Norse	Literal	English
9	**9**	**9**
Svá er sagt, at þegar er náttaði, ríða þeir Þorvaldr at bænum í Örnólfsdal.	So is said, to from-there that nightfall, ride they Thorvald to estate in Ornolfsdal.	So it is said that from there when it was nightfall Thorvald and his men rode to the estate in Ornolfsdal.
Váru þar þá allir menn í svefni.	Where there then all men in sleep.	All of the men there were asleep.
Þeir draga viðarköst at bænum ok slá í eldi.	There dragged brushwood to the-farmhouse and struck to fire.	They dragged brushwood up to the house and struck a fire.
Vakna þeir Blund-Ketill eigi fyrr en húsin loguðu yfir þeim.	Awoke there Blund-Ketill not before and house burned over them.	Blund-Ketill and his men awoke but not before the house was burning over them.
Blund-Ketill spurði, hverir þar kveikti svá heitan eld.	Blund-Ketill asked, who there kindled so threatening fire.	Blund-Ketill asked who had kindled so threatening a fire.
Þórir sagði, hverir váru.	Thorir said, who were.	Thorir said who they were.
Blund-Ketill frétti, ef nökkut skyldi ná sáttum.	Blund-Ketill heard, if something should near fulfilled.	Blund-Ketill asked if there was any chance of an agreement.
Þórir sagði, at engi er kostr annarr en brenna.	Thorir said, to none is choice other but burn.	Thorir said that there was no other choice than to burn.
Þeir skiljast nú eigi fyrr við, en hvert mannsbarn er þar inni brunnit.	They departed now not before with, but each born-man was there in burnt.	They now departed but not before each man-born inside was burned.
Hersteinn, sonr Blund-Ketills, hafði farit um kveldit til fóstra síns, er Þorbjörn hét ok var kallaðr stígandi.	Herstein, son Blund-Ketill's, had gone about evening to foster-father his, was Thorbjorn named and was called Strider.	Hersteinn, son of Blund-Ketill, had gone that evening to his foster-father, whose name was Thorbjorn and who was called Strider.
Þat er mælt, at Þorbjörn væri eigi allr jafnan, þar sem hann var sénn.	That was said, to Thorbjorn was not all equally, there as he was seen.	It is said that Thorbjorn was not quite the same as he appeared to be.
Hersteinn vaknar um morgininn ok spurði, hvárt fóstri hans vekði.	Herstein awoke about morning and asked, whether foster-father his was-awake.	Herstein awoke around morning and asked whether his foster-father was awake.
Hann kveðst vaka,	He said awake,	He said that he was awake.

The Saga of Hen-Thorir (Old Norse)

Old Norse	Literal	English
"eða hvat viltu?"	"or what will-you?"	"and what do you want?"
"Mik dreymði, at mér þótti sem faðir minn gengi hér inn, ok loguðu um hann klæðin öll, ok allr þótti mér sem hann væri eldr einn".	"Me dreamed, that to-me thought as father mine going here in, and burned about he clothes all, and all thought to-me as he was fire one".	"I dreamt, that it seemed to me that my father walked in here, and all the clothes around him burned, and it seemed to me that he was all on fire".
Þeir standa upp ok ganga út ok sjá skjótt logann.	They stood up and went out and saw quickly the-fire.	They stood up and went outside, and quickly saw the fire.
Þeir taka vápn sín ok fara hvatliga, ok váru þá allir menn á brottu, er þeir kómu þar.	They take weapons theirs and went quickly, and were then all men to away, when they came there.	Then they took their weapons and went quickly, and when they got there, all the men were gone.
Hersteinn mælti:	Herstein spoke:	Herstein spoke:
"Hér eru orðin hörmulig tíðendi, eða hvat er nú til ráða?"	"Here they-are become harm-like tidings, and what is now to decide?"	"Here has become harmful news, and what is to be done now?"
Þorbjörn svarar:	Thorbjorn answered:	Thorbjorn answered:
"Nú skal neyta þess boðs, er Tungu-Oddr hefir oft mælt, at ek skylda til hans koma, ef ek þyrfta nökkurs við".	"Now shall make-use this offer, that Tungu-Odd has often spoken, to I should to his came, if I needed someone with".	"Now I shall make use of this offer that Tungu-Odd has often spoken about, that I should come to him if I had need of someone".
Hersteinn svarar:	Herstein answered:	Herstein answered:
"Eigi þykkir mér þat vænligt".	"Not seemed to-me that hopeful".	"That does not seem to me to be that hopeful".
En þó fara þeir ok koma á Breiðabólstað ok kalla út Odd.	And though go there and come of Breidabolstad and call out Odd.	But though they went and came to Breidabolstad and called Odd outside.
Hann gengr út ok tekr við þeim vel ok spurði tíðenda.	He going out and took with them well and asked tidings.	He went out and received them well and asked what the news was.
Þeir sögðu slík, sem orðin váru.	They said such, as became were.	They said what had happened.
Hann lætr illa yfir.	He had ill over.	He felt bad over it.

The Saga of Hen-Thorir (Old Norse)

Old Norse	Literal	English
Þorbjörn karl tekr þá til orða:	Thorbjorn a-man took then to words:	The man Thorbjorn took to words:
"Á þá leið er, Oddr bóndi", sagði hann, "at þú hefir heitit mér ásjá þinni, ok vil ek nú til þess taka, at þú leggir til nökkur góð ráð ok komir til".	"So then the-way is, Odd the-farmer", said he, "to you has pledged to-me assistance you, and wish I now to this take, that you place to some good decision and come to".	"So it is this way, farmer Odd", he said, "you pledged your assistance to me, and I now wish to have some good advice to come".
Oddr kvaðst svá gera mundu.	Odd spoke so be-done would.	Odd spoke and said that he would do.
Ríða þeir nú í Örnólfsdal ok koma þar fyrir dag.	Ride there now in Ornolfsdal and come there before day.	They now rode to Ornolfsdal and got there before mid-day.
Váru þá fallin húsin ok fölskaðr mjök eldrinn.	Were then fallen the-houses and pale-burnt much the-fire.	The houses were then fallen and the fire had burnt much.
Nú ríðr Oddr at húsi einu, því er eigi var allt brunnit.	Now rode Odd to house one, because was not was all burned.	Now Odd rode to one house because it was not all burned.
Hann seilist til birkirafts eins ok kippir burt ór húsinu, ríðr síðan andsælis um húsin með loganda brandinn ok mælti:	He reached to birch-rafter one and drew away from the-house, rode then anti-sun-wise about the-house with flaming brand and spoke:	He reached for one of the birch rafters and then rode anti-sun-wise around the house with the flaming brand and spoke:
"Hér nem ek mér land, fyrir því at hér sé ek nú eigi byggðan bólstað.	"Here take I to-me land, for because to here see I now not settled building.	"Here I take the land for myself, for because I see now no settled building.
Heyri þat váttar, þeir er hjá váru".	Hear that witnesses, they that nearby they-are".	There the witnesses hear that are nearby".
Hann keyrir síðan hestinn ok ríðr í brott.	He whipped then horse and rode in away.	He then spurred his horse and rode away.
Hersteinn mælti:	Herstein spoke:	Herstein spoke:
"Hvat er nú til ráða?	"What is now to decide?	"What is the decision to be now?"
Eigi reyndist þessi vel".	Not turned-out this well".	This has not turned out well".
Þorbjörn mælti:	Thorbjorn spoke:	Thorbjorn spoke:

The Saga of Hen-Thorir (Old Norse)

Old Norse	Literal	English
"Þegi þú, ef þú mátt, hvat sem í gerist".	"Silence you, if you might, what as in became".	"Be silent if you can, whatever happens".
Hersteinn svarar ok kvaðst þat eina talat hafa, er eigi var við of.	Hersteinn answered and said that only spoken have, was not was with of.	Hersteinn answered and said that they had only spoken, which was not too much.
Útibúr var óbrunnit, þat sem varningr Austmanns var inni ok mikit fé annat.	Out-house was unburnt, that as goods Easterners was inside and much wealth other.	The storeroom was unburnt, the Easterner's goods were inside and a lot of other wealth.
Í þessu hverfr Þorbjörn karl.	In this turned Thorbjorn the-man.	At this moment, the man Thorbjorn vanished.
Nú lítr Hersteinn heim til bæjarins ok sér útibúrið opit ok út borit féit, en engan sér hann manninn.	Now looked Herstein home to dwellings and his out-house open and out carried wealth, but none his he people.	Now Herstein looked towards the dwellings and saw that his storeroom was open, and the goods being carried out, but none of his people.
Þar eru bundnar klyfjar.	There they-were bound loaded.	Then they bounded up the loads.
Þar næst heyrir hann hark mikit í túnit, sér nú, at heim eru rekin hross öll, þau er faðir hans hafði átt, sauðir ok naut ór fjósi ok allt ganganda fé.	There nearest heard he noise much in the-fields, his now to home they-were driven horses all they were father his had had, sheep and bulls about the-barn and all walking cattle.	Then he heard a great noise in the fields, and now all the horses that his father had were being driven home, sheep and bulls from the barn, and all livestock.
Síðan eru klyfjar upp hafðar ok því næst öllu á ferð snúit ok allt fémætt á brott fært.	After they-were loaded up had and accordingly near all to travelled away and all valuables to away taken.	After they had loaded up, straightaway they all travelled away, and all valuables were taken away.
Hersteinn víkr nú eftir ok sér, at Þorbjörn karl rekr féit.	Herstein turned now after and saw, that Thorbjorn a-man driving the-cattle.	Herstein now turned and went after them, and saw that the man Thorbjorn was driving the cattle.
Þeir snúa leið sinni ofan eftir heraði í Stafholtstungur ok svá út yfir Norðrá.	They turned the-ways theirs over after the-district in Stafholtstungur and so out over Norðurá.	They moved on their way over through the district in Stafholtstunga and then out over Nordura.

The Saga of Hen-Thorir (Old Norse)

Old Norse	Literal	English
# 10	# 10	# 10
Sauðamaðr Þorkels trefils ór Svignaskarði gekk þenna morgin at fé sínu.	Shepherd Thorkel Trefil about Svignaskardi went that morning to cattle his.	The shepherd of Thorkel Trefil of Svignaskard went that morning to his cattle.
Hann sér, hvar þeir fara ok reka alls kyns fénað.	He saw where they fared and drove all kinds-of cattle.	He saw where they travelled and drove all their kins' cattle.
Hann segir þetta Þorkatli, en hann svarar:	He said that Thorkel, and he answered:	He told Thorkel, and he answered:
"Veit ek hverju gegna mun.	"Know I each going should.	"I know how it should go forward.
Þat munu vera Þverhlíðingar, vinir mínir.	That would being Þverhlíðingar, friends mine.	That will be my friends of Therarhlid.
Þeir hafa vetrarnauð mikla, ok munu þeir reka hingat fé sitt,	They have winter-need much, and shall they drive here cattle his,	They have much need this winter and we shall drive his cattle here.
skal þeim þat heimilt,	shall them that allow,	they shall be allowed to.
ek hefi hey ærin,	I have hay a-year,	I have hay for a year.
eru hér ok nógar jarðir útifé".	they-were here and enough earth grazing".	There are also enough lands here for grazing.
Hann gekk út, er þeir kómu í tún, ok fagnar þeim ok býðr allan greiða, slíkan sem þeir vilja þegit hafa.	He went out, as they came to the-plot, and gave them and invited all assistance, such as they wished receive have.	He went out when they came to the field, and welcomed them and offered them all the favours they wanted.
Varla náðu þeir at stíga af baki, svá var bóndi beinn við þá.	Rarely reached there that leapt of horseback, so was the-farmer hospitable with then.	They barely managed to get off the back of their horses, than the farmer was right at them.
Þorbjörn mælti:	Thorbjorn spoke:	Thorbjorn spoke:
"Mikit er nú um beina þinn, ok væri mikit undir, at þú efndir þetta allt vel, er þú hefir heitit okkr".	"Much is now about assistance yours, and was much under, to you fulfilment that all well, that you has pledged us".	"There is much that now depends on your assistance, and it would be well undertaken, if you did all this well, what you promised us".

The Saga of Hen-Thorir (Old Norse)

Old Norse	Literal	English
"Veit ek erendi þitt, at féit mun hér skulu eftir vera, ok skortir hér eigi jörð nóga ok góða".	"Know I errand yours, that cattle will here should after being, and shortage here not the-earth enough and good".	"I know your errand, that the cattle will be here after, and there is no shortage of good enough earth".
Þorbjörn mælti:	Thorbjorn spoke:	Thorbjorn spoke:
"Þiggja munum vit þat".	"Accept shall with that".	"I shall accept that".
Þá víkr hann Þorkatli hjá húsunum ok mælti:	Then took he Thorkel aside the-house and spoke:	Then he took Thorkel beside the house and spoke:
"Tíðendi mikil eru at segja".	"Tidings great there-are to say".	"There are great tidings to tell".
Þorkell spurði, hver þau væri.	Thorkel asked, who they was.	Thorkell asked what they were.
"Blund-Ketill bóndi var brenndr inni í nótt",	"Blund-Ketill the-farmer was burned in about the-night",	"Blund-Ketil the farmer was burned during the night",
sagði Þorbjörn.	said Thorbjorn.	said Thorbjorn.
"Hverjir gerðu þat níðingsverk?"	"Who did that low-deed?"	"Who did that low-deed?"
sagði Þorkell.	said Thorkel.	said Thorkel.
Þorbjörn sagði þá allt, sem farit hafði,	Thorbjorn said then all, as gone had,	Thorbjorn told him all that had happened.
"ok þarf Hersteinn nú þinna heillaráða".	"and needed Herstein now your good-advice".	"and now Herstein needs your good advice".
Þorkell mælti:	Thorkel spoke:	Thorkel spoke:
"Eigi þætti mér ráðit, hvárt ek mynda svá skjótt á boð brugðizt hafa, ef ek hefða þetta vitat fyrr.	"Not seems to-me advised, if I should so quickly to offer accustomed have, if I had that known before.	"It does not seem to me well advised that I should have been so quick with my offer, if I had known that before.
En mínum ráðum vil ek nú láta fram fara, ok förum nú til matar fyrst".	But my advice will I now allow from going and let-us-go now to feed first".	But my counsel I will now go along with, and let us go now and eat first".
Þeir játtuðu því.	They affirmed accordingly.	They affirmed accordingly.
Þorkell trefill var þá mjök fámáligr ok nökkut hugsi,	Thorkel Trefill was then much of-few-words and somewhat thoughtful.	Thorkel Trefil was then very much of few words and somewhat thoughtful.

The Saga of Hen-Thorir (Old Norse)

Old Norse	Literal	English
ok er þeir váru mettir, lætr hann taka hesta þeira.	And when they were full-of-food had he brought horses theirs.	And when they were full of food he had their horses brought.
Síðan taka þeir vápn sín ok stíga á bak.	Then took they weapons theirs and mounted on back.	Then they took their weapons and mounted on the backs.
Ríðr Þorkell fyrir þann dag ok mælti áðr, at vel skyldi geyma fjárins í haganum, en gefa vel því, sem inni var.	Rode Thorkel before that day and spoke before, that well should retain cattle in the-pastures, and given well accordingly, as in was.	Thorkel rode in front that day and said before that the cattle in the pastures should be as well kept as those inside.
Þeir ríða nú út á Skógarströnd á Gunnarsstaði.	They rode now out to Skogarstrand in Gunnarsstadirr.	They now rode out to Skogarstrand in Gunnarsstadir.
Þat er innarliga á Ströndinni.	That which lying-in of The-strand.	Tha was lying far in from the strand.
Þar bjó sá maðr, er Gunnarr hét ok var Hlífarson, mikill maðr ok sterkr ok inn mesti garpr.	There lived so a-man, who Gunnar named and was son-of-Hlifar, big man and strong and the most brave-strong.	There lived a man named Gunnar the son of Hlifar, a big strong man and the most brave.
Hann átti systur Þórðar gellis, er Helga hét.	He married sister-of Thord Gellir, who Helgi named.	He married the sister of Thord Gellir who was named Helgi.
Gunnarr átti tvær dætr.	Gunnar had two daughters.	Gunnar had two daughters.
Hét önnur Jófríðr, en önnur Þuríðr.	Named one Jofrid, and another Thurid.	One named Jofrid and another Thurid.
Þeir koma þar síð dags og stíga af baki fyrir ofan hús.	There come there late day and leapt of horseback before above the-house.	They arrived there late in the day, dismounted from horseback above the house.
Vindr var á norðan ok heldr kalt.	Wind was in the-north and rather cold.	The wind was in the north and rather cold.
Þorkell gengr at durum ok klappar, en húskarl gengr til hurðar ok heilsar vel þeim, sem kominn var, ok spyrr, hverr hann væri.	Thorkel went to the-door and knocked, but the-housekeeper went to the-door-beam and greeted well them, as come was, and asked, who he was.	Thorkel went to the door and knocked, but the housekeepet went to the door beam and greeted them well, and asked who he was.
Þorkell kvað hann eigi vita mundu at gerr, þó at hann segði honum,	Thorkel spoke he not knowing would if done, though that he said him,	Thorkel said that he would not know, even if he told him.
"ok bið Gunnar út ganga".	"and bid Gunnar out going".	"and ask Gunnar to come out".

The Saga of Hen-Thorir (Old Norse)

Old Norse	Literal	English
Hann kvað Gunnar kominn í rekkju.	He spoke Gunnar come in bed.	He said that Gunnar had gone to bed.
Hann biðr hann segja, at maðr vill hitta hann.	He asked him to-say, to man wishes to-meet him.	He asked him to say that a man wishes to meet him.
Húskarl gerir svá, gengr inn ok segir Gunnari, at maðr vill hitta hann.	The-housekeeper did so, going in and said Gunnar, that man will to-meet he.	The housekeeper did so, went in and told Gunnar that a man wished to meet him.
Gunnarr spurði, hverr hann væri.	Gunnar asked, who he was.	Gunnar asked who he was.
Húskarl kvaðst þat eigi vita,	The-housekeeper spoke that not knowing,	The housekeeper said that he did not know.
"en mikill er hann vexti".	"and much was he grown".	"but he was great and large grown".
Gunnarr mælti:	Gunnar spoke:	Gunnar spoke:
"Far þú ok seg honum, at hann sé hér í nátt".	"Go you and say to-him, that he bed here about the-night".	"Go and say to him that he should bed here for the night".
Húskarl ferr ok gerir sem Gunnarr bauð, en Þorkell kvaðst eigi vilja þiggja boð af þrælum, heldr at bónda sjálfum.	The-housekeeper went and did as Gunnar bid, but Thorkel spoke not wished to-accept the-invitation of a-thrall, rather to the-farmer himself.	The housekeeper went and did as Gunnar asked, but Thorkel said that he did not wish to accept the invitation of a thrall rather than from the farmer himself.
Húskarl segir, at þat væri sannligra,	The-housekeeper said, that it was true-like,	The housekeeper said that it might well be so.
"en eigi hefir Gunnarr vana til þess at standa upp um nætr.	"but not has Gunnar custom to this to stand up about the-night.	"but Gunnar is not accustomed to getting up in the night.
Gerðu annathvárt",	Do either-way",	Do one thing or the other",
sagði húskarl, "at þú far á brott eða gakk inn ok ver hér í nátt".	said the-housekeeper, "that you go to away or come in and be here in the-night".	said the housekeeper, "that you go away or come in and be here for the night".
"Gerðu annathvárt",	"Do either-way",	Do one thing or the other",
segir Þorkell, "at þú rek erendi duganda eða ek lek sverðshjöltin á nasir þér".	said Thorkel, "that you drive errand sufficiently or I lay sword's-hilt on nose to-you".	said Thorkel, "that you fulfil my errand sufficiently or I lay my sword's hilt to your nose".

The Saga of Hen-Thorir (Old Norse)

Old Norse	Literal	English
Húskarl hleypr inn ok rekr aftr hurðina.	The-housekeeper ran in and drove after the-door-beam.	The housekeeper ran in and drove the door bean behind.
Gunnarr spurði, hví hann færi svá óðliga.	Gunnar asked, why he went so wildly.	Gunnar asked why he went so wildly.
Hann sagðist eigi vildu tala fleira við inn komna mann,	He said not wished to-talk more with the come man,	He said that he did not wish to talk anymore with the man who had come.
"því at hann er mjök hastorðr".	"because to him was much harsh-spoken".	"because that he was much too harshly spoken".
Gunnarr reis þá upp ok gekk út í túnit.	Gunnar rose then up and went out into the-enclosure.	Gunnar then got up and went out into the enclosure.
Hann var í skyrtu ok línbrókum, möttul yfir sér ok svarta skó á fótum, sverð í hendi.	He was in shirt and linen-breeches, mantle over him and black shoes of feet, sword in hand.	He was in a shirt and linen breeches, with a cloak over him, and black shoes on his fee, and a sword in hand.
Hann fagnar vel Þorkatli ok biðr hann inn ganga.	He greeted well Thorkel and bid he inside going.	He greeted Thorkel well and invited him to go inside.
Hann segir, at þeir váru fleiri saman.	He said, that they were more together.	He said that there were still more of them together.
Gunnarr gengr út í túnit, en Þorkell þrífr í hurðarhringinn ok rekr aftr hurðina.	Gunnar went out into the-enclosure, but Thorkel deftly to the-door-ring and drove behind the-door-beam.	Gunnar went out into the enclosure but Thorkel quickly went to the door ring and pulled the door to.
Þeir ganga þá á bak húsunum.	There to-go then of back the-house.	They then went to the back of the house.
Gunnarr heilsar þeim.	Gunnar greeted them.	Gunnar greeted them.
Þorkell sagði:	Thorkel said:	Thorkel said:
"Setjumst vér niðr, því at vér eigum margt at tala við þik Gunnarr".	"Let-us-sit we down, because that we have many to say with you Gunnar".	"Let us sit down, because we have much to discuss with you Gunnar".
Þeir gera svá, setjast niðr á tvær hendr honum ok svá nær, at þeir sátu á skikkjunni, er Gunnarr hafði yfir sér.	They did so, sitting down on two hands his and so close, that they sat on cloak, that Gunnar had over himself.	They did so, sitting on the left hand and the right hand of him, and so close that they sat on the cloak that Gunnar had over himself.

The Saga of Hen-Thorir (Old Norse)

Old Norse	Literal	English
Þorkell mælti þá:	Thorkel spoke then:	Thorkel spoke then:
"Svá er háttat, Gunnarr bóndi, at hér er sá maðr í ferð með mér, er Hersteinn heitir, sonr Blund-Ketills.	"So is the-way, Gunnar the-farmer, that here was seen man in travelled with to-me, was Herstein was-named, son Blund-Ketill.	"This is the way it is, farmer Gunnar, there is a man travelling with me that is named Herstein, the son of Blund-Ketil.
Er eigi því erendi at leyna, at hann vill biðja dóttur þinnar, Þuríðar.	Is not therefore errand to hide, that he will invite daughter yours, Thorid.	There is no point in hiding the fact that he wishes to ask for the hand of your daughter Thurid.
Hefi ek ok fyrir þessa sök með honum farit, at ek vildi eigi, at þú vísaðir manninum frá, því at mér sýnist happaráð it mesta.	Have I and for this reason with him travelling, to I wish not, to you turn-away the-man from, because to to-me seems happy-decision the most.	I have travelled with him for this reason, that you do not turn this man away, because to me it seems to be the most happy decision.
Þykkir mér ok miklu varða, at eigi sé óvirt þetta mál ok mín tillög eða seint svarat".	Seemed to-me and much concern, that not see unworthy that matter and mine proposal or coldly answered".	It is a matter of deep concern to me, and also my matter, that the proposal is not seen as unworthy or answered coldly".
Gunnarr mælti:	Gunnar spoke:	Gunnar spoke:
"Eigi em ek einhlítr um svör þessa máls, ok vil ek ráðast um við móður hennar ok svá við dóttur mína ok einkum við Þórð gelli, frænda hennar.	"Not am I sufficient about answer this matter, and wish I arrange about with mother hers and so with daughter mine and especially with Thord Gellir, kinsman hers.	"I am not sufficient to answer this matter, and I will arrange with her mother and with my daughter and especially with Thord Gellir her kinsman.
En góðar einar fréttir höfum vér til þessa manns ok svá til föður hans, ok er þetta ásjámál".	And good Einar news have we to this man and so to father his, and was that matter-consideration".	But we have heard good things of this man and also of his father, and this is a matter of consideration".
Þá svarar Trefill:	Then answered Trefill:	Then Trefill answered:
"Svá skaltu til ætla, at vér munum eigi lengi vánbiðlar vera konunnar, ok þykkjumst vér eigi minnr sjá fyrir þinni sæmð en várri.	"So shall-you to suppose, that we shall not longer hope-abide being the-woman, and think we not less seems for your honour than ours.	"So should you suppose that we shall not longer be abiding in hope of the woman, and we think this is no less an honour to you than to us.

The Saga of Hen-Thorir (Old Norse)

Old Norse	Literal	English
Þykkir mér ok kynligt um svá vitran mann sem þú ert, at þú virðir slíka hluti fyrir þér, svá vel sem boðit er.	Seems to-me also strange about so wise man as you are that you value such part for to-you so well as invitation is.	It also seems to me strange, since you are such a wise man and you respect such things for yourself, as well as they are offered.
Höfum vér ok svá at eins heiman gert ferð vára, at eigi mun til einskis ætlat,	Have we also so to one's home made journey further that not should to nothing intend.	We have also made such a long journey from home, that it should not be for nothing.
ok mun ek, Hersteinn, veita þér slíkt lið, sem þú vill, at þetta fari fram, ef hann kann eigi at sjá, hvat honum sómir".	and should I, Herstein, grant you such company, as you will, that that goes from, if he know not that see, what him honourable".	And Herstein, I shall grant you such assistance as you wish in order for this to go forward, if he cannot see what is honourable to him".
Gunnarr svarar:	Gunnar answered:	Gunnar answered:
"Þat fæ ek eigi skilit, hví þér látið svá brátt at þessu eða haldið við heitan sjálfa, því at mér lízt þetta mjök jafnræði, en einskis ills örvænti ek frá yðr, ok mun ek þat ráð upp taka at rétta fram höndina",	"That get I not understand why you let so soon that this or holding with threatening myself because that to-me appears that much equally and nothing ill desperation I from you and should I that decision up take that rights from hand",	"What I don't understand is why you wish it to happen so soon, or hold with threatening me, because to me it appears very much equal, but in vain do I despair of you, and I should take the decision to extend my hand".
ok svá gerir hann, en Hersteinn nefnir sér vátta ok fastnar sér konu.	and so did he, then Herstein named his witnesses and betrothed himself the-woman.	And so he did, then Herstein named his witnesses and betrothed himself to the woman.
Eftir þetta standa þeir upp ok ganga inn.	After that stood they up and went in.	After that they stood up and went in.
Er þeim veittr beini góðr.	Were they given benefit good.	They were well looked after.
Nú spyrr Gunnarr tíðenda.	Now asked Gunnar news.	Now Gunnar asked the news.
Þorkell segir, at þeir hafi nú eigi annat nýligar frétt en brennu Blund-Ketills.	Thorkel said, that they had now not other newer news than the-burning Blund-Ketill's.	Thorkell said that they had no newer news than the burning of Blund-Ketill.
Gunnarr spurði, hverr því olli.	Gunnar asked who therefore caused.	Gunnar asked, who therefore caused it.
Þorkell segir, at Þorvaldr Oddsson var upphafsmaðr at ok Arngrímr goði.	Thorkel said, that Thorvald son-of-Odd was the-instigators to and Arngrim chieftain.	Thorkel said that Thorvald son of Odd was the instigator and also Arngrim the chieftain.

The Saga of Hen-Thorir (Old Norse)

Old Norse	Literal	English
Gunnarr svaraði fá, lastaði lítt, enda lofaði eigi.	Gunnar answered a-few, blame little, end praised not.	Gunnar gave his answer, blamed little and praised not.

11

Old Norse	Literal	English
Þegar um morgininn í ár er Gunnarr á fótum ok gengr at Þorkatli ok bað þá klæðast.	From-there about morning in early was Gunnar on feet and went to Thorkel and asked then to-dress.	Early in the morning, Gunnar was on his feet and went to Thorkel and asked him to get dressed.
Þeir gera svá, ganga síðan til snæðings.	There be-done so, to-go then to eating.	They did so, and then went to eat.
Eru þá ok búnir hestar þeira, ok stíga þeir á bak.	They-were then and prepared horses theirs, and mounted they on back.	Then their horses were ready, and they mounted on the back.
Ríðr Gunnarr fyrir inn með firðinum.	Rode Gunnar before in with fjord.	Gunnar rode in front along the fjord.
Þá váru íslög mikil.	Then was ice-bound much.	Then it was very much ice-bound.
Eigi létta þeir fyrr en þeir koma í Hvamm til Þórðar gellis, ok fagnar hann þeim vel ok spurði tíðenda.	Not let-up there before and there come in Hvamm to Thord Gellir, and gave he them well and asked tidings.	They did not let up before they came to Hvamm to Thord Gellir and he received them well and asked the news.
Þeir sögðu slíkt, er þeim líkaði.	There said such, was them liked.	They told him so as they liked.
Gunnarr heimtir Þórð á mál ok segir, at þar er í för Hersteinn, sonr Blund-Ketills, ok Þorkell trefill.	Gunnar got Thord of matter and said, that there was in journey Herstein, son Blund-Ketill, and Thorkel Trefill.	Gunnar got on to the matter with Thord and said what was happening with Herstein son of Blund-Ketill and Thorkel Trefill,
"Er þat erendi þeira, at Hersteinn mælir til mægða við mik, en til samfara við Þuríði dóttur mína, eða hversu ráðligt lízt þér þat?	"Are that errand theirs, to Herstein discussing to marriage with me, but to together-travelling with Thurid daughter mine, or how-so advise appears to-you that?	"Is it their business that Hersteinn is recommending me as a father-in-law, but for marriage with my daughter Thurid, or how advisable do you think it is?
Maðr er vænn ok gerviligr.	Man is handsome and accomplished.	The man is handsome and accomplished.

The Saga of Hen-Thorir (Old Norse)

Old Norse	Literal	English
Hann skortir ok eigi fé, því faðir hans hefir þat mælt, at hann myndi af hendi láta búit, en Hersteinn tæki við".	He shortage and not wealth, because father his has that said, that he would of hand let place, but Herstein take with".	He is not short of wealth because of his father has said that he would leave the estate, then Herstein would take over".
Þórðr svarar:	Thord answered:	Thord answered:
"Vel er mér við Blund-Ketill, því at einn tíma, er við Tungu-Oddr deildum á alþingi um þrælsgjöld, er dæmðust á hendr honum, ok fór ek at heimta í foraðsillu veðri ok vér þrír saman ok kómum um nótt til Blund-Ketills, ok var oss þar allvel fagnat, ok þar várum vér viku.	"Well am to-me with Blund-Ketill, because that one time, that with Tungu-Odd shared at the-assembly about servant-fees, were judged to hand him, and went I to insist in abominable weather and we three together and came about night to Blund-Ketill's, and were us there all-well celebrating, and there were we a-week.	"I am fine with Blund-Ketill, because of that time when Tungu-Odd and I were arguing at the assembly about servant fees, and it was judged to his hand, and I went to insist in bad weather, and the three of us came in the night to Blund-Ketill's and we were well received there and stayed for a week.
Hann skipti við oss hestum, en gaf mér góð stóðhross.	He exchanged with us horses, and gave to-me good stallions.	He exchanged horses with us, but gave me good stallions.
Slíkt reynda ek af honum, en þó lízt mér svá á, at eigi muni því misráðit, þó at eigi sé þessu keypt".	Such experience I of him, but though appears to-me so as, to not should because mis-advised, though to not see this bought".	That was my experience of him, but though it appears to me that it would not be mis-advised not to conclude this matter".
"Svá máttu til ætla",	"So might to suppose",	"So might you suppose",
segir Gunnarr, "at eigi mun hon föstnuð öðrum manni, þó at henni bjóðist, því at mér lízt sjá maðr vaskligr ok vel boðinn ok mikil hætta í, hversu til tekst, ef þessum manni er frá vísat".	said Gunnar, "to not should her betrothe other man, though that her offered, because to to-me appears see the-man bold and well invited and much danger in, how-so to take, if this people was from turn-away".	said Gunnar, "that she should not be betrothed to any other man though she is offered, because it appears to me that he is a bold man with a good offer, and there is great danger from these people if they are turned away".
Eftir þat gengr Gunnarr til fundar við dóttur sína, því at hon var með Þórði á fóstri, ok fréttir hana eftir, hversu henni var um gefit.	After that went Gunnar to meet with daughter his, because to she was with Thord in fostering, and news hers after, how-so to-her was about given.	After that Gunnar went to meet with his daughter because she was being fostered with Thord, and the news after her, and how she was given to the idea.
Hon svarar, at eigi er henni svá mikil manngirnð í hug, at henni þætti jafngott at sitja heima,	She answered, that not was she so greatly men-desiring in thought, to her seemed equal-good to settle at-home,	She replied that she didn't have so much love for people, and in her mind that she would just as well sit at home,

The Saga of Hen-Thorir (Old Norse)

Old Norse	Literal	English
"því at ek á kost góðrar forsjá, þar sem Þórðr er, frændi minn.	"because to I in provided-for well custody, there as Thord who, kinsman mine.	"because I have the advantage of good guardianship, where Thord is my kinsman.
En ykkarn vilja mun ek gera um þetta ok annat".	But your wish should I do about this and other-things".	But according to your will, I will do about this and other things".
Nú elr Gunnarr á málit við Þórð ok segir, at honum lízt þetta ráð allsæmiligt.	Now came Gunnar to the-matter with Thord and said, to him appeared that counsel decent.	Now Gunnar came to the matter with Thord and said to him that it appeared to be good counsel.
Þórðr svarar:	Thord answered:	Thord answered:
"Hví skaltu eigi gefa honum dóttur þína, ef þér líkar?"	"Why shall-you not to-give him daughter yours, if you like?"	"Then why not give him your daughter if you like?"
Gunnarr svarar:	Gunnar answered:	Gunnar answered:
"Því at eins gef ek hana, at þat sé jafnvel þinn vili sem minn".	"Because to one give I her to that being equal-good your will as mine".	"Because I will give her if your will is as good as mine".
Þórðr kvað beggja þeira ráð þetta vera skyldu.	Thord said both theirs counsel that being would.	Thord said that both of them agreed that this was a duty.
"Ek vil",	"I wish",	"I will",
sagði Gunnarr, "at þú, Þórðr, fastnir Hersteini konuna".	said Gunnar, "that you, Thord, betrothe Herstein a-wife".	said Gunnar, "that you, Thord, betrothe Herstein a wife".
Þórðr svarar:	Thord answered:	Thord answered:
"Sjálfr skaltu þat gera at fastna dóttur þína".	"Self shall-you that do to betrothe daughter yours".	"You yourself shall betrothe your own daughter".
Gunnarr svarar:	Gunnar answered:	Gunnar answered:
"Mér þykkir meiri virðing í, at þú fastnir hana, því at þat samir betr".	"To-me seems more worthy to, that you betrothe her, because to that same better".	"It seems to me more worthy that you to betrothe her because it will be better".
Þórðr lét nú þetta leiðast, ok fóru nú festar fram.	Thord had now that lay, and went now fixed from.	Now Thord let it lie and it was fixed upon.
Þá mælti Gunnarr:	Then spoke Gunnar:	Then Gunnar spoke:

The Saga of Hen-Thorir (Old Norse)

Old Norse	Literal	English
"Bið ek enn, at þú látir hér vera boðit í Hvammi, ok mun þá gert verða með mestri sæmð".	"Ask I but, to you let here being the-wedding in Hvamm, and should then done worthy with the-most honour".	"But I ask, that you let the wedding me here in Hvamm, and then it should be done worthily with the most honour".
Þórðr bað hann því ok ráða, ef honum þætti svá betr.	Thord bid him accordingly and advised, if he seemed so better.	Thord agreed with him accordingly and was advised that it seemed better.
Gunnarr segir:	Gunnar said:	Gunnar said:
"Svá munum vér til ætla, at vér látim þegar vera á viku fresti".	"So should we to intend, to we let from-there being one week from-now".	"So we should intend to it, that we have from there being one week from now".
Eftir þat stíga þeir á bak ok snúa á ferð, ok víkr Þórðr á götu með þeim ok spurði enn, ef nökkut væri nýtt at segja.	After that mounted their on back and turned to travelled, and week Thord and the-path with them and asked but, if any was new to say.	After that they mounted on horseback and turned on their way, and Thord turned to the path with them and asked again if there was any news.
Gunnarr svarar:	Gunnar answered:	Gunnar answered:
"Ekki höfum vér nú nýligar frétt en brennu Blund-Ketills bónda".	"Not have we now new news but the-burning Blund-Ketill the-farmer".	"We do not have any news newer than the burning of Blund-Ketill the farmer".
Þórðr spurði, hversu þat varð.	Thord asked, how-so that became.	Thord asked how it had happened.
En Gunnarr sagði allan atburðinn um brennuna ok hverr henni olli ok svá, hverir þat gerðu.	But Gunnar said all at-carried about the-burning and who he that-caused and so, who that did.	Then Gunnar told the whole story about the fire and who caused it and who did it.
Þórðr mælti:	Thord spoke:	Thord spoke:
"Eigi myndi þessu gjaforði svá skjótt ráðit hafa verit, ef ek hefða þetta vitat, ok þykkizt þér nú allmjök hafa komizt fyrir mik í viti ok beittan brögðum í þessu.	"Not should this reserved so quickly advised had been, if I have that known, and seems to-you now all-much have come for me in wit and cunning strategy in this.	"This would not have been possible with such a quick decision if I had known about it, and now you're pretty sure you've outsmarted me and used cunning strategy in this.
En þó þykkir mér eigi víst, at þér séð yðr einhlítir at þessu máli".	But though seems to-me not certain, to you see-you your sufficient to this the-matter".	But even so, I don't think you are of one mind on this matter".
Gunnarr mælti:	Gunnar spoke:	Gunnar spoke:

The Saga of Hen-Thorir (Old Norse)

Old Norse	Literal	English
"Þar er gott til trausts at ætla sem þú ert, enda er þér nú skylt at veita mági þínum, en vér erum skyldir at veita þér, því at margir heyrðu, at þú fastnaðir konuna ok þetta var allt við þitt ráð gert,	"There is good to trust to suppose as you are, concluded are you now should to grant son-in-law yours, but we are obliged to grant to-you, because to many heard, that you betrothed the-woman and that was all with your consent done,	"There is good for trust to believe in you, since you are now obliged to provide for your son-in-law, and we are obliged to provide for you, because many people heard that you caught the woman and this was all arranged by you,
ok er nú vel, at þér reynið eitt sinn, hverr yðar drjúgastr er höfðingjanna, því at þér hafið lengi úlfsmunni af etizt".	and as now well, to to-you test one they, who your greatly are chieftain, because to to-you have long wolves mouth of".	and now it is good that you try for once which of you is the best of the chieftains, because you have had a wolf's mouth for eating for a long time".

12

Nú skiljast þeir, ok er Þórðr inn reiðasti, ok þykkir honum þeir hafa gabbat sik.	Now parted they, and was Thord the most-angry, and seemed him they have fooled him.	Now they parted and Thord was angry as could be, and it seemed that they had fooled him.
En þeir ríða nú fyrst á Gunnarsstaði ok þykkjast allvel leikit hafa, at þeir höfðu komit Þórði í málit með sér, ok váru nú allkátir.	But they rode now first to Gunnarsstadir and considered all-well played have, that they had come Thord to the-matter with his, and were now merry.	But they now rode first to Gunnarsstadir and thought that they had played their hand very well in bringing Thord into the matter and they were now merry.
Eigi ríða þeir nú suðr at sinni, en bjóða mönnum til boðs ok sækja í Hvammi at ákveðnum tíma.	Not rode they now south to they but invited men to the-wedding and sought to Hvamm to certain time.	They did not ride to the south, but they invited men to the wedding and returned to Hvamm at the appointed time.
Hafði Þórðr þar margt fyrirboðsmanna ok skipar mönnum í sæti um kveldit.	Had Thord there many invited-people and ordered people in seated about evening.	Thord had many invited people there and ordered them to their seats in the evening.
Sat hann sjálfr á annan bekk ok Gunnarr, mágr hans, ok hans menn, en Þorkell trefill hjá brúðguma á annan bekk ok þeira boðsmenn.	Sat he himself on opposite bench and Gunnar, son-in-law his, and his men, and Thorkel Trefill beside bridegroom on opposite bench and theirs invited-people.	He himself sat on the second bench, and his brother-in-law Gunnar and his men, while Thorkell Trefill with the groom on the second bench and their attendants.
Brúðir skipuðu pall.	The-bride appointed platform.	The bride was on the appointed platform.

The Saga of Hen-Thorir (Old Norse)

Old Norse	Literal	English
Ok svá sem borð váru sett ok allir menn í sæti komnir, þá stökk Hersteinn brúðgumi fram yfir borðit ok gengr þar at, sem einn steinn stóð.	And so when the-tables were set and all people in seats came, then sprang Herstein the-bridegroom from over the-tables and going there that, as one stone stood.	And when the tables were set and all the people came to their seats, Herstein the bridegroom strode over the tables and went to where a stone stood.
Hann steig öðrum fæti upp á steininn ok mælti:	He stepped other foot up of the-stone and spoke:	He stepped one foot up on the stone and spoke:
"Þess strengi ek heit",	"This binding I pledge",	"This binding I pledge",
sagði hann, "at áðr alþingi er úti í sumar, skal ek hafa fullsekðat Arngrím goða eða sjálfdæmi ella".	said he, "that before the-assembly is out this summer, shall I have fully-outlawed Arngrim the-chieftain or self-judgement otherwise".	he said, "that before the assembly is finished this summer, I shall have Arngrim the chieftain fully outlawed, or the right to make my own judgement".
Síðan stígr hann í sæti sitt.	Then climbed he in seat his.	Then he climbed to his seat.
Gunnarr stökk þá fram ok mælti:	Gunnar sprang then from and spoke:	Gunnar then sprang up and spoke:
"Þess strengi ek heit",	"This binding I pledge",	"This binding I pledge",
sagði hann, "at áðr alþingi er úti í sumar, skal ek hafa sótt til útlegðar Þorvald Oddsson eða hafa sjálfdæmi ella".	said he, "that before the-assembly is out this summer, shall I have sought to outlawry Thorvald son-of-Odd or have self-judgement otherwise".	he said, "that before the assembly is finished this summer I shall have sought outlawry for Thorvald son of Odd, or have self-judgement".
Upp stígr hann undir borð ok mælti til Þórðar:	Up climbed he under the-table and spoke to Thord:	He climbed back under the table and spoke to Thord:
"Hví sitr þú, Þórðr, ok mælir eigi um?	"Why sit you, Thord, and speak not about?	"Why do you sit Thord and no speak out?
Vitum vér, at slíkt er þér í hug sem oss".	Know we, that such is to-you in thought as us".	We know that you have the same thought as us".
Þórðr svarar:	Thord answered:	Thord answered:
"Kyrrt mun þat at sinni".	"Peace should that that yours".	"It should be still in mind".
Gunnarr svarar:	Gunnar answered:	Gunnar answered:

The Saga of Hen-Thorir (Old Norse)

Old Norse	Literal	English
"Ef þú vill, at vér talim fyrir þik, þá er þat til reiðu,	"If you wish, that we talk for you, then is that to readily,	"If you wish that we talk for you, then that can readily be done".
en vitum vér, at þú ætlar þér Tungu-Odd".	and know we, that you intend you Tungu-Odd".	But we know what you intend for Tungu-Odd".
Þórðr mælti:	Thord spoke:	Thord spoke:
"Þér skuluð ráða yðrum ummælum, en ek mun því ráða, hvat ek tala.	"You should rule your about-the-matter, and I should therefore rule, what I told.	"You should settle your announcements, and I will decide what I say.
Endið þetta vel, sem þér hafið um mælt".	End that well, as you have about said".	End it well, what you have said about".
Eigi var til nýlundu fleira at boðinu, en þó fór þat allsköruliga fram, ok er þat þraut, fór hverr, sem fyrir lá,	Not was to news more than the-wedding but though went that all-clear from and was that away went each as before laying.	There was no more news of the wedding, except that it went well from then on, and when it was over, each went as they had been before.
ok líðr vetrinn af hendi.	and passed the-winter of hand.	And the winter passed on.
Ok er várar safna þeir at sér mönnum ok fara suðr til Borgarfjarðar ok koma í Norðrtungu ok stefna Arngrími til þings í Þingnes ok Hænsa-Þóri.	And when spring raised they to his men and went south to Borgafjord and came to North-Tongue and summoned Arngrim to the-assembly in Assembly-headland and Hen-Thorir.	And when spring came, they gathered their men and went south to Borgarfjord and came to North-Tongue and summoned Arngrim to the assembly at Thingnes along with Hen-Thorir.
Nú skilst Hersteinn frá liðinu með þrem tigum manna, þangat sem hann sagði inn síðasta náttstað verit hafa Þorvalds Oddssonar, því at hann var þá farinn af vist sinni.	Now parted Herstein from the-company with three tens men, from-there as he said the last night-quarters been have Thorvald's son-of-Odd, because that he was then travelling of hospitality his.	Now Herstein separated from the company with thirty men to where he said that the last night's lodgings had been Thorvald Oddsson's, because he had then left his place.
Nú er ókyrrt í heraðinu ok mikil umræða ok samandráttr liðs af hvárratveggja hendi.	Now is un-quiet in the-district and much about-discussion and gathering company of each-way arms.	Now there was unquiet in the district and much discussion about and gathering of companies to arms on either side.

The Saga of Hen-Thorir (Old Norse)

Old Norse	Literal	English
13	**13**	**13**
Þat varð til tíðenda, at Hænsa-Þórir hvarf brott ór heraðinu við tólfta mann, þegar hann spurði, hverir í málit váru komnir, ok fréttist alls ekki til hans.	That was to the-news, to Hen-Thorir disappeared away from the-district with twelve men, from-there he learned, each in the-matter were come, and enquired all not to his.	It was news that Hen-Thorir disappeared away from the district with twelve men, as soon as he learned who were coming to the case, and no one could find out anything about him.
Oddr safnar nú liði um dalina, Reykjardal hvárntveggja ok Skorradal, ok um allar sveitir fyrir sunnan Hvítá, ok þó hafði hann margt ór öðrum sveitum.	Odd gathered now company about the-valleys, Reykjardal either-way and Skorradal, and about all areas for the-south Hvita and though had he many about other countryside.	Now Odd gathered a company from either side of the valleys, Reyjardal and Skorradal, and all about the areas south of Hvita and also many others in the countryside.
Arngrímr goði safnaði mönnum um Þverárhlíð ok Norðrárdal at sumum hluta.	Arngrim chieftain collected men about Þverarhlíd and Norduradal to some parts.	Arngrim the chieftain gathered men around some parts of Thverarhlid and Norduradal.
Þorkell trefill safnaði mönnum it neðra um Mýrar ok Stafholtstungur, ok suma Norðrdæla hefir hann með sér, því at Helgi, bróðir hans, bjó í Hvammi, ok hefir hann hann með sér.	Thorkel Trefill gathered men then lower about Myrar and Stafholtstunga, and some Norðurdæla had he with him, because that Helgi, brother his, lived in Hvamm, and had he he with him.	Thorkel Trefill then gathered men around lower Myrar and Stafholtstunga and had some in Norduradal with him because his brother Helgi lived in Hvamm and he was with him.
Nú safnar Þórðr gellir liði vestan ok hefir eigi margt lið.	Now gathered Thord Gellir company west and had not many company.	Now Thord Gellir gathered a company in the west, but not a large company.
Hittast nú þessir allir, er í váru málinu, ok hafa alls tvau hundruð manna, ríða nú ofan fyrir útan Norðrá ok yfir á at Eyjavati fyrir ofan Stafholt ok ætla yfir Hvítá, þar sem heitir Þrælastraumr.	Met now these all, are in were this-case, and had all two hundred men, rode now over for outside Norðura and over about to Eyjavaði before above Stafholt and suppose over White-water, there as was-named Thraelastraum.	Now all who were involved in this case met, and had two hundred men in all, and they rode over outside Nordura and over to Eyjavadi above Stafholt, intending to cross over Hvita at a place named Thraelastraum.
Þá sjá þeir mannaferð mikla fyrir sunnan ána.	Then see there journey-of-men much before from-the-south river.	They they saw the journey of a great body of men from the south river.
Er þar Tungu-Oddr ok nær fjögur hundruð manna,	Were there Tungu-Odd and nearly four hundreds people,	Tungu-Odd was there with nearly four hundred people.

The Saga of Hen-Thorir (Old Norse)

Old Norse	Literal	English
gæða nú ferðina ok vilja fyrr koma til vaðsins,	increased now travelling and wish before come to wading-water,	They increased their travelling and wished to come to the water first.
hittast nú við ána, ok hlaupa þeir Oddr af baki ok verja vaðit, en þeim Þórði gengr ógreitt framreiðin ok vildu gjarna komast á þingit.	meet now with river, and ran there Odd off horseback and guarded the-ford, that they Thord went obstructed riding-on and wished willingly to-come to the-assembly.	They now met at the river, and Odd's men leapt from horseback and guarded the ford so that Thord and his men were obstructed from riding on, though they wished to come to the assembly.
Slær nú í bardaga, ok verða þegar áverkar.	Struck now in battle, and become from-there injuries.	Now there was a battle, and injuries came from it.
Fellu fjórir menn af Þórði.	Fell many men of Thord.	Many of Thord's men fell.
Þar fell Þórólfr refr, bróðir Álfs ór Dölum, virðuligr maðr, ok hverfa nú frá við svá búit.	There fell Thorolf Refur, brother-of Alf of Dölum, worthy man, and turned-back now from with so done.	There fel Thorolf Refur, the brother of Alf of Dolum, a worthy man, and when this was done they turned back.
Einn maðr féll af Oddi, en þrír urðu mjök sárir.	One man fell of Odd, but three became much wounded.	One of Odd's men fell, and three became much wounded.
Þórðr snýr nú málinu til alþingis.	Thord turned now this-case to the-assembly.	Thord turned this case over to the national assembly.
Þeir ríða nú heim vestr, ok þykkir mönnum mjök hallazt hafa metorð vestanmanna.	They rode now home west, and seemed men much slanted had reputation the-western-men.	Now they rode west to home, and the men from the west seemed to have had their reputation slanted.
Nú ríðr Oddr á þingit.	Now rode Odd to the-assembly.	Now Odd rode to the assembly.
Hann sendi heim þræla sína með hross.	He sent home servants his with horses.	He sent his servants home with horses.
Jórunn, kona hans, spurði tíðenda er þeir kómu heim.	Jorunn, wife his, asked the-news when they came home.	Jorunn his wife asked for news when they came home.
Þeir kváðust engi segja kunna önnur en þau, at sá maðr var einn kominn vestan ór Breiðafirði, at svara kunni Tungu-Oddi, ok var hans hljómr ok rödd sem griðungr gelldi.	They said nothing to-say could other-than that they, to saw man was one come west about Breidafjord, to answer could Tungu-Odd, and was his sound and voice as a-bull bellowing.	They said that there was nothing that they could say other than that they saw a man who had come from the west around Breidafjord who could answer Tungu-Odd "and his sound and voice was like that of a bull bellowing".

The Saga of Hen-Thorir (Old Norse)

Old Norse	Literal	English
Hon kvað þat engi tíðendi, þótt honum væri svarat sem öðrum manni, en kvað þó þat hafa gerzt at tíðendum, at eigi væri líkligra til.	She said that no news, thought he was answered as other men, but spoke though that have done to news, to not was likely to.	She said that this was not news even though he was answered as other men, but said that this news was not very likely.
"Var þar ok bardagi",	"Was there also a-battle",	"There was also a battle",
sögðu þeir, "ok fellu fimm menn alls, en margir urðu sárir".	said they, "and fell five men in all, but many became wounded".	they said, "and five men fell in all but many became wounded".
En áðr gátu þeir þess at engu.	But before got they this to nothing.	But before they got nothing of this.
Nú líðr þingit, ok verðr þar eigi til tíðenda.	Now passed the-assembly, and became there not to the-news.	Now the assembly passed and there came no news.
En er þeir mágar koma heim vestr, skipta þeir bústöðum,	But when they father-and-son came home west, exchanged they residences,	But when the father and son came home to the west, they exchanged residences.
ferr Gunnarr í Örnólfsdal, en Hersteinn tekr Gunnarsstaði.	went Gunnar to Ornolfsdal, but Herstein took Gunnarsstað.	Gunnar went to Ornolfsdal, but Herstein took Gunnarsstadir.
Eftir þetta lætr Gunnarr færa til sín vestan við þann allan, sem Örn austmaðr hafði átt, ok flytja heim í Örnólfsdal.	After that had Gunnar brought to him west wood that all, which Orn the-eastern-man had owned, and carried home to Ornolfsdal.	After that Gunnar had all of the wood which Orn the Easterner had owned brought to him and carried home to Ornolfsdal.
Tekr hann til síðan ok húsar upp bæinn í annat sinn, því at Gunnarr var allra manna hagastr.	Took he to then and house-built up dwellings about another he, because that Gunnar was all man the-best.	He then took building up the dwellings about him, because Gunnar was the best of all men.
Hann var ok um allt atgervismaðr ok manna bezt vígr ok inn vaskasti í öllu.	He was and about all dynamic-man and people the-best spear-man and the boldest of all.	He was dynamic in all ways, and was the best with a spear, and the boldest of all.

14

Nú líða stundir fram allt til þess, at menn ríða til þings.	Now passed awhile from all to this, that men rode to the-assembly.	Now a while passed from all this until the men rode to the assembly.

The Saga of Hen-Thorir (Old Norse)

Old Norse	Literal	English
Er nú mikill viðbúnaðr í heruðunum.	Was now much preparation among the-districts.	There was now much preparation among the districts.
Ríða nú hvárirtveggju ákafa fjölmennir.	Ride now each-side eager crowd.	There now rode an eager crowd on either side.
Ok er þeir Þórðr gellir koma á Gunnarsstaði, er Hersteinn sjúkr ok má eigi fara til þings.	And when they Thord Gellir came to Gunnarsstað, was Herstein sick and may not travel to the-assembly.	And when Thord Gellir and his men came to Gunnarsstadir, Herstein was sick and unable to travel to the assembly.
Selr hann nú öðrum í hendr sakirnar.	Sold he now other in hand the-sake.	He handed over his part in the lawsuits.
Eftir váru hjá honum þrír tigir manna.	After were beside him three tens men.	Thirty men stayed behind beside him.
Nú ríðr Þórðr til þings.	Now rode Thord to the-assembly.	Now Thord rode to the assembly.
Hann safnar at sér vinum sínum ok frændum ok kemr snemma til þings,	He gathered that him friends his and kinsmen and came early to the-assembly,	He gathered his friends and kinsmen and soon came to the assembly.
en þingit var þá undir Ármannsfelli.	but the-assembly was then from Armannsfell.	But the assembly was then held from Armannsfell.
Ok svá sem flokkar koma, hefir Þórðr liðsdrátt mikinn.	And so as groups come, had Thord assembling-troops greatly.	And as the groups arrived, Thord had a great assembling of troops.
Nú er sén ferð Tungu-Odds.	Now was seen travelled Tungu-odd's.	Now when Tungu-Odd's company was seen travelling.
Ríðr Þórðr þá í mót honum ok vill eigi, at hann nái þinghelginni.	Riding Thord then in meeting him and willed not that he got-to the-assembly.	Then Thord rode to meet him and wished that he did not get to the sanctuary of the assembly.
Oddr ríðr með þrjú hundruð manna.	Odd rode with three hundred men.	Odd rode with three hundred men.
Þeir Þórðr verja þingit, ok slær þá þegar í bardaga.	They Thord blocked the-assembly and struck then from-there in battle.	Thord and his men blocked the assembly and then struck them in battle.
Tekst brátt mannfall, en allmargir urðu sárir.	Take soon men-fallen, and all-many became wounded.	Soon men were taken and fell, and many became wounded.

The Saga of Hen-Thorir (Old Norse)

Old Norse	Literal	English
Þar fellu sex menn af Oddi, því at Þórðr var miklu fjölmennari.	There fell six men of Odd, because that Thord was great following-men.	Six of Odd's men fell there, because Thord had a great following of men.
Þetta sjá góðgjarnir menn, at þau vandræði myndi af standa, ef þingheimrinn berðist, at seint myndi bætr bíða.	That saw benevolent men that they difficulty would of withstand if the-asembly fought to late should reconciliation bid.	Benevolent men then saw that there would be difficulty to withstand if the assembly fought, so they asked for a reconciliation.
Er þá gengit í milli, ok verða skildir, ok snúit málum til sættar, ok var Oddr ofrliði borinn ok varð undan at láta, fyrir því at bæði var, at hann þótti þyngra málahlut eiga at flytja, enda varð hann aflvani fyrir liðs sakar.	Was then went to between and became shields and turned matters to settle and was Odd outnumbered bore and became give-way to allow for because to both was to he seemed heavy case-load had to carry conclude became he overpowered for the-company sake.	Then they came to an agreement, then the shields were turned, and things were settled, and Odd was overmatched and had to give in, because both of them thought he had a more difficult case to deal with, and he became overpowered for the sake of the company against him.
Var þá þat mælt, at Oddr myndi tjalda á brottu ór þinghelgi, en ganga til dóma ok at nauðsynjum sínum, fara með sik spakliga, sýna enga þrjózku né hans menn.	Was then that spoke to Odd should tent in away about the-assembly but going to the-court and to necessities his, went with himself heavily, show no belligerance not his men.	It was then declared that Odd should set his tent away from the assembly, but go about his business in the court, this went heavily with him, and he was to show no belligerence nor were any of his men.
Sitja menn nú yfir málum ok leita at sætta þá.	Sat men now over the-matter and let to settle then.	Men now sat over the matter and had to settle it then.
[Þórðr gellir talaði þá langa tölu ok snjalla at Lögbergi ok tjáði þat, hversu illa at mönnum gegndi þat at fara í ókunnig þing at sækja um víg eða harma sinna at reka, ok sagði nú, hversu mikit at honum varð fyrir, áðr hann gat þessu máli til skila komit, ok kvað mörgum manni mein mundu at verða þessu vandræði, ef eigi væri bætr á ráðnar,	[Thord Gellir said then long told and ingeniously that Law-Mountain and expressed that, how-so ill that men might that it go in unknown assembly that sought about slaying or regret his that driven, and said now, how-so much that him became before, already he got this the-matter to return coming, and spoke many people injury would that become this trouble, if not was compensated of ruling,	[Thord Gellir then spoke a long and clever speech to Lögberg and expressed how bad it was for men to go to an unfamiliar assembly to ask for a battle or to carry out their grievances, and now said how much had happened to him before he could this matter came to an end, and he said that many people would be hurt by this trouble, if things were not improved,
"fyrir því",	"before therefore",	"before therefore",

The Saga of Hen-Thorir (Old Norse)

Old Norse	Literal	English
sagði hann, "at hér til hafa þat lög verit, at sakar skal sækja á því þingi, er næst er vetfanginu".	said he, "that here to to-have that law been, that sake shall seek of therefore the-assembly, that nearest was known-to-hand".	he said, "that until now it has been the law that cases should be brought to the nearest assembly".
En þá er landinu var skipt í fjórðunga, var svá skipat, at þrjú váru þing í fjórðungi hverjum, nema í Norðlendingafjórðungi váru fjögur ok því svá, at þeir urðu eigi á annat sáttir.	And then was the-land was shared in quarters, was so exchanged, that three were assembly in the-fourth everyone, except in Northern-Quarter were four and therefore so, that there became not of another settled.	But when the country was divided into quarters, it was arranged in such a way that there were three assemblies in each quarter, except in the Northern Quarter where there were four, and so they were not satisfied with anything else.
Þeir, er váru fyrir norðan Eyjafjörð, vildu eigi þangat sækja þing, enda eigi í Skagafjörð, þeir er fyrir vestan váru.	There, where was before north Eyjafjord, wished not from-there sought the-assembly, end not in Skagafjord, there was before the-west was.	Those who were to the north of Eyjafjörður did not want to attend the assembly there, because they were not in Skagafjörður, they were to the west.
En þó skyldi jafnan dóm nefna á alþingi ór þeira fjórðungi sem ór einhverjum öðrum.	But though should equally deemed mention in the-assembly for there quarter as for each other.	However, even so, a judgment should be mentioned in the Althing for that quarter that belonged to someone else.
Af því skal einn maðr þaðan sitja fyrir forráðsgoðorð, at þeir goðar vildu allir setit hafa.	Of therefore shall one man from-there sit before custody-chieftain, that there chieftains wished all settled to-have.	Therefore, one person from there shall sit for guardianship, that the good people all wanted to have a seat.
En síðan váru sett fjórðungsþing.	And then were set quarter-assembly.	But then quarterly meetings were held.
Svá sagði mér Úlfhéðinn Gunnarsson.	So said to-me Ulfhedin son-of-Gunnar.	So it was told to me by Ulfhedinn Gunnarsson.
Nú er setit at málunum],	Now was settled that matter],	Now that matter was settled],
ok horfir Oddi þungliga fyrir þat mest, at mikit ofrefli var í móti.	and looked Odd heavily for that most, to much overwhelming was in meeting.	and Oddi regretted the fact that there was a lot of overreaction in the meeting.

The Saga of Hen-Thorir (Old Norse)

Old Norse	Literal	English
# 15	# 15	# 15
En nú skal segja nökkut af Hersteini, at honum létti brátt sóttarinnar, er þeir riðu til þingsins.	But now shall say some of Herstein, to him left soon sickness, when they rode to the-assembly.	But new shall be told something of Herstein, that he was soon be relieved of his illness, when they rode to the parliament.
Ferr hann þá í Örnólfsdal.	Went he then to Ornolfsdal.	He then went to Ornolfsdal.
Þat var einn morgin snemma, at hann var í smiðju, því at hann var manna hagastr á járn.	That was one morning soon, that he was in workshop, because that he was people the-best at iron.	It was early one morning, that he was in the smithery, because he was the best of all people at smithing.
Þá kemr þar bóndi einn, sá er Örnólfr hét, ok sagði svá:	Then came there the-farmer one, saw was Ornolf named, and said so:	Then a farmer came there, whose name was Ornolfr, and said so:
"Sjúk er kýr mín",	"Sick is cow mine",	"My cow is sick",
sagði hann, "ok bið ek þik, Hersteinn, at þú farir at sjá hana.	said he, "and ask I you, Herstein, that you travel and see her.	he said, "and I ask you, Herstein, that you travel and see her.
Þykkir oss nú gott, at þú ert aftr kominn, ok höfum vér þá nökkut svá iðgjöld föður þíns, er oss varð at mestu gagni".	Seemed us now good, that you are returned come, and have we then some so recompensed father yours, that us became to most useful".	It seems good to us that you are back, and we have some of your father's compensation, which was of great use to us".
Hersteinn svarar:	Herstein answered:	Herstein answered:
"Eigi hirði ek um kú þína, ok kann ek eigi at sjá, hvat henni er til meins".	"Not shepherd I about cow yours, and can I not to see, what her is to harm".	I am not a shepherd for your cow, and I can not see, what is her harm".
Bóndi svarar:	The-farmer answered:	The farmer answered:
"Mikill er þó munr, at faðir þinn gaf mér kúna, en þú vill eigi sjá hana".	"Much is though difference, that father your given to-me the-cow, but you will not see her".	"There is much difference, than the cow your father gave me, but you will not see her".
Hersteinn svarar:	Herstein answered:	Herstein answered:
"Ek gef þér aðra kú, ef þessi deyr".	"I give to-you another cow, if this-one dies".	"I will give you another cow if this one dies".

The Saga of Hen-Thorir (Old Norse)

Old Norse	Literal	English
Bóndi svarar:	The-farmer answered:	The farmer answered:
"Þat vil ek fyrst þiggja, at þú sjáir þessa".	"That will I first receive, to you see this-one".	"The first that I wish to receive is that you see this one".
Hersteinn sprettr þá upp ok verðr hermt við ok gengr út ok bóndinn með honum, snúa síðan í veg til skógar.	Herstein sprang then up and became angry with and went out and the-farmer with him, turned then the way to the-woods.	Herstein then sprang up and became angry at this, and walked out of the smith and the farmer went with him, turned away and went to the woods.
Liggr þar ein sneiðigata ok skógrinn á tvær hendr.	Lying there along the-path and forests on two hands.	Lying there along the path there were forests on either side.
Ok er Hersteinn ferr klifgötuna, nemr hann staðar.	And when Herstein went cliff-path, took he to-stand.	And when Herstein went to the cliff-path, he came to a stand.
Hann var allra manna skyggnstr.	He was of-all people keen-eyed.	He was the keenest eyed of all people.
Hann mælti þá:	He spoke then:	He then spoke:
"Kom þar fram skjöldr í skóginum".	"Come there from the-shield in the-woods".	"Come there from behind the shield in the woods".
Bóndi þagði.	The-farmer silent.	The farmer remained silent.
Hersteinn mælti:	Herstein spoke:	Herstein spoke:
"Hefir þú svikit mik, hundrinn þinn?	"Have you betrayed me, mongrel you?	"Have you betrayed me, you mongrel?
Nú ef þú ert í nökkurum særum at leyna, þá leggst þú niðr í götuna ok tala eigi orð,	Now if you are in somewhat wounded to hiding, then lay you down on the-path and speak not words,	Now if you have some wounds to hide, then you lie down on the path and don't speak a word,
en ef þú gerir eigi þetta, þá mun ek drepa þik".	but if you do not that, then shall I kill you".	and if you do not, then I shall kill you".
Bóndinn leggst þá niðr, en Hersteinn snýr heim ok kallar á menn sína.	The-farmer laid then down, then Herstein turned home and called to men his.	The farmer then laid down, then Herstein turned home and called to his men.
Þeir taka vápn sín ok fara þegar í skóginn ok finna Örnólf í götunni.	They took weapons theirs and went from-there to the-woods and found Ornolf on the-path.	They took their weapons and immediately went to the forest and found Ornolf on the path.

The Saga of Hen-Thorir (Old Norse)

Old Norse	Literal	English
Þeir biðja hann fara með sér þangat, sem mælt var, at þeir skyldu finnast.	They bid him to-go with them from-there, as said was, to they should meet.	They asked him to go with them from there, where it was said, that they should meet.
Nú fara þeir, þar til er þeir koma í eitt rjóðr.	Now went they, there to where they came to a clearing.	Now they went to where they came to a clearing.
Þá mælti Hersteinn til Örnólfs:	Then spoke Herstein to Ornolf:	Then Herstein spoke to Ornolf:
"Eigi vil ek skylda þik til at tala, en far nú sem fyrir þik var lagit".	"Not will I should you to to speak, but go now as for you were laying".	"I don't want to oblige you to talk, but go now as was arranged for you".
Bóndi hleypr þá upp á hól einn ok blístrar hátt.	The-farmer leapt then up on the-hill one and whistled loudly.	The farmer then ran up the hill alone and whistled loudly.
Síðan hlaupa þar fram tólf menn, ok var þar Hænsa-Þórir fyrir flokki,	Then ran there from twelve men, and was there Hen-Thorir before the-flock,	Then twelve men ran forward there, and Hen-Thorir was there in front of the group,
en þeir Hersteinn taka þessa menn höndum ok drepa.	but they Herstein took these men in-hand and death.	but then Herstein and his men took these man in hand and killed them.
Höggr Hersteinn sjálfr höfuð af Þóri ok hefir með sér, ríða nú síðan suðr til þings ok segja þar þessi tíðendi.	Struck Herstein himself head of Thorir and had with him, rode now then south to the-assembly and say there these tidings.	It was Herstein himself who struck the head off Thorir and took it with him, they now rode to the assembly and told them of this news.
Verðr Hersteinn ágætr mjök af þessu verki ok fær af virðing mikla, sem ván var at.	Became Herstein honoured much of this work and accomplishment of worthiness great, as expected was to.	Herstein became very much honoured for his work, and accomplishment of great worthiness, as was expected.
Nú er setið yfir málum manna, ok verða þær málalyktir, at Arngrímr goði verðr sekr fullri sekð ok allir þeir, er at brennunni váru, nema Þorvaldr Oddsson,	Now was settled over the-matter people, and became there concluded, to Arngrim the-chieftain became outlawed fully well and all they, who at the-burning were, taken Thorvald son-of-Odd,	Now the cases of the men were being discussed, and they concluded that Arngrím the chieftain would be fully outlawed and all those who were at the burning, except Thorvald Oddson,
hann skyldi vera útan þrjá vetr ok eiga þá útkvæmt.	he should being outside three winters and have then out-freed.	he should go out of the land for three winters and then be free.
Gefit var fé fyrir hann ok svá til farningar öðrum mönnum.	Given was money for him and so to the-faring other men.	Money was given for him and to the faring of other men.

The Saga of Hen-Thorir (Old Norse)

Old Norse	Literal	English
Þorvaldr fór útan um sumarit ok var leiddr upp á Skotlandi ok þjáðr þar.	Thorvald went abroad about summer and was led up to Scotland and enthralled there.	Thorvald went abroad about summer and was led up to Scotland and was enslaved there.
Nú eftir þetta var slitit þinginu, ok þykkir mönnum Þórðr vel ok sköruliga hafa fylgt þessum málum.	Now after that was settled the-assembly, and thought men Thord well and boldly have followed this matter.	Now after that the assembly was settled, and men thought that Thord had followed the matter boldly and well.
Arngrímr goði fór ok útan um sumarit, ok er þat eigi á kveðit, hversu mikit fé goldit var.	Arngrim the-chieftain went and abroad about summer, and was that not not spoken, how-so much wealth paid was.	Arngrim the chieftain went abroad about summer, and it was not spoken about how much wealth was paid over.
Lýkr á þá leið þessum málum.	Ended so then passed this matter.	And so the matter passed and was ended.
Ríða menn síðan heim af þingi, en þeir fara útan, svá sem mælt var, er sekir váru.	Rode men then home from the-assembly, and those journeying out, so as spoken were, who outlawed were.	Men then rode home from the assembly, and those journeying out, who were outlawed.

16

Gunnarr Hlífarson sitr nú í Örnólfsdal ok hefir húsat vel.	Gunnar son-of-Hlifar sat now at Ornolfsdal and had housed well.	Gunnar son of Hlifar settled now at Ornolfsdal and house himself well.
Hann hafði selför, ok var mannfátt heima.	He had cattle-keeping, and was lack-of-people at-home.	He had cattle keeping, and there were few people at home.
Jófríðr, dóttir Gunnars, átti sér tjald úti, því at henni þótti þat ódaufligra.	Jofrid, daughter Gunnar's, had herself a-tent outside, because to her thought that less-dreary.	Jofrid, Gunnar's daughter, had herself a tent outside, because she found this less dull.
Einn dag berr svá til, at Þóroddr, sonr Tungu-Odds, ríðr í Þverárhlíð.	One day befell so to, that Thorodd, son-of Tungu-Odd, rode to Þverarhlíð.	One day it happened, that Thorodd, son of Tungu-Odd, rode to Thverarhlid.
Hann kemr at Örnólfsdal um farinn veg ok gengr inn í tjaldit til Jófríðar.	He came to Ornolfsdal about travelling way and went in to tent to Jofrid.	He came to Ornolfsdal while travelling on his way and went in to Jofrid's tent.
Hon heilsar honum vel.	She greeted him well.	She greeted him well.

The Saga of Hen-Thorir (Old Norse)

Old Norse	Literal	English
Hann sezt niðr hjá henni, ok taka þau tal sín á milli, ok í því kemr sveinn frá selinu ok biðr Jófríði taka ofan klyfjar með sér.	He sat down beside her, and took they talking theirs in between, and so because came a-boy from mountain-pasture and asked Jofrid take off pack-loads with him.	He sat down beside her, and they took to talking together, when there came a boy from the mountain pasture, who asked Jofrid to help unpack the horses with him.
Þóroddr ferr til ok tekr ofan klyfjarnar, en sveinninn ferr síðan á brott ok kemr til sels.	Thorodd went to and took above pack-loads, but the-boy went then to away and came to summer-pasture.	Thorodd went with him to unload the packs, but the boy then went away and came to the summer pasture.
Gunnarr spyrr, hví honum yrði nú svá fljótt.	Gunnar asked, how he could now so quickly.	Gunnar asked him how he had done it so quickly.
Hann svarar engu.	He answered nothing.	He did not answer.
Gunnarr spurði:	Gunnar asked:	Gunnar asked:
"Sástu nökkut til tíðenda?"	"Saw-you anything to news?"	"Did you see anything of news?"
"Alls eigi",	"All not",	"Not at all",
kvað sveinninn.	spoke the-boy.	said the boy.
"Nei",	"No",	"No",
sagði Gunnarr, "þannig ertu í bragði sem nökkut hafi þér fyrir augu borit, þat sem þér þykkir umræðu vert, ok seg mér, ef svá er,	said Gunnar, "that-way are-you you looking as something have you for eyes bear, that as to-you seemed about-discussion worth, and say to-me, if so is,	Gunnar said, "the way you look, is like something your eyes bear, that you seemed worthy of discussion, and tell me if it is.
eða er nökkut manna komit til bæjarins?"	or is some man come to the-estate?"	or did a man come to the estate?"
"Engan sá ek kominn",	"None saw I come",	"I saw none coming",
sagði sveinninn.	said the-boy.	said the boy.
"Þú munt nú segja verða",	"You should now say be",	"You should now say",
sagði Gunnarr ok tók sviga einn mikinn ok ætlar at berja piltinn með.	said Gunnar and took whip one great and intended to beat the-boy with.	said Gunnar, and took a great whip and intended to beat the boy with it.

The Saga of Hen-Thorir (Old Norse)

Old Norse	Literal	English
Eigi fekk hann af honum heldr en áðr.	Not got he of him rather than before.	Yet he got nothing out of him rather than before.
Eftir þat fekk Gunnarr sér hest ok hleypr á bak ok ríðr skyndiliga ofan til vetrhúsa með hlíðinni.	After that got Gunnar his horse and leapt on back and rode suddenly above to winter-house along the-hillside.	After that Gunnar got his horse and leapt on its back, and rode suddenly up to the winter house along the hillside.
Jófríðr getr at líta ferð föður síns ok sagði Þóroddi ok biðr hann ríða í brott.	Jofrid caught to company travelled father hers and told Thorodd and bid he ride then away.	Jofrid caught sight of the company of her father's travelling and told Thorodd and bid that he then ride away.
"Vilda ek gjarna, at eigi hlytist illt af mér".	"Wish I will, to not result-in ill of me".	"I wish that nothing ill result because of me".
Þóroddr segist munu bráðliga ríða.	Thorodd said would soon ride.	Thorodd said he would ride soon enough.
Gunnarr berr fljótt at ok hleypr af baki, gengr þegar inn í tjaldit.	Gunnar bore quickly to and leaping off horseback, went from-there the to the-tent.	Gunnar bore quickly towards and leapt off horseback, and went from there to the tent.
Þóroddr heilsar honum vel, en Gunnarr tók kveðju hans ok spurði síðan, hví hann væri þar kominn.	Thorodd greeted him well, and Gunnar took greeting his and asked then, why he was there come.	Thorodd greeted him well, and Gunnar took his greeting and then asked, why he had come there.
Þóroddr sagði, at svá bar til um ferðir hans,	Thorodd said, that so bore to about journey his,	Thorodd said that he was about his journey,
"ok vil ek þó eigi gera þetta til fjandskapar við þik.	"and wish I though not be-done that to hostility with you.	"and I wish though for there not to be hostility with you.
En vita vil ek, hverju þú vill svara mér, ef ek bið Jófríðar, dóttur þinnar".	And knowing wish I, each you will answer to-me, if I ask Jofrid, daughter yours".	And I wish to know, how you will answer me, if I ask for the hand of Jofrid, your daughter".
Gunnarr svarar:	Gunnar answered:	Gunnar answered:
"Eigi mun ek gifta þér dóttur mína við þessa meðferðina.	"Not should I give you daughter mine with this with-goings-on.	"I should not give you my daughter with these goings on.
Hefir nú ok í odda staðizt með oss um hríð".	Has now and on a-spear-point standing with us about awhile".	And also there has been a spear-point between us for a while".
Síðan reið Þóroddr heim.	Then rode Thorodd home.	Then Thorodd rode home.

The Saga of Hen-Thorir (Old Norse)

Old Norse	Literal	English
# 17	# 17	# 17
Þat var einn dag, at Oddr segir, at eigi myndi illa fallit at hafa nökkurar landsnytjar af Örnólfsdal,	That was one day, that Odd said, that not should ill fall to have some-of produce of Ornolfsdal,	It was one day that Odd said that it wouldn't be a bad idea to have a few pieces of land from Ornolfsdal,
"þar er aðrir menn hafa setzt á eigur mínar at röngu".	"there as other men have sat in ownership mine to wrong".	"there where other people have settled on my property by mistake".
Konur sögðu þat til liggja.	Women said that to remained.	The women said that this was a good idea.
"Gerist fé harðla nytlétt ok mun þá miklu betr mjólka, ef svá er breytt".	"Was cattle hard of-little-milk and should then much better milk, if so was changed".	"If cattle becomes hard and of little milk, it will milk much better if this is changed".
"Þá skal þangat fénu halda",	"Then shall from-there cattle hold",	"Then that's where the cattle should be kept",
sagði Oddr, "því at þar eru hagar góðir".	said Odd, "because that there they-were pasture good".	said Oddr, "because there are good pastures".
Þá sagði Þóroddr:	Then said Thorodd:	Then Thorodd said:
"Ek mun bjóðast til at fylgja fénu, ok mun þá ógengiligra þykkja".	"I should offer to that follow cattle, and should then less-likely regarded".	"I will offer to follow the cattle, and it will make it less likely regarded".
Oddr segist þat gjarna vilja, ok fara þeir nú með fénu.	Odd said that gladly wish, and go there now with cattle.	Oddr says he would like to, and now they go with the cattle.
Ok er þeir eru langt komnir, segir Þóroddr, at þeir skulu þangat halda fénu, at þeir fá versta haga ok skermsl eru mest.	And as they they-were long coming, said Thorodd, to they should from-there hold cattle, that they got worst pasture and barren-ground they-were the-most.	And when they had come a long way, Thorodd said that should keep the cattle there, where they got the worst grazing and the most barren ground.
Nú líðr nóttin af hendi, ok reka þeir heim féit um morgininn.	Now passed the-night of hand, and drove they home cattle about morning.	Now the night passed, and they drove the cattle home around morning.

The Saga of Hen-Thorir (Old Norse)

Old Norse	Literal	English
Ok er konur hafa mjólkat, þá kveða þær aldri jafnilla nýtzt hafa sem nú, ok er þessa eigi oftar freistat.	And when women had milking then said then never equal used have as now and was this not more tried.	And when the women did the milking, they said that never had they had to try as hard to milk then, and this was not tried again.
Líða nú svá stundir fram.	Passed now so awhile from.	And so a while passed.
Þat var einn morgin snemma at Oddr kemr at máli við Þórodd, son sinn:	It was one morning early that Odd came to the-matter with Thorodd, son his:	It was early one morning that Odd spoke to Thorod, his son:
"Þú skalt fara ofan í sveit ok safna mönnum, ok vil ek nú reka menn af eignum várum, en Torfi skal fara upp um Hálsa ok gera þeim í kunnleika um þenna fund.	"You shall go above in company and raised men, and wish I now driven men of owning ours, but Torfi shall travel up about Halsa and do them to make-known about this find.	"You shall go down into the countryside and gather men, and now I want to drive men from our property, but Torfi shall go up through Hals and let them know about this meeting.
Vér skulum hittast við Steinsvað".	We shall meet with Steinsvað".	We shall all meet at Steinsvad".
Þeir gera nú svá, safna liði.	There be-done now so, raised company.	They did so, and now raised a company.
Fá þeir Þóroddr níu tigi manna, ríða síðan til vaðsins.	Got they Thorodd nine tens a-man, ride then to the-ford.	Thorodd and his men got ninety men, and rode to the ford.
Þeir Þóroddr koma fyrri til vaðsins.	There Thorodd come before to wading-water.	Thorodd's party was the first to arrive there at the ford.
Hann biðr þá ríða fyrir,	He asked then ride before,	He asked them to ride on,
"en ek vil bíða föður míns".	"that I will abide father mine".	"but I will wait for my father".
Ok er þeir koma at garði í Örnólfsdal, er Gunnarr at gera hlass.	And was there come that farmyard in Ornolfsdal, was Gunnar that be-done heavy-load.	And when they came to the farmyard at Ornolfsdal, Gunnar was loading a cart with a heavy load.
Nú ræðir sveinn um, er var með Gunnari:	Now discussed the-boy about, that was with Gunnar:	Now the boy that was with Gunnar spoke:
"Menn fara at bænum eigi allfáir saman".	"Men travel to the-estate not very-few together".	"There are men travelling to the estate, and not just a few of them all together".
"Já",	"Yes",	"Yes",

The Saga of Hen-Thorir (Old Norse)

Old Norse	Literal	English
sagði Gunnarr, "svá er þat",	said Gunnar, "so is it",	said Gunnar, "so it is",
ok gengr heim til bæjarins ok tók boga, því at hann skaut allra manna bezt af honum, ok er þar helzt til jafnat, er var Gunnarr at Hlíðarenda.	and went home to the-estate and took a-bow, because that he shot of-all people the-best of him, and was there rather to equal, as was Gunnar of Hlidarendi.	and he went home to the farmhouse and took a bow, because he was the best shot of all men, and was equal only to Gunnar of Hlíðarendi.
Hann hafði þá húsat vel bæinn, en gluggr var á útihurðinni, svá at inn mátti rétta ok út höfuð sitt.	He had then a-house well built, but window was in the-front-door, so to in might straighten and out head his.	He had a well built house, but there was a window in the front door, so that one might straighten out his head.
Hann stóð við hurðina með bogann.	He stood with the-door-beam with a-bow.	He stood with the door beam with a bow.
Nú kemr Þóroddr at bænum ok gengr at durum við fá menn ok spyrr, ef Gunnarr vill nökkura sætt bjóða.	Now came Thorodd to the-house going to the-door with a-few men and asked if, Gunnar Wished some settlement invitation invite.	Now Thorodd came to the house and went to the door with a few men and asked if Gunnar could be invited to make some sort of atonement.
Hann svarar:	He answered:	He answered:
"Ek veit eigi, at ek eiga nökkut at bæta,	"I know not, that I own something that atone-for,	"I do not know that I have anythng to atone for,
en hitt væntir mik, áðr þér fáið mitt vald, at griðkonur mínar muni stungit hafa nökkura þína félaga svefnþorni, áðr ek hníga í gras".	but find expect me, before you get of-me power, that handmaidens mine shall pierce have some of-your companions sleep-thorn, before I bite the grass".	but expect this of me, that before you overpower me, that my handmaidens shall have pierced some of your companions with sleep-thorn before I bite the grass".
Þóroddr svarar:	Thorodd answered:	Thorodd answered:
"Satt er þat, at þú ert afbragð flestra manna nú, þeira sem uppi eru,	"True is it, that you are outstanding the-most of-people now, they as about-standing they-are,	"It's true, that you are the most outstanding of people now, among those who are outstanding,
en þó má koma svá margt lið í móti þér, at þú fáir eigi móti staðit, því at faðir minn ríðr at garði með mikit lið ok ætlar at drepa þik".	but though may come so many company to meet to-you, that you get not with stand, because that father mine rides to the-path with much company and intend that killed you".	but there may come so many men to meet you, that you will not withstand, because my father is riding the path with a great company and intends to kill you".

The Saga of Hen-Thorir (Old Norse)

Old Norse	Literal	English
Gunnarr svarar:	Gunnar answered:	Gunnar answered:
"Vel er þat, en þat mynda ek vilja, at ek hefða mann fyrir mik, áðr ek hníga at velli.	"Well was that, but that should I wish, to I have man before me, before I slump to fields.	"That is all well, but I wish to take a man with me before I slump into the fields.
En eigi gruna ek þat, þótt faðir þinn haldi lítt sættirnar".	And not suspect I that, thought father your holds little the-settlement".	And I suspect that your father hold little of the same sentiment".
"Hina leið er",	"Then passed was",	"Then it is this way",
sagði Þóroddr, "at vér viljum gjarna sættast, ok rétt nú fram höndina með góðum vilja þínum ok gift mér Jófríði, dóttur þína".	said Thorodd, "that we wish-to gladly reconcile, and right now from hand with good wish yours and marry to-me Jofrid, daughter yours".	said Thorodd, "that we wish to gladly reconcile, right now by handshake, and with your good wishes, that I will marry your daughter Jofrid".
Gunnarr svarar:	Gunnar answered:	Gunnar answered:
"Eigi kúgar þú dóttur mína af mér.	"Not cower you daughter mine of to-me.	"I will not be cowed by you to give you my daughter".
En eigi væri þat fjarri jafnaði boðit sakar þín, því at þú ert góðr drengr".	But not was that far-from equal offer sake yours, because that you are good fellow".	But it wouldn't be far off an equal match if you offered, because you are a good fellow".
Þóroddr svarar:	Thorodd answered:	Thorodd answered:
"Eigi mun þat svá virt af góðgjörnum mönnum, ok kann ek mikla þökk fyrir, at þú takir þenna kost með þeim máldögum, sem því hæfir".	"Not should that so worth of good-doing men, and know I much thanks before, that you take this choose with them agreement, as therefore have".	"It will not be so respected by benevolent people, and I would be very grateful if you take this option with the agreement as appropriate".
Ok nú við umtölur vina sinna ok þat annars, at honum þótti Þóroddr jafnan vel farit hafa með sínu máli, þá verðr þat af, at Gunnarr réttir fram höndina, ok lúka svá þessu máli.	And now with about-talking friends his and that others, to him thought Thorodd equal well going have with his the-matter, then worthy that of, that Gunnar righted from hand, and concluded so this the-matter.	And now with the prsuasion of his friends and others, he thought Thorodd equally well going in this matter, and then worthy, that Gunnar extended out his hand, and so the matter was concluded.
Nú í þessu kemr Oddr í tún, ok snýr Þóroddr þegar í mót feðr sínum ok spyrr, hvat hann ætlar.	Now in this came Odd to the-yard, and turned Thorodd from-there in meeting father his and asked, what he intended.	Now at this Odd came to the field, and Thorodd immediately turned to face his father and asked what he was up to.

The Saga of Hen-Thorir (Old Norse)

Old Norse	Literal	English
Hann kveðst ætla at brenna bæinn ok svá mennina.	He said intended to burn dwellings and so men.	He said that he intended to burn the house, and so men.
Þóroddr svarar:	Thorodd answered:	Thorodd answered:
"Á aðra leið er nú komit málinu, ok erum við Gunnarr nú sáttir",	"About other passes then now coming the-matter, and we-are with Gunnar now settled",	"Now things have taken a different turn, and Gunnar and I are now satisfied".
ok segir nú allt, hvé komit er.	and said now all, how come was.	and he told him how everything had happened.
"Heyr hér á endemi",	"Hear here of shame",	"Hear here of shame",
segir Oddr.	said Odd.	said Odd.
"Væri þér þá verra at eiga konuna, þótt Gunnarr væri drepinn áðr, er mestr var várr mótstöðumaðr?	"Was to-you then worse to have this-woman, thought Gunnar was killed before, that most was our enemy?	"Would it be worse for you to have the woman, even though Gunnar was killed first, who was our greatest opponent?
Ok höfum vér illt at verki at hefja þik".	And have we ill that work that heaved you".	And we have done ill work in raising you".
Þóroddr svarar ok mælti:	Thorodd answered and spoke:	Thorodd answered and spoke:
"Við mik skaltu nú fyrst berjast, ef eigi kemr öðru við".	"With me shall-you now first battle, if not came another with".	"Fight with me first, if nothing else".
Ganga menn nú í milli ok sætta þá feðga.	To-go men now in among and settle then father-and-son.	People now went between them and reconciled the father and son.
Urðu þær málalykðir, at Jófríðr er gefin Þóroddi, ok líkar Oddi stórilla,	Became there conclusions, that Jofrid was given-to Thorodd, and disliked Odd greatly,	They concluded that Jofrid be given to Thorodd, and Oddi disliked this very much,
fara nú heim við svá búit.	went now home with so settled.	they now travelled home with the matter settled.
Eftir þat sitja menn at boði, ok unir Þóroddr allvel sínu ráði.	After that sat men that announced, and satisfied Thorodd all-well his counsel.	After that men sat at the wedding-feast, and Thorodd was very satisfied with his counsel.

The Saga of Hen-Thorir (Old Norse)

Old Norse	Literal	English
Ok at vetri afliðnum ferr Þóroddr útan, því at hann hafði spurt, at Þorvaldr, bróðir hans, var í höftum, ok vildi leysa hann með fé.	And to winter passed went Thorodd travelled-out, because to he had learned, that Thorvald, brother his, was in bondage, and wished release him with wealth.	And as winter passed, Thorodd travelled out, because he had learned that Thorvald, his brother, was in bondage, and he wished to release him with wealth.
Hann kemr til Nóregs ok kom eigi út síðan ok hvárrgi þeira bræðra.	He came to Norway and came not out then and neither theirs brothers.	He came to Norway and did not come back, and neither did his brother.
Oddr tók nú at eldast mjök.	Odd took now to old-age much.	Odd now took very much to old age.
Ok er hann spurði þat, at hvárrgi sona hans myndi til koma, tók hann sótt mikla, ok er at honum tók at þröngva, mælti hann við vini sína, at þeir mundi flytja hann upp á Skáneyjarfjall, þá er hann væri dauðr, ok kvaðst hann þaðan vildu sjá yfir tunguna alla,	And as he learned that, to neither sons his should to come, took he sickness much, and when to him took to heavily, spoke he with friends his, that there would carry he up of Skaney-Fell, then was he was dead, and spoke he from-there wished see over The-Tongue all,	And when he learned that neither of his sons would come back, he took great pains, and when he began to strain, he said to his friends that they would carry him up to Skaneyjarfjall when he was dead, and he said from there he wanted to see over the whole of Tungu,
ok svá var gert.	and so was done.	And so it was done.
En Jófríðr Gunnarsdóttir var síðan gefin Þorsteini Egilssyni at Borg ok var inn mesti kvenskörungr.	But Jofrid Daughter-of-Gunnar was then married Thorstein son-of-Egil of Burg and was the most noblest-women.	But Jofrid, daughter of Gunnar was then married to Thorstein, son of Egil of Burg, and was the noblest of women.
Ok lýkr þar Hænsa-Þóris sögu.	And ends there Hen-Thorir saga.	And here ends the saga of Hen-Thorir.

Word List *(Old Norse to English)*

Old Norse	English
A, a	
aðra	another, other
aðrir	other
af	from, from, of, of, off
afar	great
afbragð	outstanding
affærði	taken-away
afliðnum	passed
aflvani	overpowered
aftr	after, behind, returned
ala	bore
aldri	never, never
algjafta	hay-feed
alla	all
allan	all
allar	all
allfáir	very-few
allgott	all-good
allir	all, all
allkátir	merry
alllítil	all-little
alllítit	all-little
allmargir	all-many
allmjök	all-much
allr	all, all
allra	all, of-all
alls	all, all, in-all
allsæmiligt	decent
allsköruliga	all-clear
allt	all, all
Allvel	all-well, all-well
almæltra	all-matters
alþingi	the-assembly, the-assembly
alþingis	the-assembly
alþýðu	the-people
andsælis	anti-sun-wise
Annan	next, opposite
annarr	another, one, other, other-than
annarra	other
annarrra	other, others
annars	others
annat	another, other, other-things
annathvárt	either-way
anntu	care
Arngrím	Arngrim (name)
Arngrími	Arngrim (name)
Arngrímr	Arngrim (name)
Arngríms	Arngrim (name)
Arngrímsson	Son-of-Arngrim (name)
at	and, as, at, at, if, in, in, it, it, of, of, than, that, that, the, the-door, to, to
atburðinn	at-carried
atgervismaðr	dynamic-man
auðga	wealthy
auðgastr	wealthy
auðigr	wealthy-man
auðmaðr	wealthy-man, wealthy-man
augu	eyes
austmaðr	the-eastern-man
Austmanninum	the-Eastern-Men (name)
Austmanns	Easterners (name)
Austmenn	the-Easterners (name), the-Easterners (name)
Á, á	
á	a, about, and, as, at, for, from, in, not, of, on, one, out, over, so, to
ábyrgð	risk
áðr	already, before
ágætr	honoured
ákafa	eager
ákveðnum	appointed, meeting
Álfs	alf

69

Word List (Old Norse to English)

Old Norse	English
áminnast	remember
án	without
ána	river
ár	early
Ármannsfelli	Armannsfell (place)
ásjá	assistance, assistance
ásjámál	matter-consideration
áþekkr	similar
átt	had, have, own, owned
átta	had
átti	had, married
áttu	had
áverkar	injuries
ávíta	to-rebuke

Æ, æ

æfar	great
ærin	a-year
ærit	necessary
ætla	intend, intended, suppose
ætlak	suppose
ætlar	intend, intended
ætlat	intend, intended
ætlum	intend

B, b

bað	asked, bid
báðum	both
bæ	dwelling
bæði	both
bæinn	built, dwellings
bæja	homes
bæjarins	dwellings, the-estate
bæjunum	the-towns
bænum	estate, farmhouse, the-estate, the-farm, the-house
bærinn	the-farm
Bærr	dwelling
bæta	atone-for
bætr	compensated, reconciliation
bak	back
baki	horseback
bannir	banned
bar	bore
bardaga	battle
bardagi	a-battle
barn	child
barnfóstr	child-foster, foster-child
barnfóstri	child-fostering
barnfóstrinu	child-fostering
bauð	bid, invited, offered
beggja	both
beina	assistance
beini	benefit
beinn	hospitable
beittan	cunning
bekk	bench
bera	carried
berðist	fought
berja	beat
berjast	battle
berr	befell, bore
berum	bear
Betr	better
betra	better
betri	better
bezt	best, the-best
bezti	best
Bið	ask, bid
bíða	abide, bid
biðja	ask-for, bid, invite, invited
biðr	asked, bid
binda	bound
birkirafts	birch-rafter
bjó	lived
bjóða	invite, invited
bjóðast	offer
bjóðist	offered
björg	help
bjuggu	dwelt
blístrar	whistled
blóð	blood

70

Word List (Old Norse to English)

Old Norse	English
Blund-Katli	Blund-Ketill (name)
Blund-Ketill	Blund-Ketill (name)
Blund-Ketills	Blund-Ketill (name), Blund-Ketill's (name)
Blund-Ketillsson	Son-of-Blund-Ketill (name)
blunds	Blund (name)
Blundsvatn	Blundsvatn (name)
boð	offer, the-invitation
boði	wedding-feast
boðinn	invited
boðinu	the-wedding
boðit	invitation, offer, offered, the-wedding
boðs	offer, the-wedding
boðsmenn	invited-people
boga	a-bow, bow
bogann	a-bow
bólstað	building
bónda	the-farmer
Bóndi	the-farmer
bóndinn	the-farmer
bönnum	banning
borð	the-table, the-tables
borðit	the-tables
borðum	the-table
Borg	Burg (place)
Borgarfirði	Borgafjord (place)
Borgarfjarðar	Borgafjord (place)
Borgarfjörð	Borgafjord (place)
borinn	bore
borit	bear, carried
börn	children
bráðliga	soon
bræðra	brothers
bragði	looking
brandinn	brand
brátt	soon
braut	away
Breiðabólstað	Breidabolstad (place)
Breiðafirði	Breidafjord (place)
breiðskeggs	Broad-Beard (name)
brenna	burn
brenndr	burned
Brenni	burn
brennu	the-burning
brennuna	the-burning
brennunni	the-burning
breytt	changed
bróðir	brother, brother-of
brögðum	strategy
brott	away
brottu	away
brúðguma	bridegroom
brúðgumi	the-bridegroom
Brúðir	the-bride
brugðit	broken
brugðizt	accustomed
brunnit	burned, burnt
bú	preprations
búa	prepare
búi	farm
búin	ready
búit	done, dwelled, place, prepared, settled
bundnar	bound
búnir	prepared
burt	away
bústöðum	residences
býðr	bids, invited
byggðan	settled
býr	farm

D, d

Old Norse	English
dælt	dealt
dæmðust	judged
dætr	daughters
dag	day
daginn	the-day
dags	day
dagverðar	breakfast
dalina	the-valleys
dauðr	dead
deildum	shared
deyja	die
deyr	dies
Dölum	Dölum (place)
dóm	deemed
dóma	judgement
dóttir	daughter

Word List (Old Norse to English)

Old Norse	English
dóttur	daughter
draga	dragged, dragging
dreng	fellow
drengiligt	manly
drengr	fellow
drepa	death, kill, killed
drepinn	killed
drepit	knock
dreymði	dreamed
drjúgastr	greatly
duga	be-helping, helping
duganda	sufficiently
durum	the-door, with
dyrr	the-door

E, e

Old Norse	English
eða	and, or
ef	Gunnar (name), if
efndir	fulfilment
eftir	after
Egilssyni	Son-of-Egil (name)
eiga	had, have, not, own
eigi	not
eigin	own
eignum	owning
eigu	our-own
eigum	have, own
eigur	ownership
ein	along
eina	only
einar	Einar (name)
einhlítir	sufficient
einhlítr	sufficient
einhverjum	each
einkis	nothing
einkum	especially
einmánuðr	one-month
Einn	one
eins	one, one's
einskis	nothing
einu	one
eitt	a, once, one
eitthvert	something
ek	I
ekki	not
ekr	drives
eld	fire
eldast	old-age
eldi	fire
eldr	fire
eldrinn	the-fire
ella	otherwise
elr	came
em	am
en	and, but, than, that, then, while
enda	conclude, concluded, end
endemi	shame
Endið	end
enga	no, none
engan	none
engi	no, none, not, nothing
engu	nothing
engum	none
enn	but, in
er	am, are, as, is, is-it, is-that, said, that, then, was, were, when, where, which, who
erendi	errand
Erni	Orn (name)
ert	are
ertu	are-you
eru	there-are, they-are, they-were
erum	are, we-are
Esjubergi	Esyuberg (place)
eta	eating
etizt	eating
Eyjafjörð	Eyjafjord (place)
Eyjavati	Eyjavaði (place)

F, f

Old Norse	English
fá	a-few, get, got, men
faðir	father
fæ	get
fær	accomplishment

Word List (Old Norse to English)

Old Norse	English
færa	brought
færi	went
færra	fewer
fært	taken
fæti	foot
fagnaði	celebration
fagnar	gave, greeted
fagnat	celebrating
fáið	get
fáir	get
fala	bargain
falli	falls
fallin	fallen
fallit	fall
fámáligr	of-few-words
fámennr	few-men
fann	found
Far	go
fara	go, going, journeying, sent, to-go, travel, travelled, travelling, went
fari	goes
farinn	travelling
farir	travel
farit	going, going-away, gone, travelling, went
farmönnum	travelling-men
farningar	the-faring
fast	fast
fást	getting
fastna	betrothe
fastnaðir	betrothed
fastnar	betrothed
fastnir	betrothe
Fátt	few
fé	cattle, money, wealth
feðga	father-and-son
feðgar	father-and-son
feðr	father
fegnir	celebrating
féit	cattle, the-cattle, wealth
fekk	got
félaga	companions
félagar	followers

Old Norse	English
fell	fell
féll	fell
Fellr	fell
Fellu	fell
fémætt	valuables
fémunum	goods
fénað	cattle
fengr	getting
fénu	cattle
ferð	journey, to-travel, travel, travelled, travelled-from
ferðina	travelling
ferðir	journey
ferðum	travel
ferr	goes, travelling, went
festar	fixed
fimm	five
finna	found
finnast	meet
firðinum	fjord
firn	abomination
Fitjum	Fitiar (place)
fjandmaðr	fiend-man
fjandskapar	hostility
fjár	cattle
fjárins	cattle
Fjarri	far, far-from
fjárviðtökunni	wealth-with-betokened
fjögur	four
fjölði	many
fjölmennari	following-men
fjölmennir	crowd
fjóra	four
fjórðunga	quarters
fjórðungi	quarter, the-fourth
fjórðungsþing	quarter-assembly
fjórir	many
fjósi	the-barn
fleiprir	babble
fleira	more
fleiri	more
flestra	the-most
fljótt	quickly
flokkar	groups

Word List (Old Norse to English)

Old Norse	English
flokki	the-flock
flutningar	moving
flytizt	move
flytja	carried, carry
flytr	brought
fóðr	fodder
föður	father
fölskaðr	pale-burnt
föng	got
fór	for, goes, travelled, went
för	journey
foraðsillu	abominable
forkast	fodder
fornum	the-older
forráðsgoðorð	custody-chieftain
forráðsmaðr	manager
forsjá	custody
fóru	went
förum	let-us-go
föstnuð	betrothe
fóstra	foster-father
fóstrar	foster
fóstri	foster, foster-father, fostering
föt	bed-clothing
fótum	feet
frá	from
frænda	kinsman
frændi	a-kinsman, kinsman
frændum	kinsmen
fram	from
framreiðin	riding-on
frásögn	from-said
freistat	tempted
frekust	most-often
fresti	from-now
frétt	news
frétti	heard
fréttir	news
fréttist	enquired
fréttu	asked
frítt	free
fullri	fully
fullsekðat	fully-outlawed
fúnar	rots
fund	find, meet
fundar	meet
fundit	found
Fylgðu	follow
fylgi	following
fylgja	follow
fylgt	followed
fyrir	before, for, from
fyrirboðsmanna	invited-people
fyrr	before
fyrra	before
fyrri	before
fyrst	first

G, g

Old Norse	English
gabbat	fooled
gæða	increased
gæfumaðr	lucky-man
gaf	gave, given
gagni	useful
gakk	come
Gakktu	go-you
ganga	go, going, to-go, went
ganganda	going, walking
garða	farmyard
garði	farmyard, the-farmyard, the-path, yard
garpr	brave-strong
gat	got
gátu	got
gef	give
gefa	give, given, to-give
gefast	be-given
gefin	given-to, married
gefit	given
gefr	gave
gegna	going
gegndi	might
gegni	suits
gegnir	goes
Geirs	Geir's (name)
Geirshlíð	Geir's-Slope (place)
gekk	went

Word List (Old Norse to English)

Old Norse	English
gelldi	bellowing
gelli	Gellir (name)
gellir	Gellir (name)
gellis	Gellir (name)
gengi	going
gengit	went
gengr	going, to, went
Ger	do, make
gera	be-done, did, do, make
Gerast	be
gerð	made
gerði	went
gerðist	became
gerðu	did, do
gerir	did, do
gerist	became, was
gerr	do, done
gert	done, made
gerviligr	accomplished
gerzt	done
getr	caught, may
geyma	keep, retain
gift	marry
gifta	give
gisti	guest
gistingu	guest, guesting
gjafar	gifts
gjaforði	reserved
gjálgrun	idle-talk
gjarna	gladly, will, willingly
gluggr	window
góð	good
goða	the-chieftain
góða	good
goðar	chieftains
góðar	good
góðgjarnir	benevolent
góðgjörnum	good-doing
goði	chieftain, the-chieftain
góðir	good
góðr	good
góðrar	well
góðu	good
góðum	good
Gói.	Gói (month, February)
goldit	paid
gólfinu	the-floor
gólfit	the-floor
gott	good
götu	the-path
götuna	the-path
götunni	the-path
græddist	gained
græðir	accumulated
Græðist	gathered
gras	grass
grasvöxtr	hay-crop
greiða	assistance
greiðliga	quite
greinir	article
griðkonur	handmaidens
griðungr	a-bull
gruna	suspect
grunaði	mistrust
grunar	suspect
Gunnar	Gunnar (name)
Gunnari	Gunnar (name)
Gunnarr	Gunnar (name), wished
Gunnars	Gunnar's (name)
Gunnarsdóttir	Daughter-of-Gunnar (name)
Gunnarsson	Son-of-Gunnar (name)
Gunnarsstaði	Gunnarsstadir (place)
Gunnvaldr	Gunnvald (name)

H, h

Old Norse	English
hæfir	have
hæns	hens
Hænsa-Þóri	Hen-Thorir (name)
Hænsa-Þórir	Hen-Thorir (name)
Hænsa-Þóris	Hen-Thorir (name)
hætta	danger
hafa	had, have, to-have
hafðar	had
hafði	had
hafðist	had

Word List (Old Norse to English)

Old Norse	English	*Old Norse*	English
hafi	had, harbour, have, having	*heimilast*	right
		heimilt	allow
hafið	have	*heimleiðis*	home-ways
hafim	have	*heimta*	insist
hafir	have	*heimtir*	got
haft	had, have	*heit*	pledge
haga	pasture	*heitan*	threatening
haganum	the-pastures	*heitir*	named, was-named
hagar	pasture	*heitit*	pledged
hagastr	the-best	*heldr*	either, rather
halda	hold	*heldust*	rather
haldi	holds	*Helga*	Helgi (name)
haldið	holding	*Helgason*	Son-of-Helgi (name)
hálft	half-of	*Helgavatni*	Helgivatn (place)
hallazt	slanted	*Helgi*	Helgi (name)
Hálsa	Halsa (place)	*Helgu*	Helgi (name)
hana	her, hers	*Helzt*	held, rather
handa	hand	*hendi*	arms, hand
handsalar	hands-over	*hendr*	hand, hands
Hann	he, him	*hennar*	hers
hans	his	*henni*	he, her, she, to-her
happaráð	happy-decision	*hér*	here
harðla	hard	*heraða*	districts
hark	noise	*heraði*	district, the-district
harma	regret	*heraðinu*	the-district
hart	roughly	*heraðit*	the-district
hásetar	sailors	*heraðsins*	district
hastorðr	harsh-spoken	*heraðsstjórn*	district-administration
hátt	loudly	*hermt*	angry
háttat	the-way	*hérna*	here
haust	autumn	*Hersteini*	Herstein (name)
hausti	autumn	*Hersteinn*	Herstein (name)
haustit	autumn	*heruð*	districts
hefða	had, have	*heruðunum*	the-districts
hefðu	had	*hest*	horse
hefi	have	*hesta*	horses
hefir	had, has, have	*hestar*	horses
hefja	heaved, raising	*hestinn*	horse
heiði	the-heath	*hestinum*	horse
heillaráða	good-advice	*hestum*	horses
heilli	fairly	*hét*	named
heilsar	greeted	*hey*	hay
heilsat	greeted	*heybjörg*	haystacks
heim	home	*heyin*	haystacks
heima	at-home, home	*heyit*	hay, the-hay
heiman	from-home, home		

Word List (Old Norse to English)

Old Norse	English	Old Norse	English
heyjum	hay	Höfn	the-harbour
heykost	hay-supply	höfnina	the-harbour
heyleigur	hay-allowance	höfninni	the-port
Heyr	hear	Hófst	began
heyra	heard	höftum	bondage
heyrðu	heard	höfuð	head
Heyri	hear	höfuðburðr	head-bearing
heyrir	heard	höfum	have
heybroti	hay-need	Höggr	struck
Hina	then	Högnasonar	Son-of-Hogni (name)
hingat	here	hól	the-hill
hinkr	hang-back	hon	her, she
hirði	shepherd	hönd	hand
hitt	find, it	höndina	hand
hitta	to-meet	höndum	hands, in-hand
Hittast	found, meet	honum	he, him, his, to-him
hitti	met	horfir	looked
hittir	met	hörmulig	harm-like
hjá	aside, beside, by, nearby	hörmuligt	tragic
		hóti	a-good-deal
hjálp	help	hratt	quickly
hjálpa	help	hríð	awhile
hlammanda	The-Stamper (name)	Hrómundi	Hromund (name)
hlass	heavy-load	hross	horses
hlaupa	ran	hrossa	horses
hleypir	ran	hrossum	horses
hleypr	leaping, leapt, ran	hrossunum	the-horses
Hlíðarenda	Hlidarendi (place)	húðir	hides
Hlíðina	The-Slope (place)	hug	mind, thought
hlíðinni	the-hillside, the-slope	hugða	thought
Hlífarson	Son-of-Hlifar (name)	hugðist	thought
hljómr	sound	hugnar	to-mind
hljóp	ran	hugr	thoughts
hljótast	to-get	hugsa	consider
hljótist	to-get	hugsi	thoughtful
hlut	part	hundrað	a-hundred
hluta	lot, parts	hundrinn	mongrel
hluti	part	hundruð	hundred, hundreds
hlutr	lot	hurð	the-door
hlýða	obeyed	hurðar	the-door-beam, the-doors
hlytist	result-in		
hlýtr	must	hurðarhringinn	the-door-ring
hníga	bite, slump	hurðina	the-door-beam
höfðingjanna	chieftain	hús	the-house
höfðingjar	chieftains	húsakost	house-choice
höfðu	had	húsar	house-built

Word List (Old Norse to English)

Old Norse	English
húsat	a-house, housed
húsi	house
húsin	house, the-house, the-houses
húsinu	the-house
húskarl	the-housekeeper
húsum	house
húsunum	the-house
Hvamm	Hvamm (place)
Hvammi	Hvamm (place)
hvar	where
hvarf	disappeared
hvárirtveggju	each-side
hvárntveggja	either-side
hvárratveggja	each-way
hvárrgi	neither
hvárt	if, whether, which
hvat	what
hvatliga	quickly
hve	how
hvé	how
hver	who
hverfa	turned-back
hverfr	turned
hverir	each, who
Hverjir	who
hverju	each, how, how-so
hverjum	everyone
hvern	each
hverr	each, how, who
hversu	how, how-so
hvert	each, which
hví	how, why
Hvítá	Hvita (place)
hyggja	considered, think
hyggst	seems

I, i

iðgjöld	recompensed
illa	ill
illbýli	ill-harm
ills	ill
illt	ill
Illu	ill

Old Norse	English
illum	evil
inn	in, inside, the
innarliga	lying-in
inni	in, inside
ins	the
it	the, then

Í, í

í	a, about, among, as, at, in, into, of, on, so, the, then, this, to, you
íslög	ice-bound

J, j

Já	yes
jafnaðarmaðr	an-even-man
jafnaði	equal
jafnan	equal, equally
jafnat	equal
jafngott	equal-good
jafnilla	equally
jafnmikinn	equally-great
jafnræði	equally
jafnvel	equal-good
jarðir	earth
járn	iron
játtuðu	affirmed
Jófríðar	Jofrid (name)
Jófríði	Jofrid (name)
Jófríðr	Jofrid (name)
jól	yule
jörð	the-earth
Jórunn	jorun, Jorunn (name)

K, k

kaldr	cold
Kalla	call, called
kallaðr	called
kallar	called
kalt	cold

Word List (Old Norse to English)

Old Norse	English
kann	can, know
Kannast	knew
kappsamr	zealous
karl	a-man, the-man
kaup	buying, deal
kaupa	purchase, to-buy
kaupdrengr	merchant
kaupin	the-purchase
kaupir	bought
kaupmenn	trading-men
kaupmönnum	the-trading-men
kaupskap	goods
kaupstefnur	trading-post
kaupum	trading
kemr	came, comes
kennt	known
kennumst	knowing
Ketilssonar	Son-of-Ketil (name)
keypt	bought
keypti	bought
keyrir	whipped
kippir	drew
kjósa	choose
klæðast	to-dress
klæðin	clothes
klappar	knocked
klifgötuna	cliff-path
klyfjar	loaded, pack-loads, the-load
klyfjarnar	pack-loads
köldu	cold
kom	came, come
koma	came, come
komast	to-come
kominn	come
komir	come
komit	came, come, comes, coming
komizt	come
komna	come
komnir	arrived, came, come, coming
Kómu	came
kómum	came
kona	wife, woman
konu	a-wife, the-woman
konuna	a-wife, the-woman, this-woman
konunnar	the-woman
konur	the-women, women
kost	choice, choose, provided-for
kosti	cost
kostr	choice
krefr	needed
kú	cow
kúgar	cower
kúgast	to-be-oppressed
kúna	the-cow
kunna	could
kunni	could
kunnleika	make-known
kvað	said, spoke
kvaðst	said, spoke
kváðust	said
Kvámu	coming
kveða	said
kveðit	spoken
kveðju	greeting
kveðst	said
kveikti	kindled
kveld	evening
kveldi	evening
kveldit	evening
kvenskörungr	noblest-women
kynligt	strange, wonder
kyns	kinds-of
kýr	cow
kyrrt	peace

L, l

Old Norse	English
lá	laying
lætr	had
lag	lay
lagði	became
lagi	laying
lagit	laying
land	land, lands, the-land
landi	the-land
landinu	the-land

Word List (Old Norse to English)

Old Norse	English
landseta	tenants
landsetar	tenants
landseti	a-tenant
landsetum	the-tenants
landshorna	lands-corners
landsnytjar	produce
langa	long
langt	long
lastaði	blame
láta	allow, allowed, have, let
látið	let
látim	let
látin	spoken-of
látir	let
Láttu	let
látum	allow
launar	are-repaid
laut	leant
legði	leave
leggir	place
leggja	grant
leggst	laid, lay
leið	passed, passes, the-way, the-ways
leiða	lead
leiðast	lay
leiddr	led
leiðrétta	have-right
leigulanda	tenant-farms
leikit	played
leikr	like
leita	let
lek	lay
lengi	long, longer
lét	had
Letja	discourage
létt	light
létta	let-up
létti	left
léttir	remained
leyna	conceal, hiding
leysa	redeem, release
leyst	release
lézt	let
lið	company
líða	passed
liði	company
liðinu	the-company
líðr	passed
liðs	company, the-company
liðsdrátt	assembling-troops
liðsinni	assistance
liggja	remained
Liggr	lying
líkaði	liked
líkar	disliked, like
líkara	likely
líkligra	likely
línbrókum	linen-breeches
líta	company
lítil	little
lítill	little
lítils	little
lítit	little
lítr	looked
lítt	little
lízt	appeared, appears, behold, seems
lofaði	praised
lög	law
loganda	flaming
logann	the-fire
Lögbergi	Law-Mountain (place)
lögðu	laid
lögmálsstaðinn	law-matter-standing
loguðu	burned
loku	locked
löndum	the-lands
Löngu	long
lúka	concluded
lúkist	end
Lýgr	lies
Lýkr	ended, ends
lýsa	proclaim

M, m

Old Norse	English
má	may
maðr	a-man, man, the-man

Word List (Old Norse to English)

Old Norse	English
mægða	marriage
mælir	discussing, speak
mælt	said, spoke, spoken
mælti	said, spoke
mætir	met
mætti	may
mágar	father-and-son
mági	son-in-law
mágr	son-in-law
mál	matter, matter
mála	the-matter
málahlut	case-load
málalykðir	concluded, conclusions
máldögum	agreement
máli	the-matter
málinu	the-matter, this-case
málit	the-matter
máls	matter
málum	matter, matters, the-matter
málunum	matter
mann	man, men
manna	a-man, man, men, of-people, people
mannaða	manly
mannaferð	journey-of-men
mannfall	men-fallen
mannfátt	lack-of-people
Mannferðin	men-travelling
manngirnð	men-desiring
manni	man, men, people
manninn	people
manninum	the-man
manns	man
mannsbarn	born-man
marga	many
margir	many
margt	many
mat	food
matar	feed
matast	eat
mátt	might
mátti	might
máttrinn	power
máttu	as-might, might
með	along, between, with
meðferðina	with-goings-on
mega	be-able-to
mein	injury
meins	harm
meir	more
meira	more
meiri	greater, more
menn	and, men
mennina	men
mér	I, me, my, to-me
mest	most, the-most
mesta	most
mestan	mostly
mesti	most
mestr	most
mestri	the-most
mestu	most
metorð	reputation
mettir	full-of-food
miðla	share
mik	me
mikil	great, greatly, much
mikill	big, much
mikinn	great, greatly, much
mikit	much
mikla	great, much
miklu	great, much
milli	among, between
mín	mine, my
mína	mine
mínar	mine
mínir	mine
minn	mine
minna	my
minnr	less
míns	mine, my
mínu	mine
mínum	mine, my
misgöngin	tide-change
misráðit	mis-advised
mitt	mine, of-me
mjök	much
mjólka	milk
mjólkat	milked

Word List (Old Norse to English)

Old Norse	English
móður	mother
mönnum	men, people
morgin	morning, the-morning
morgininn	morning
mörgum	many
mót	meeting, towards
mótgangi	meeting-going
móti	meet, meeting, to-meet, with
mótstöðumaðr	enemy
möttul	mantle
mun	shall, should, will, would
mund	time
mundi	would
mundu	would
muni	shall, should, would
munir	would
munr	difference
munt	might, should, would
muntu	should-you
munu	shall, would
munuð	shall
munum	shall, should
Mynda	should, would
myndi	should, would
Mýrar	Myrar (place)

N, n

Old Norse	English
ná	near
náðu	reached
nær	close, nearly
næst	near, nearest
nætr	the-night
nái	can-get
náinn	near
náir	brought
nasarnar	his-nose
nasir	nose
nátt	the-night
náttaði	nightfall
náttar	nightfall
náttstað	night-quarters
nauðamikill	need-much
nauðsynjum	necessities
nauðsynligra	need-like
naut	bulls
nautum	cattle
né	not
neðra	lower
nefna	mention
nefnir	named
Nei	no
neita	refuse
nem	take
nema	except, taken, unless
nemr	took
nenni	bother
Nes	The-Headland (place)
neyta	make-use
níðingsverk	low-deed
niðr	down
níu	nine
njóta	enjoy
nóga	enough
nógar	enough
nökkur	some
nökkura	any, settlement, some, someone
nökkurar	some-of
nökkurs	some, someone
nökkuru	somewhat
nökkurum	somewhat
nökkut	any, anything, some, something, somewhat
norðan	north, the-north
Norðlendingafjórðungi	Northern-Quarter (place)
norðr	north
Norðrá	Norðura (place), Norðurá (place), North-River (place)
Norðrárdal	Norduradal (place), North-River-Valley (place)
Norðrdæla	Norðurdæla (place)
Norðrtungu	North-Tongue (place)
Nóregs	Norway (place)
nótt	night, the-night
nóttin	the-night
nú	now, then

Word List (Old Norse to English)

Old Norse	English
nýligar	new, newer
nýligra	newer
nýlundu	news
nytlétt	of-little-milk
nýtra	more-helpful
nýtt	new
nýtzt	new

O, o

Old Norse	English
Odd	Odd (name)
odda	a-spear-point
Oddi	Odd (name)
Oddr	Odd (name)
Odds	Odd's (name)
Oddsson	Oddson (name), Son-of-Odd (name)
Oddssonar	Son-of-Odd (name)
of	of
ofan	above, off, over
ofar	above
ofrefli	overwhelming
ofrliði	outnumbered
oft	often
oftar	often
og	and
ok	also, and, asked, going
okkarr	ours
okkr	us
olli	caused, that-caused
opit	open
orð	word, words
orða	words
orðin	became, become
orðit	words
orðsjúkr	word-sickened
oss	us, we
otar	pushed

Ó, ó

Old Norse	English
óágengiligra	less-likely
óbirgr	un-stocked
óbrunnit	unburnt
ódælla	uneasy
ódaufligra	less-dreary
óðliga	wildly
ófyrirsynju	unexpected
ógreitt	obstructed
ójafnað	un-equally
ókunnig	unknown
ókyrrt	un-quiet
ólíkligt	unlike
ór	about, for, from, of, out-from, out-of
órlausna	solution
órlausnar	a-solution
ósinn	inlet
ópokkasælli	disliked
óvináttu	un-friendship
óvingan	difficulty
óvinir	enemies
óvinsældin	unpopularity
óvinsældir	unpopularity
óvirt	unworthy

Ö, ö

Old Norse	English
öðru	another, anything
öðrum	other, others
öfund	envy
öll	all
öllu	all
öllum	all
önnur	another, one, other, other-than, the-other
Önundarson	Son-of-Onund (name)
ör	an-arrow
örkola	a-burn-out
Örlygssonar	Son-of-Orlyg (name)
Örn	Orn (name)
Örnólf	Ornolf (name)
Örnólfr	Ornolf (name)
Örnólfs	Ornolf (name)
Örnólfsdal	Ornolfsdal (place)
örvænt	surely
örvænti	desperation

Word List (Old Norse to English)

Old Norse	English
P, p	
pall	platform
pallinum	the-seat
pening	money
piltinn	the-boy
R, r	
ráð	consent, counsel, decision
ráða	advised, decide, rule
ráðast	arrange
ráði	counsel
ráðit	advised
ráðligt	advise
ráðnar	ruling
ráðs	plan
ráðum	counsel, instructions
ræðir	discussed
ræna	steal
rænt	robbed
rænti	robbed
rán	robbery
rangt	wrong
ráni	robbery
ránit	robbery, the-robbery
ránsmaðr	robber-man
Rauða-Bjarnarson	Son-of-Rauda-Bjarni (name)
rauðr	red
Raun	torment
refr	Refur (name)
reið	rode
reiðasti	most-angry
reiðu	readily
reikar	wandered, wanders
reikunarmaðr	a-roaming-man
reip	ropes
reis	rose
rek	drive
reka	drive, driven, drove
rekin	driven
rekkju	bed
rekr	driving, drove
rétt	right
rétta	rights, straighten
réttir	right, righted
réttist	straightened-up
réttr	right
réttu	rights
Reykjardal	Reykjardal (place)
reynast	turn-out
reynda	experience
reyndar	seen
reyndist	turned-out
reynið	test
ríða	ride, rode
ríðr	rides, rode
riðu	rode
ríkismunr	powerful
rjóðr	clearing
rödd	voice
röngu	wrong
rúm	room
S, s	
sá	saw, seen, so
sækja	seek, sought
sæmð	honour
sæmðr	honoured
særum	wounded
sæti	seat, seated, seats
sætt	invitation
sætta	settle, settled
sættar	settle
sættast	reconcile
sættirnar	the-settlement
sætzt	seen
safna	gathered, raised
safnaði	collected, gathered
safnar	gathered
sagði	said, said-to, spoke, told, told
sagðist	said
sagt	said, told, told
sakar	sake
sakirnar	the-sake

84

Word List (Old Norse to English)

Old Norse	English
sama	same, the-same
saman	together
samandráttr	gathering
samfara	together-travelling
samir	same
sannast	surely
sannligra	true-like
sannligt	right
sárir	wounded
sárr	wounded
Sástu	saw-you
Sat	sat
satt	true, truly
sáttir	settled
sáttum	fulfilled
sátu	sat
Sauðamaðr	shepherd
sauðir	sheep
sé	as, bed, being, is, see
séð	see-you
seg	say
segði	said
segir	said
segist	said
segja	said, say, to-say
seilist	reached
seint	coldly, late
sekð	well
sekðir	penalty
sekir	outlawed
sekr	outlawed
seldi	selling
selför	cattle-keeping
seli	sell
selinu	mountain-pasture
selja	sell
Selr	sold
sels	summer-pasture
sem	as, when, where, which, who
sém	see
sén	seen
sendi	sent
sénn	seen
sér	are, herself, him, himself, his, saw, them
setið	settled
setit	settled
setjast	sitting
Setjumst	let-us-sit
sett	set
seturúm	a-seat
setzt	sat
sex	six
sezt	sat
sið	traditions
síð	late
Síðan	after, since, than, then
síðasta	last
síðr	side
sígast	sank
sik	him, himself, his, themselves, to-him
silfr	silver
sín	him, his, theirs
sína	his, theirs
sinn	he, his, they, yours
sinna	his
sinni	his, theirs, they, yours
síns	hers, his
sínu	his
sínum	his
siti	sit
Sitja	sat, settle, sit
sitr	sat, sit
sitt	his, the
sjá	saw, see, seems
sjáir	see
sjálfa	myself
sjálfdáðum	self-judgement
sjálfdæmi	self-judgement
Sjálfir	ourselves
sjálfr	himself, self
sjálfum	himself
Sjúk	sick
sjúkr	sick
Skagafjörð	Skagafjord (place)
skal	shall

Word List (Old Norse to English)

Old Norse	English
skalt	shall
skaltu	shall-you
Skáneyjarfjall	Skaney-Fell (place)
skapi	mood
skapir	mind
skapsmunum	disposition
skaut	shot
Skeggjasonar	Skeggja's-sons (name)
skermsl	barren-ground
skikkjunni	cloak
skila	return
skildir	shields
skilðust	separated
skilit	understand
skiljast	departed, parted
skilst	parted
skip	a-ship
skipar	ordered
skipat	exchanged
skipkvámuna	the-ship-arrival
skipt	shared
skipta	exchanged, this-exchange
skipti	exchanged
skipuðu	appointed
skjöldr	the-shield
skjótar	soon
skjótt	quickly
skó	shoes
skógar	the-woods
skógarnef	woods-outskirts
Skógarströnd	Skogarstrand (place)
skóginn	the-woods
skóginum	the-woods
skógrinn	forests
skömm	shame
Skorradal	Skorradal (place)
skorta	be-short-of
skortir	shortage
sköruliga	boldly
Skotlandi	Scotland (place)
skuldir	debts
skulu	shall, should
skuluð	should
skulum	shall
skyggnstr	keen-eyed
skylda	should
skyldi	should
skyldir	obliged
skyldr	should
skyldu	should, would
skylt	should
skyndiliga	suddenly
skyrtu	shirt
slá	struck
Slær	struck
slátrat	slaughter, slaughtered
slík	such
slíka	such
slíkan	such
slíkr	such
slíkt	such
slíku	such
slitit	settled
smiðju	workshop
snæðings	eating
snauðr	poor
sneiðigata	the-path
snemma	early, soon
snjalla	ingeniously
snúa	turned
snúit	away, turned
snýr	turned
sögðu	said
sögu	saga
sök	reason
sölu	sell
sölur	sell
sóma	honour
sómir	honourable
son	son
sona	sons
sonr	son, son-of, sons
sonu	sons
sótt	sickness, sought
sóttarinnar	sickness
spakliga	profoundly
spark	trampling
spillist	get-spoiled
sprettr	sprang

Word List (Old Norse to English)

Old Norse	English
spurði	asked, learned
spurt	learned
spyrja	to-learn
spyrjast	heard
spyrr	asked, if
stað	place
staðar	to-stand
staddr	standing
staðinn	there
staðit	stand
staðizt	standing
Stafholt	Stafholt (place)
Stafholtstungur	Stafholtstungur (place)
stakkar	stacks
standa	stand, stood, withstand
stefna	agreement, direct, summoned
stefnir	summoned
steig	stepped
steininn	the-stone
steinn	stone
Steinsvað	Steinsvað (place)
stendr	are-standing
sterkr	strong
stíga	leapt, mounted
stígandi	Strider (name)
stígr	climbed
stigu	stepping
stóð	stood
stóðhross	stallions
stofu	the-main-room
stökk	sprang
stökkr	heels
stórauðigr	rich
stórfé	great-fee
stórilla	greatly
stórmikit	great
stórmjök	a-great-much
streng	the-string
strengi	binding
Ströndinni	the-strand
strykr	struck
stund	awhile
stundir	awhile
stungit	pierce
stýrimaðr	the-steersman
stýrimann	the-steersman
suðr	south
suma	some
sumar	summer
sumarit	summer
sumarkaup	summer-market
sumri	summer
sumum	some
sunnan	from-the-south, the-south
svá	so
svara	answer, answered
svaraði	answered
svarar	answered, answers
svarat	answered
svarta	black
svefni	sleep
svefnþorni	sleep-thorn
sveininum	the-boy
sveinn	a-boy, the-boy
Sveinninn	the-boy
sveit	company
sveitir	areas
sveitum	countryside
sverð	sword
sverðshjöltin	sword's-hilt
sviga	whip
Svignaskarði	Svignaskard (place), Svignaskardi (place)
svikit	betrayed
svör	answer
sýna	show
syni	son
sýnist	seems
sýnt	seemed
systur	sister-of

T, t

Old Norse	English
tæki	take
tak	take
taka	take, taken, took
takir	take

Word List (Old Norse to English)

Old Norse	English
tal	talking
tala	say, speak, told, to-talk
Talaði	said
talast	talked
talat	spoken
talim	talk
tek	take
tekit	received, taken
tekr	took
tekst	take
tíðenda	news, the-news, tidings
tíðendi	news, the-news, tidings
tíðendum	news
tigi	tens
tigir	tens
tigu	ten, tens
tigum	tens
til	to, until
tilgangr	point
tillag	proposal
tillög	proposal, suggestions
tíma	time
tjá	expressed
tjáði	expressed
tjald	a-tent
tjalda	tent
tjaldit	tent, the-tent
tók	took
tókt	took
tólf	twelve
tólfta	twelve
tölu	told
töluð	told
töluðu	talked
Torfi	Torfi (name)
traust	trust
trausts	trust
trefill	Trefill (name)
trefils	Trefil (name)
troðinn	trodden
tún	the-plot, the-yard
tunguna	The-Tongue (place)
Tungu-Odd	Tungu-Odd (name)
Tungu-Oddi	Tungu-Odd (name)
Tungu-Oddr	Tungu-Odd (name)
Tungu-Odds	Tungu-Odd (name), Tungu-odd's (name)
Tungu-Oddsdóttur	Daughter-of-Tungu-Odd (name)
túnit	enclosure, the-enclosure
tvá	two
tvær	two
tvau	two
tveir	two
tysvar	twice

Þ, þ

Old Norse	English
þá	then
þaðan	from-there
þær	there, they
þætti	seemed, seems
þagði	silent
þagnar	silenced, silent
þakkar	thanked
þangat	from-there, there
þann	that, then
þannig	that-way
þar	there
þarf	need, needed
Þat	it, that, the
þau	them, they
þegar	already, from-there
Þegi	silence
þegit	receive
þegna	thanes
þeim	them, they
þeir	their, there, they, those
þeira	their, theirs, there, they
þenna	that, then, this
þér	to-you, to-your, you
þess	this
þessa	these, this, this-one
þessi	these, this, this-one
þessir	these
þessu	this

Word List (Old Norse to English)

Old Norse	English
þessum	this
þetta	that, then, this
þiggja	accept, receive, to-accept
þik	you
þín	yours
þína	of-your, your, yours
þing	assembly, assemtbly, the-assembly
þingheimrinn	the-asembly
þinghelgi	the-assembly
þinghelginni	the-assembly-sanctuary
þingi	the-assembly
þinginu	the-assembly
þingit	the-assembly
Þingnes	Assembly-headland (place)
þings	the-assembly
þingsins	the-assembly
þinn	you, your, yours
þinna	your
þinnar	yours
þinni	you, your, yours
þíns	yours
þínu	yours
þínum	yours
þitt	your, yours
þjáðr	enthralled
þjófr	thief
þó	then, though
þökk	thanks
Þorbjörn	Thorbjorn (name), Thorbjorn (name)
Þórð	Thord (name), Thord (name)
Þórðar	Thord (name)
Þórði	Thord (name)
Þórðr	Thord (name)
Þorgeirs	Thorgeir (name)
Þóri	Thori (name), Thorir (name)
Þórir	Thorir (name)
Þóris	Thori (name), Thori's (name)
Þórissonar	Son-of-Thori (name)
Þorkatli	Thorkel (name), Thorkel (name)
Þorkell	Thorkel (name)
Þorkels	Thorkel (name), Thorkel's (name)
Þórodd	Thorodd (name)
Þóroddi	Thorodd (name)
Þóroddr	Thorodd (name)
Þórólfr	Thorolf (name)
þorri	drought
þorrnaði	dried
Þorsteini	Thorstein (name)
Þorvald	Thorvald (name)
Þorvaldr	Thorvald (name)
Þorvalds	Thorvald's (name)
þótt	thought
þótti	seemed, thought
þóttumst	thought
þræla	servants
Þrælastraumr	Thraelastraum (place)
þrælsgjöld	servant-fees
þrælum	a-thrall
þraut	away
þrem	three
þriðja	third
þrífr	deftly
þrír	three
þrjá	three
þrjózku	belligerance
þrjú	three
þröngt	presses
þröngva	heavily
þú	you
þungliga	heavily
þungt	difficulty
þurfa	need
þurfti	needed
Þuríðar	Thorid (name)
Þuríði	Thurid (name)
Þuríðr	Thurid (name)
Þverárhlíð	Þverarhlíd (place), Þverarhlíð (place)
Þverhlíðingar	Þverhlíðingar (place)
því	accordingly, because, therefore
þvílíka	as-you-like

Word List (Old Norse to English)

Old Norse	English
þykkir	seemed, seems, thought
Þykkist	thought
þykkizt	seems
þykkja	regarded
þykkjast	considered, to-see
þykkjumst	think, we-think
þyngra	heavy
þyrfta	needed
þyrfti	needs

U, u

Old Norse	English
Uggir	dread
um	about
umhugat	about-concern
umkvæði	about-speaking
ummælum	about-the-matter, announcements
umræða	about-discussion
umræðu	about-discussion
umsjá	protection
umtölur	about-talking
undan	from, give-way
undir	along, from, under, undertaken
uni	win
unir	satisfied
unnit	win
upp	up
upphafsmaðr	the-instigators
uppi	about-standing
upptefldir	uprooted
urðu	became

Ú, ú

Old Norse	English
Úlfarssonar	Son-of-Ulf (name)
Úlfhéðinn	Ulfhedin (name)
úlfsmunni	wolves-mouth
Úlfssonar	Son-of-Ulf (name)
út	out
útan	abroad, beyond, out, outside, travelled-out
útarliga	out-lying
útgöngu	to-come-out
úti	out, outside
Útibúr	out-house
útibúrið	out-house
útifé	grazing
útihurðinni	the-front-door
útkvæmt	out-freed
útlegðar	outlawry

V, v

Old Norse	English
vaðit	the-ford
vaðsins	the-ford
vænligt	hopeful
vænn	handsome
væntir	expect
væri	was, were, would-be
vaka	awake
Vakna	awoke
vaknar	awoke
Valbrandsson	Son-of-Valbrand (name)
vald	power
váligra	woeful
Valþjófssonar	Son-of-Valthjof (name)
ván	expected
vana	custom
vánbiðlar	hope-abide
vanða	custom
vandræði	difficulty, trouble
vándum	trouble
vanr	used-to
vápn	weapons
var	was, were
vára	further
várar	spring
varð	became, was
varða	a-concern, concern
varði	expected
varðveita	safeguard
varit	the-situation
varla	rarely
varnaði	keeping
varning	wares

Word List (Old Norse to English)

Old Norse	English
varningr	goods
várr	our, out
várri	ours, provisions
váru	our, they-are, wares, was, were, where
várum	our, ours, were
vasast	entangle-with
vaskasti	boldest
vaskligr	bold
Vatni	Vatn (Water) (place)
vátta	witnesses
váttar	witnesses
veðri	weather
veg	the-way, way
veinan	wailing
Veit	knew, know
veita	give, grant
veitir	provide
veitt	given
veitti	gave
veittr	given
veiztu	know-you
vekði	was-awake
vel	well
velli	fields
venja	accustomed
ver	be
vér	we, we-are
vera	being
verð	the-price, the-worth
verða	be, became, become, worthy
verði	became
verðr	became, worth, worthy
verit	been
verja	blocked, guarded
verki	work
verkmanna	work-men
verr	worse
verra	worse
verri	worse
verst	the-worst
versta	worst
vert	worth
vesölð	misery
vestan	the-west, west
vestanmanna	the-western-men
vestr	west
vetfanginu	known-to-hand
vetr	winter, winters
vetrarnauð	winter-need
vetrhúsa	winter-house
vetri	winter
vetrinn	the-winter, winter
vexti	grown
við	a-few, with, wood
víða	with
viðarköst	brushwood
viðbúnaðr	preparation
Víðfari	Vidfari (name), Vidfari (name)
Víðimýri	Vidimyr (place)
viðrbúningr	with-laid
viðskiptum	dealings
víg	slaying
vígr	spear-man
víkr	took, turned, week
viku	a-week, week
Vil	will, wish
Vilda	will, wish
vildi	wish, wished
vildu	wished
vili	will
vilja	willed, wish, wished
viljum	wish-to
vill	some, will, wills, wish, wishes
vilt	will
viltu	will-you
vin	friend
vina	friends
vináttu	friendship
Vindr	wind
vinfengi	friendship
vini	friends
vinir	friends
vinsælasti	most-popular
vinsæll	befriended, popular
vinum	friends
virðing	worthiness, worthy
virðir	value

Word List (Old Norse to English)

Old Norse	English
virðuligr	worthy
virt	worth
vísaðir	turn-away
vísat	turn-away
vissa	knew
vissi	knew, to-know
vist	hospitality
víst	certain, certainly, knowing, known
vistaðist	guested
Vit	with
vita	certainly, know, knowing
vitat	known
viti	knew, wit
vitr	wise
vitran	wise
vitu	know
Vitum	know
völu	goods
vörzlu	vouch

Y, y

yðar	your
yðr	to-you, you, your, yours
yðrum	your
yfir	over
ykkarn	your
yrði	could

Ý, ý

Ýmisst	or

Word List *(English to Old Norse)*

English	Old Norse

A, a

English	Old Norse
a	á, eitt, í
a-battle	bardagi
abide	bíða
abominable	foraðsillu
abomination	firn
about	á, í, ór, um
about-concern	umhugat
about-discussion	umræða, umræðu
about-speaking	umkvæði
about-standing	uppi
about-talking	umtölur
about-the-matter	ummælum
above	ofan, ofar
a-bow	boga, bogann
a-boy	sveinn
abroad	útan
a-bull	griðungr
a-burn-out	örkola
accept	þiggja
accomplished	gerviligr
accomplishment	fær
accordingly	því
accumulated	græðir
accustomed	brugðizt, venja
a-concern	varða
advise	ráðligt
advised	ráða, ráðit
a-few	fá, við
affirmed	játtuðu
after	aftr, eftir, Síðan
a-good-deal	hóti
a-great-much	stórmjök
agreement	máldögum, stefna
a-house	húsat
a-hundred	hundrað
a-kinsman	frændi
alf	Álfs
all	alla, allan, allar, allir, allr, allra, alls, allt, öll, öllu, öllum
all-clear	allsköruliga
all-good	allgott
all-little	alllítil, alllítit
all-many	allmargir
all-matters	almæltra
all-much	allmjök
allow	heimilt, láta, látum
allowed	láta
all-well	Allvel
along	ein, með, undir
already	áðr, þegar
also	ok
am	em, er
a-man	karl, maðr, manna
among	í, milli
an-arrow	ör
and	á, at, eða, en, menn, og, ok
an-even-man	jafnaðarmaðr
angry	hermt
announcements	ummælum
another	aðra, annarr, annat, öðru, önnur
answer	svara, svör
answered	svara, svaraði, svarar, svarat
answers	svarar
anti-sun-wise	andsælis
any	nökkura, nökkut
anything	nökkut, öðru
appeared	lízt
appears	lízt
appointed	ákveðnum, skipuðu
are	er, ert, erum, sér
areas	sveitir
are-repaid	launar
are-standing	stendr
are-you	ertu
Armannsfell (place)	Ármannsfelli
arms	hendi
Arngrim (name)	Arngrím, Arngrími, Arngrímr, Arngríms
a-roaming-man	reikunarmaðr

Word List (English to Old Norse)

English	Old Norse	English	Old Norse
arrange	ráðast	bargain	fala
arrived	komnir	barren-ground	skermsl
article	greinir	battle	bardaga, berjast
as	á, at, er, í, sé, sem	be	Gerast, ver, verða
a-seat	seturúm	be-able-to	mega
a-ship	skip	bear	berum, borit
aside	hjá	beat	berja
ask	Bið	became	gerðist, gerist, lagði, orðin, urðu, varð, verða, verði, verðr
asked	bað, biðr, fréttu, ok, spurði, spyrr		
ask-for	biðja	because	því
as-might	máttu	become	orðin, verða
a-solution	órlausnar	bed	rekkju, sé
a-spear-point	odda	bed-clothing	föt
assembling-troops	liðsdrátt	be-done	gera
assembly	þing	been	verit
Assembly-headland (place)	Þingnes	befell	berr
		before	áðr, fyrir, fyrr, fyrra, fyrri
assemtbly	þing		
assistance	ásjá, beina, greiða, liðsinni	befriended	vinsæll
		began	Hófst
as-you-like	þvílíka	be-given	gefast
at	á, at, í	be-helping	duga
at-carried	atburðinn	behind	aftr
a-tenant	landseti	behold	lízt
a-tent	tjald	being	sé, vera
at-home	heima	belligerance	þrjózku
a-thrall	þrælum	bellowing	gelldi
atone-for	bæta	bench	bekk
autumn	haust, hausti, haustit	benefit	beini
awake	vaka	benevolent	góðgjarnir
away	braut, brott, brottu, burt, snúit, þraut	be-short-of	skorta
		beside	hjá
a-week	viku	best	bezt, bezti
awhile	hríð, stund, stundir	betrayed	svikit
a-wife	konu, konuna	betrothe	fastna, fastnir, föstnuð
awoke	Vakna, vaknar	betrothed	fastnaðir, fastnar
a-year	ærin	better	Betr, betra, betri
		between	með, milli
		beyond	útan
		bid	bað, bauð, bið, bíða, biðja, biðr

B, b

babble	fleiprir	bids	býðr
back	bak	big	mikill
banned	bannir	binding	strengi
banning	bönnum	birch-rafter	birkirafts

Word List (English to Old Norse)

English	Old Norse
bite	hníga
black	svarta
blame	lastaði
blocked	verja
blood	blóð
Blund (name)	blunds
Blund-Ketill (name)	Blund-Katli, Blund-Ketill, Blund-Ketills
Blund-Ketill's (name)	Blund-Ketills
Blundsvatn (name)	Blundsvatn
bold	vaskligr
boldest	vaskasti
boldly	sköruliga
bondage	höftum
bore	ala, bar, berr, borinn
Borgafjord (place)	Borgarfirði, Borgarfjarðar
Borgarfjord (place)	Borgarfjörð
born-man	mannsbarn
both	báðum, bæði, beggja
bother	nenni
bought	kaupir, keypt, keypti
bound	binda, bundnar
bow	boga
brand	brandinn
brave-strong	garpr
breakfast	dagverðar
Breidabolstad (place)	Breiðabólstað
Breidafjord (place)	Breiðafirði
bridegroom	brúðguma
Broad-Beard (name)	breiðskeggs
broken	brugðit
brother	bróðir
brother-of	bróðir
brothers	bræðra
brought	færa, flytr, nái r
brushwood	viðarköst
building	bólstað
built	bæinn
bulls	naut
Burg (place)	Borg
burn	brenna, Brenni
burned	brenndr, brunnit, loguðu
burnt	brunnit
but	en, enn
buying	kaup
by	hjá

C, c

English	Old Norse
call	Kalla
called	kalla, kallaðr, kallar
came	elr, kemr, kom, koma, komit, komnir, Kómu, kómum
can	kann
can-get	nái
care	anntu
carried	bera, borit, flytja
carry	flytja
case-load	málahlut
cattle	fé, féit, fénað, fénu, fjár, fjárins, nautum
cattle-keeping	selför
caught	getr
caused	olli
celebrating	fagnat, fegnir
celebration	fagnaði
certain	víst
certainly	víst, vita
changed	breytt
chieftain	goði, höfðingjanna
chieftains	goðar, höfðingjar
child	barn
child-foster	barnfóstr
child-fostering	barnfóstri, barnfóstrinu
children	börn
choice	kost, kostr
choose	kjósa, kost
clearing	rjóðr
cliff-path	klifgötuna
climbed	stígr
cloak	skikkjunni
close	nær
clothes	klæðin
cold	kaldr, kalt, köldu
coldly	seint
collected	safnaði

Word List (English to Old Norse)

English	Old Norse
come	gakk, kom, koma, kominn, komir, komit, komizt, komna, komnir
comes	kemr, komit
coming	komit, komnir, Kvámu
companions	félaga
company	lið, liði, liðs, líta, sveit
compensated	bætr
conceal	leyna
concern	varða
conclude	enda
concluded	enda, lúka, málalykðir
conclusions	málalykðir
consent	ráð
consider	hugsa
considered	hyggja, þykkjast
cost	kosti
could	kunna, kunni, yrði
counsel	ráð, ráði, ráðum
countryside	sveitum
cow	kú, kýr
cower	kúgar
crowd	fjölmennir
cunning	beittan
custody	forsjá
custody-chieftain	forráðsgoðorð
custom	vana, vanða

D, d

English	Old Norse
danger	hætta
daughter	dóttir, dóttur
Daughter-of-Gunnar (name)	Gunnarsdóttir
Daughter-of-Tungu-Odd (name)	Tungu-Oddsdóttur
daughters	dætr
day	dag, dags
dead	dauðr
deal	kaup
dealings	viðskiptum
dealt	dælt
death	drepa
debts	skuldir

English	Old Norse
decent	allsæmiligt
decide	ráða
decision	ráð
deemed	dóm
deftly	þrífr
departed	skiljast
desperation	örvænti
did	gera, gerðu, gerir
die	deyja
dies	deyr
difference	munr
difficulty	óvingan, þungt, vandræði
direct	stefna
disappeared	hvarf
discourage	Letja
discussed	ræðir
discussing	mælir
disliked	líkar, óþokkasælli
disposition	skapsmunum
district	heraði, heraðsins
district-administration	heraðsstjórn
districts	heraða, heruð
do	Ger, gera, Gerðu, gerir, gerr
Dölum (place)	Dölum
done	búit, gerr, gert, gerzt
down	niðr
dragged	draga
dragging	draga
dread	Uggir
dreamed	dreymði
drew	kippir
dried	þorrnaði
drive	rek, reka
driven	reka, rekin
drives	ekr
driving	rekr
drought	þorri
drove	reka, rekr
dwelled	búit
dwelling	bæ, Bærr
dwellings	bæinn, bæjarins
dwelt	bjuggu
dynamic-man	atgervismaðr

Word List (English to Old Norse)

English	Old Norse

E, e

English	Old Norse
each	einhverjum, hverir, hverju, hvern, hverr, hvert
each-side	hvárirtveggju
each-way	hvárratveggja
eager	ákafa
early	ár, snemma
earth	jarðir
Easterners (name)	Austmanns
eat	matast
eating	eta, etizt, snæðings
Einar (name)	einar
either	heldr
either-side	hvárntveggja
either-way	annathvárt
enclosure	túnit
end	enda, Endið, lúkist
ended	Lýkr
ends	lýkr
enemies	óvinir
enemy	mótstöðumaðr
enjoy	njóta
enough	nóga, nógar
enquired	fréttist
entangle-with	vasast
enthralled	þjáðr
envy	öfund
equal	jafnaði, jafnan, jafnat
equal-good	jafngott, jafnvel
equally	jafnan, jafnilla, jafnræði
equally-great	jafnmikinn
errand	erendi
especially	einkum
estate	bænum
Esyuberg (place)	Esjubergi
evening	kveld, kveldi, kveldit
everyone	hverjum
evil	illum
except	nema
exchanged	skipat, skipta, skipti
expect	væntir
expected	ván, varði
experience	reynda
expressed	tjá, tjáði
eyes	augu
Eyjafjord (place)	Eyjafjörð
Eyjavaði (place)	Eyjavati

F, f

English	Old Norse
fairly	heilli
fall	fallit
fallen	fallin
falls	falli
far	Fjarri
far-from	fjarri
farm	búi, býr
farmhouse	bænum
farmyard	garða, garði
fast	fast
father	faðir, feðr, föður
father-and-son	feðga, feðgar, mágar
feed	matar
feet	fótum
fell	fell, féll, Fellr, Fellu
fellow	dreng, drengr
few	Fátt
fewer	færra
few-men	fámennr
fields	velli
fiend-man	fjandmaðr
find	fund, hitt
fire	eld, eldi, eldr
first	fyrst
Fitiar (place)	Fitjum
five	fimm
fixed	festar
fjord	firðinum
flaming	loganda
fodder	fóðr, forkast
follow	Fylgðu, fylgja
followed	fylgt
followers	félagar
following	fylgi
following-men	fjölmennari
food	mat
fooled	gabbat

Word List (English to Old Norse)

English	Old Norse	English	Old Norse
foot	fæti	given	gaf, gefa, gefit, veitt, veittr
for	á, fór, fyrir, ór		
forests	skógrinn	given-to	gefin
foster	fóstrar, fóstri	give-way	undan
foster-child	barnfóstr	gladly	gjarna
foster-father	fóstra, fóstri	go	Far, fara, ganga
fostering	fóstri	goes	fari, ferr, fór, gegnir
fought	berðist	Gói (month, February)	Gói.
found	fann, finna, fundit, Hittast	going	fara, farit, ganga, ganganda, gegna, gengi, gengr, ok
four	fjögur, fjóra		
free	frítt	going-away	farit
friend	vin	gone	farit
friends	vina, vini, vinir, vinum	good	góð, góða, góðar, góðir, góðr, góðu, góðum, gott
friendship	vináttu, vinfengi		
from	á, af, frá, fram, fyrir, ór, undan, undir	good-advice	heillaráða
		good-doing	góðgjörnum
from-home	heiman	goods	fémunum, kaupskap, varningr, vöru
from-now	fresti		
from-said	frásögn	got	fá, fekk, föng, gat, gátu, heimtir
from-there	þaðan, þangat, þegar		
from-the-south	sunnan	go-you	Gakktu
fulfilled	sáttum	grant	leggja, veita
fulfilment	efndir	grass	gras
full-of-food	mettir	grazing	útifé
fully	fullri	great	æfar, afar, mikil, mikinn, mikla, miklu, stórmikit
fully-outlawed	fullsekðat		
further	vára	greater	meiri
		great-fee	stórfé

G, g

English	Old Norse	English	Old Norse
		greatly	drjúgastr, mikil, mikinn, stórilla
gained	græddist	greeted	fagnar, heilsar, heilsat
gathered	Græðist, safna, safnaði, safnar	greeting	kveðju
		groups	flokkar
gathering	samandráttr	grown	vexti
gave	fagnar, gaf, gefr, veitti	guarded	verja
Geir's (name)	Geirs	guest	gisti, gistingu
Geir's-Slope (place)	Geirshlíð	guested	vistaðist
Gellir (name)	gelli, gellir, gellis	guesting	gistingu
get	fá, fæ, fáið, fáir	Gunnar (name)	ef, Gunnar, Gunnari, Gunnarr
get-spoiled	spillist		
getting	fást, fengr	Gunnar's (name)	Gunnars
gifts	gjafar	Gunnarsstadir (place)	Gunnarsstaði
give	gef, gefa, gifta, veita	Gunnvald (name)	Gunnvaldr

Word List (English to Old Norse)

English	Old Norse

H, h

English	Old Norse
had	átt, átta, átti, áttu, eiga, hafa, hafðar, hafði, hafðist, hafi, haft, hefða, hefðu, hefir, höfðu, lætr, lét
half-of	hálft
Halsa (place)	Hálsa
hand	handa, hendi, hendr, hönd, höndina
handmaidens	griðkonur
hands	hendr, höndum
handsome	vænn
hands-over	handsalar
hang-back	hinkr
happy-decision	happaráð
harbour	hafi
hard	harðla
harm	meins
harm-like	hörmulig
harsh-spoken	hastorðr
has	hefir
have	átt, eiga, eigum, hæfir, hafa, hafi, hafið, hafim, hafir, haft, hefða, hefi, hefir, höfum, láta
have-right	leiðrétta
having	hafi
hay	hey, heyit, heyjum
hay-allowance	heyleigur
hay-crop	grasvöxtr
hay-feed	algjafta
hay-need	heyþroti
haystacks	heybjörg, heyin
hay-supply	heykost
he	Hann, henni, honum, sinn
head	höfuð
head-bearing	höfuðburðr
hear	Heyr, Heyri
heard	frétti, heyra, heyrðu, heyrir, spyrjast
heaved	hefja
heavily	þröngva, þungliga

English	Old Norse
heavy	þyngra
heavy-load	hlass
heels	stökkr
held	Helzt
Helgi (name)	Helga, Helgi, Helgu
Helgivatn (place)	Helgavatni
help	björg, hjálp, hjálpa
helping	duga
hens	hæns
Hen-Thorir (name)	Hænsa-Þóri, Hænsa-Þórir, Hænsa-Þóris
her	hana, henni, hon
here	hér, hérna, hingat
hers	hana, hennar, síns
herself	sér
Herstein (name)	Hersteini, Hersteinn
hides	húðir
hiding	leyna
him	hann, honum, sér, sik, sín
himself	sér, sik, sjálfr, sjálfum
his	hans, honum, sér, sik, sín, sína, sinn, sinna, sinni, síns, sínu, sínum, sitt
his-nose	nasarnar
Hlidarendi (place)	Hlíðarenda
hold	halda
holding	haldið
holds	haldi
home	heim, heima, heiman
homes	bæja
home-ways	heimleiðis
honour	sæmð, sóma
honourable	sómir
honoured	ágætr, sæmðr
hope-abide	vánbiðlar
hopeful	vænligt
horse	hest, hestinn, hestinum
horseback	baki
horses	hesta, hestar, hestum, hross, hrossa, hrossum
hospitable	beinn
hospitality	vist
hostility	fjandskapar

Word List (English to Old Norse)

English	Old Norse
house	húsi, húsin, húsum
house-built	húsar
house-choice	húsakost
housed	húsat
how	hve, hvé, Hverju, hverr, hversu, hví
how-so	hverju, hversu
Hromund (name)	Hrómundi
hundred	hundruð
hundreds	hundruð
Hvamm (place)	Hvamm, Hvammi
Hvita (place)	Hvítá

I, i

English	Old Norse
I	ek, mér
ice-bound	íslög
idle-talk	gjálgrun
if	at, ef, hvárt, spyrr
ill	illa, ills, illt, Illu
ill-harm	illbýli
in	á, at, enn, í, inn, inni
in-all	alls
increased	gæða
ingeniously	snjalla
in-hand	höndum
injuries	áverkar
injury	mein
inlet	ósinn
inside	inn, inni
insist	heimta
instructions	ráðum
intend	ætla, ætlar, ætlat, ætlum
intended	ætla, ætlar, ætlat
into	í
invitation	boðit, sætt
invite	biðja, bjóða
invited	bauð, biðja, bjóða, boðinn, býðr
invited-people	boðsmenn, fyrirboðsmanna
iron	járn
is	er, sé
is-it	er
is-that	Er
it	at, hitt, Þat

J, j

English	Old Norse
Jofrid (name)	Jófríðar, Jófríði, Jófríðr
jorun	Jórunn
Jorunn (name)	Jórunn
journey	ferð, ferðir, för
journeying	fara
journey-of-men	mannaferð
judged	dæmðust
judgement	dóma

K, k

English	Old Norse
keen-eyed	skyggnstr
keep	geyma
keeping	varnaði
kill	drepa
killed	drepa, drepinn
kindled	kveikti
kinds-of	kyns
kinsman	frænda, frændi
kinsmen	frændum
knew	Kannast, Veit, vissa, vissi, viti
knock	drepit
knocked	klappar
know	kann, veit, vita, vitu, Vitum
knowing	kennumst, víst, vita
known	kennt, víst, vitat
known-to-hand	vetfanginu
know-you	veiztu

L, l

English	Old Norse
lack-of-people	mannfátt
laid	leggst, lögðu
land	land
lands	land
lands-corners	landshorna

Word List (English to Old Norse)

English	Old Norse
last	síðasta
late	seint, síð
law	lög
law-matter-standing	lögmálsstaðinn
Law-Mountain (place)	Lögbergi
lay	lag, leggst, leiðast, lek
laying	lá, lagi, lagit
lead	leiða
leant	laut
leaping	hleypr
leapt	hleypr, stíga
learned	spurði, spurt
leave	legði
led	leiddr
left	létti
less	minnr
less-dreary	ódaufligra
less-likely	óágengiligra
let	láta, látið, látim, látir, Láttu, leita, lézt
let-up	létta
let-us-go	förum
let-us-sit	Setjumst
lies	Lýgr
light	létt
like	leikr, líkar
liked	líkaði
likely	líkara, líkligra
linen-breeches	línbrókum
little	lítil, lítill, lítils, lítit, lítt
lived	bjó
loaded	klyfjar
locked	loku
long	langa, langt, lengi, Löngu
longer	lengi
looked	horfir, lítr
looking	bragði
lot	hluta, hlutr
loudly	hátt
low-deed	níðingsverk
lower	neðra
lucky-man	gæfumaðr
lying	Liggr
lying-in	innarliga

M, m

English	Old Norse
made	gerð, gert
make	Ger, gera
make-known	kunnleika
make-use	neyta
man	maðr, mann, manna, manni, manns
manager	forráðsmaðr
manly	drengiligt, mannaða
mantle	möttul
many	fjölði, fjórir, marga, margir, margt, mörgum
marriage	mægða
married	átti, gefin
marry	gift
matter	mál, máls, málum, málunum
matter-consideration	ásjámál
matters	málum
may	getr, má, mætti
me	mér, mik
meet	finnast, fund, fundar, hittast, móti
meeting	ákveðnum, mót, móti
meeting-going	mótgangi
men	fá, mann, manna, manni, menn, mennina, mönnum
men-desiring	manngirnð
men-fallen	mannfall
mention	nefna
men-travelling	Mannferðin
merchant	kaupdrengr
merry	allkátir
met	hitti, hittir, mætir
might	gegndi, mátt, mátti, máttu, munt
milk	mjólka
milked	mjólkat
mind	hug, skapir
mine	mín, mína, mínar, mínir, minn, míns, mínu, mínum, mitt
mis-advised	misráðit

Word List (English to Old Norse)

English	Old Norse
misery	vesölð
mistrust	grunaði
money	fé, pening
mongrel	hundrinn
mood	skapi
more	fleira, fleiri, meir, meira, meiri
more-helpful	nýtra
morning	morgin, morgininn
most	mest, mesta, mesti, mestr, mestu
most-angry	reiðasti
mostly	mestan
most-often	frekust
most-popular	vinsælasti
mother	móður
mountain-pasture	selinu
mounted	stíga
move	flytizt
moving	flutningar
much	mikil, mikill, mikinn, mikit, mikla, miklu, mjök
must	hlýtr
my	mér, mín, minna, míns, mínum
Myrar (place)	Mýrar
myself	sjálfa

N, n

English	Old Norse
named	heitir, hét, nefnir
near	ná, næst, náinn
nearby	hjá
nearest	næst
nearly	nær
necessary	ærit
necessities	nauðsynjum
need	þarf, þurfa
needed	krefr, þarf, þurfti, þyrfta
need-like	nauðsynligra
need-much	nauðamikill
needs	þyrfti
neither	hvárrgi
never	aldri
new	nýligar, nýtt, nýtzt
newer	nýligar, nýligra
news	frétt, fréttir, nýlundu, tíðenda, tíðendi, tíðendum
next	Annan
night	nótt
nightfall	náttaði, náttar
night-quarters	náttstað
nine	níu
no	enga, engi, Nei
noblest-women	kvenskörungr
noise	hark
none	enga, engan, engi, engum
Norðura (place)	Norðrá
Norðurá (place)	Norðrá
Norduradal (place)	Norðrárdal
Norðurdæla (place)	Norðrdæla
north	norðan, norðr
Northern-Quarter (place)	Norðlendingafjórðungi
North-River (place)	Norðrá
North-River-Valley (place)	Norðrárdal
North-Tongue (place)	Norðrtungu
Norway (place)	Nóregs
nose	nasir
not	á, Eiga, eigi, ekki, Engi, né
nothing	einkis, einskis, engi, engu
now	nú

O, o

English	Old Norse
obeyed	hlýða
obliged	skyldir
obstructed	ógreitt
Odd (name)	Odd, Oddi, Oddr
Odd's (name)	Odds
Oddson (name)	Oddsson
of	á, af, at, í, of, ór
of-all	allra
off	af, ofan

Word List (English to Old Norse)

English	Old Norse
offer	bjóðast, boð, boðit, boðs
offered	bauð, bjóðist, boðit
of-few-words	fámáligr
of-little-milk	nytlétt
of-me	mitt
of-people	manna
often	oft, oftar
of-your	þína
old-age	eldast
on	á, í
once	eitt
one	á, Annarr, Einn, eins, einu, eitt, önnur
one-month	einmánuðr
one's	eins
only	eina
open	opit
opposite	annan
or	eða, Ýmisst
ordered	skipar
Orn (name)	Erni, Örn
Ornolf (name)	Örnólf, Örnólfr, Örnólfs
Ornolfsdal (place)	Örnólfsdal
other	aðra, aðrir, annarr, annarra, annarrra, Annat, öðrum, önnur
others	annarrra, annars, öðrum
other-than	annarr, önnur
other-things	annat
otherwise	ella
our	várr, váru, várum
our-own	eigu
ours	okkarr, várri, várum
ourselves	Sjálfir
out	á, út, útan, úti, várr
out-freed	útkvæmt
out-from	ór
out-house	Útibúr, útibúrið
outlawed	sekir, sekr
outlawry	útlegðar
out-lying	útarliga
outnumbered	ofrliði
out-of	ór

English	Old Norse
outside	útan, úti
outstanding	afbragð
over	á, ofan, yfir
overpowered	aflvani
overwhelming	ofrefli
own	átt, eiga, eigin, Eigum
owned	átt
ownership	eigur
owning	eignum

P, p

pack-loads	klyfjar, klyfjarnar
paid	goldit
pale-burnt	fölskaðr
part	hlut, hluti
parted	skiljast, skilst
parts	hluta
passed	afliðnum, leið, líða, líðr
passes	leið
pasture	haga, hagar
peace	kyrrt
penalty	sekðir
people	manna, manni, manninn, mönnum
pierce	stungit
place	búit, leggir, stað
plan	ráðs
platform	pall
played	leikit
pledge	heit
pledged	heitit
point	tilgangr
poor	snauðr
popular	vinsæll
power	máttrinn, vald
powerful	ríkismunr
praised	lofaði
preparation	viðbúnaðr
prepare	búa
prepared	búit, búnir
preprations	bú
presses	þröngt
proclaim	lýsa

Word List (English to Old Norse)

English	Old Norse
produce	landsnytjar
profoundly	spakliga
proposal	tillag, tillög
protection	umsjá
provide	veitir
provided-for	kost
provisions	várri
purchase	kaupa
pushed	otar

Q, q

English	Old Norse
quarter	fjórðungi
quarter-assembly	fjórðungsþing
quarters	fjórðunga
quickly	fljótt, hratt, hvatliga, skjótt
quite	greiðliga

R, r

English	Old Norse
raised	safna
raising	hefja
ran	hlaupa, hleypir, hleypr, hljóp
rarely	varla
rather	heldr, heldust, helzt
reached	náðu, seilist
readily	reiðu
ready	búin
reason	sök
receive	þegit, þiggja
received	tekit
recompensed	iðgjöld
reconcile	sættast
reconciliation	bætr
red	rauðr
redeem	leysa
Refur (name)	refr
refuse	neita
regarded	þykkja
regret	harma
release	leysa, leyst
remained	léttir, liggja

English	Old Norse
remember	áminnast
reputation	metorð
reserved	gjaforði
residences	bústöðum
result-in	hlytist
retain	geyma
return	skila
returned	aftr
Reykjardal (place)	Reykjardal
rich	stórauðigr
ride	ríða
rides	ríðr
riding-on	framreiðin
right	heimilast, rétt, réttir, réttr, sannligt
righted	réttir
rights	rétta, réttu
risk	ábyrgð
river	ána
robbed	rænt, rænti
robber-man	ránsmaðr
robbery	rán, ráni, ránit
rode	reið, ríða, ríðr, riðu
room	rúm
ropes	reip
rose	reis
rots	fúnar
roughly	hart
rule	ráða
ruling	ráðnar

S, s

English	Old Norse
safeguard	varðveita
saga	sögu
said	er, kvað, kvaðst, kváðust, kveða, kveðst, mælt, mælti, sagði, sagðist, sagt, segði, segir, segist, segja, sögðu, Talaði
said-to	sagði
sailors	hásetar
sake	sakar
same	sama, samir

Word List (English to Old Norse)

English	Old Norse	English	Old Norse
sank	sígast	shortage	skortir
sat	Sat, sátu, setzt, sezt, Sitja, sitr	shot	skaut
		should	mun, muni, munt, munum, Mynda, myndi, skulu, skuluð, skylda, skyldi, skyldr, skyldu, skylt
satisfied	unir		
saw	sá, sér, sjá		
saw-you	Sástu		
say	seg, segja, tala		
Scotland (place)	Skotlandi	should-you	muntu
seat	sæti	show	sýna
seated	sæti	sick	Sjúk, sjúkr
seats	sæti	sickness	sótt, sóttarinnar
see	Sé, sém, Sjá, sjáir	side	síðr
seek	sækja	silence	Þegi
seemed	sýnt, þætti, þótti, þykkir	silenced	þagnar
		silent	þagði, þagnar
seems	hyggst, lízt, sjá, sýnist, þætti, Þykkir, þykkizt	silver	silfr
		similar	áþekkr
		since	síðan
seen	reyndar, sá, sætzt, sén, sénn	sister-of	systur
		sit	siti, sitja, sitr
see-you	séð	sitting	setjast
self	Sjálfr	six	sex
self-judgement	sjálfdáðum, sjálfdæmi	Skagafjord (place)	Skagafjörð
sell	seli, selja, sölu, sölur	Skaney-Fell (place)	Skáneyjarfjall
selling	seldi	Skeggja's-sons (name)	Skeggjasonar
sent	fara, sendi		
separated	skilðust	Skogarstrand (place)	Skógarströnd
servant-fees	þrælsgjöld	Skorradal (place)	Skorradal
servants	þræla	slanted	hallazt
set	sett	slaughter	slátrat
settle	sætta, sættar, sitja	slaughtered	slátrat
settled	búit, byggðan, sætta, sáttir, setið, setit, slitit	slaying	víg
		sleep	svefni
settlement	nökkura	sleep-thorn	svefnþorni
shall	mun, muni, munu, munuð, munum, skal, skalt, skulu, skulum	slump	hníga
		so	Á, í, Sá, svá
		sold	Selr
shall-you	skaltu	solution	órlausna
shame	endemi, skömm	some	nökkur, nökkura, nökkurs, nökkut, suma, sumum, vill
share	miðla		
shared	deildum, skipt		
she	henni, Hon	some-of	nökkurar
sheep	sauðir	someone	nökkura, nökkurs
shepherd	hirði, Sauðamaðr	something	eitthvert, nökkut
shields	skildir	somewhat	nökkuru, nökkurum, nökkut
shirt	skyrtu		
shoes	skó	son	son, sonr, syni

Word List (English to Old Norse)

English	Old Norse	English	Old Norse
son-in-law	mági, mágr	Steinsvað (place)	Steinsvað
son-of	sonr	stepped	steig
Son-of-Arngrim (name)	Arngrímsson	stepping	stigu
		stone	steinn
Son-of-Blund-Ketill (name)	Blund-Ketillsson	stood	standa, stóð
		straighten	rétta
Son-of-Egil (name)	Egilssyni	straightened-up	réttist
Son-of-Gunnar (name)	Gunnarsson	strange	kynligt
		strategy	brögðum
Son-of-Helgi (name)	Helgason	Strider (name)	stígandi
Son-of-Hlifar (name)	Hlífarson	strong	sterkr
Son-of-Hogni (name)	Högnasonar	struck	Höggr, slá, Slær, strykr
Son-of-Ketil (name)	Ketilssonar		
Son-of-Odd (name)	Oddsson, Oddssonar	such	slík, slíka, slíkan, slíkr, slíkt, slíku
Son-of-Onund (name)	Önundarson		
Son-of-Orlyg (name)	Örlygssonar	suddenly	skyndiliga
Son-of-Rauda-Bjarni (name)	Rauða-Bjarnarson	sufficient	einhlítir, einhlítr
		sufficiently	duganda
Son-of-Thori (name)	Þórissonar	suggestions	tillög
Son-of-Ulf (name)	Úlfarssonar, Úlfssonar	suits	gegni
		summer	sumar, sumarit, sumri
Son-of-Valbrand (name)	Valbrandsson	summer-market	sumarkaup
		summer-pasture	sels
Son-of-Valthjof (name)	Valþjófssonar	summoned	stefna, stefnir
		suppose	ætla, ætlak
sons	sona, sonr, sonu	surely	örvænt, sannast
soon	bráðliga, brátt, skjótar, snemma	suspect	gruna, grunar
		Svignaskard (place)	Svignaskarði
sought	sækja, sótt	Svignaskardi (place)	Svignaskarði
sound	hljómr	sword	sverð
south	suðr	sword's-hilt	sverðshjöltin
speak	mælir, tala		
spear-man	vígr		
spoke	kvað, kvaðst, mælt, mælti, Sagði		

T, t

English	Old Norse
spoken	kveðit, mælt, talat
spoken-of	látin
sprang	sprettr, stökk	take	nem, tæki, tak, taka, takir, tek, tekst
spring	várar		
stacks	stakkar	taken	fært, nema, taka, tekit
Stafholt (place)	Stafholt	taken-away	affærði
Stafholtstungur (place)	Stafholtstungur	talk	talim
		talked	talast, töluðu
stallions	stóðhross	talking	tal
stand	staðit, standa	tempted	freistat
standing	staddr, staðizt	ten	tigu
steal	ræna	tenant-farms	leigulanda
		tenants	landseta, landsetar

Word List (English to Old Norse)

English	Old Norse
tens	tigi, tigir, tigu, tigum
tent	tjalda, tjaldit
test	reynið
than	at, en, síðan
thanes	þegna
thanked	þakkar
thanks	þökk
that	at, en, er, þann, Þat, þenna, þetta
that-caused	olli
that-way	þannig
the	at, í, inn, ins, it, sitt, þat
the-asembly	þingheimrinn
the-assembly	alþingi, alþingis, þing, þinghelgi, þingi, þinginu, þingit, þings, þingsins
the-assembly-sanctuary	þinghelginni
the-barn	fjósi
the-best	bezt, hagastr
the-boy	piltinn, sveininum, sveinn, Sveinninn
the-bride	Brúðir
the-bridegroom	brúðgumi
the-burning	brennu, brennuna, brennunni
the-cattle	féit
the-chieftain	goða, goði
the-company	liðinu, liðs
the-cow	kúna
the-day	daginn
the-district	heraði, heraðinu, heraðit
the-districts	heruðunum
the-door	at, durum, dyrr, hurð
the-door-beam	hurðar, hurðina
the-door-ring	hurðarhringinn
the-doors	hurðar
the-earth	jörð
the-Easterners (name)	Austmenn
the-eastern-man	austmaðr
the-Eastern-Men (name)	Austmanninum
the-enclosure	túnit
the-estate	bæjarins, bænum
the-faring	farningar
the-farm	bænum, bærinn
the-farmer	bónda, Bóndi, bóndinn
the-farmyard	garði
the-fire	eldrinn, logann
the-flock	flokki
the-floor	gólfinu, gólfit
the-ford	vaðit, vaðsins
the-fourth	fjórðungi
the-front-door	útihurðinni
the-harbour	Höfn, höfnina
the-hay	heyit
The-Headland (place)	Nes
the-heath	heiði
the-hill	hól
the-hillside	hlíðinni
the-horses	hrossunum
the-house	bænum, hús, húsin, húsinu, húsunum
the-housekeeper	húskarl
the-houses	húsin
the-instigators	upphafsmaðr
the-invitation	boð
their	þeir, þeira
theirs	sín, sína, sinni, þeira
the-land	land, landi, landinu
the-lands	löndum
the-load	klyfjar
them	sér, þau, þeim
the-main-room	stofu
the-man	karl, maðr, manninum
the-matter	mála, máli, málinu, málit, málum
the-morning	morgin
the-most	flestra, mest, mestri
themselves	sik
then	en, er, Hina, í, it, nú, síðan, þá, þann, þenna, Þetta, þó
the-news	tíðenda, tíðendi
the-night	nætr, nátt, nótt, nóttin
the-north	norðan
the-older	fornum
the-other	önnur

Word List (English to Old Norse)

English	Old Norse
the-pastures	haganum
the-path	garði, götu, götuna, götunni, sneiðigata
the-people	alþýðu
the-plot	tún
the-port	höfninni
the-price	verð
the-purchase	kaupin
there	staðinn, þær, þangat, þar, þeir, þeira
there-are	eru
therefore	því
the-robbery	ránit
the-sake	sakirnar
the-same	sama
these	þessa, þessi, þessir
the-seat	pallinum
the-settlement	sættirnar
the-shield	skjöldr
the-ship-arrival	skipkvámuna
the-situation	varit
the-slope	Hlíðinni
The-Slope (place)	Hlíðina
the-south	sunnan
The-Stamper (name)	hlammanda
the-steersman	stýrimaðr, stýrimann
the-stone	steininn
the-strand	Ströndinni
the-string	streng
the-table	borð, borðum
the-tables	borð, borðit
the-tenants	landsetum
the-tent	tjaldit
The-Tongue (place)	tunguna
the-towns	bæjunum
the-trading-men	kaupmönnum
the-valleys	dalina
the-way	háttat, leið, veg
the-ways	leið
the-wedding	boðinu, boðit, boðs
the-west	vestan
the-western-men	vestanmanna
the-winter	vetrinn
the-woman	konu, konuna, konunnar
the-women	konur

English	Old Norse
the-woods	skógar, skóginn, skóginum
the-worst	verst
the-worth	verð
they	sinn, sinni, þær, Þau, þeim, þeir, þeira
the-yard	tún
they-are	eru, váru
they-were	eru
thief	þjófr
think	hyggja, þykkjumst
third	þriðja
this	í, þenna, þess, þessa, þessi, þessu, þessum, þetta
this-case	málinu
this-exchange	skipta
this-one	þessa, þessi
this-woman	konuna
Thorbjorn (name)	Þorbjörn
Thord (name)	Þórð, Þórðar, Þórði, Þórðr
Thorgeir (name)	Þorgeirs
Thori (name)	Þóri, Þóris
Thorid (name)	Þuríðar
Thorir (name)	Þóri, Þórir
Thori's (name)	Þóris
Thorkel (name)	Þorkatli, Þorkell, Þorkels
Thorkel's (name)	Þorkels
Thorodd (name)	Þórodd, Þóroddi, Þóroddr
Thorolf (name)	Þórólfr
Thorstein (name)	Þorsteini
Thorvald (name)	Þorvald, Þorvaldr
Thorvald's (name)	Þorvalds
those	þeir
though	þó
thought	hug, hugða, hugðist, þótt, Þótti, þóttumst, þykkir, Þykkist
thoughtful	hugsi
thoughts	hugr
Thraelastraum (place)	Þrælastraumr
threatening	heitan
three	þrem, þrír, þrjá, þrjú
Thurid (name)	Þuríði, Þuríðr

Word List (English to Old Norse)

English	Old Norse	English	Old Norse
tide-change	misgöngin	travelled	fara, ferð, Fór
tidings	tíðenda, tíðendi	travelled-from	ferð
time	mund, tíma	travelled-out	útan
to	á, at, gengr, í, til	travelling	fara, farinn, farit, ferðina, ferr
to-accept	þiggja	travelling-men	farmönnum
to-be-oppressed	kúgast	Trefil (name)	trefils
to-buy	kaupa	Trefill (name)	trefill
to-come	komast	trodden	troðinn
to-come-out	útgöngu	trouble	vandræði, vándum
to-dress	klæðast	true	
to-get	hljótast, hljótist	true-like	sannligra
together	saman	truly	Satt
together-travelling	samfara	trust	traust, trausts
to-give	gefa	Tungu-Odd (name)	Tungu-Odd, Tungu-Oddi, Tungu-Oddr, Tungu-Odds
to-go	fara, ganga		
to-have	hafa		
to-her	henni	Tungu-odd's (name)	Tungu-Odds
to-him	honum, sik	turn-away	vísaðir, vísat
to-know	vissi	turned	hverfr, snúa, snúit, snýr, víkr
told	sagði, sagt, tala, tölu, töluð		
		turned-back	hverfa
to-learn	spyrja	turned-out	reyndist
to-me	mér	turn-out	reynast
to-meet	hitta, móti	twelve	tólf, tólfta
to-mind	hugnar	twice	tysvar
took	nemr, taka, tekr, tók, tókt, víkr	two	tvá, tvær, tvau, tveir

Þ, þ

English	Old Norse
Þverarhlíd (place)	Þverárhlíð
Þverarhlíð (place)	Þverárhlíð
Þverhlíðingar (place)	Þverhlíðingar

U, u

English	Old Norse
Ulfhedin (name)	Úlfhéðinn
unburnt	óbrunnit
under	undir
understand	skilit
undertaken	undir
uneasy	ódælla
un-equally	ójafnað
unexpected	ófyrirsynju

English	Old Norse
to-rebuke	ávíta
Torfi (name)	Torfi
torment	Raun
to-say	segja
to-see	þykkjast
to-stand	staðar
to-talk	tala
to-travel	ferð
towards	mót
to-you	þér, yðr
to-your	þér
trading	kaupum
trading-men	kaupmenn
trading-post	kaupstefnur
traditions	sið
tragic	hörmuligt
trampling	spark
travel	fara, farir, ferð, ferðum

Word List (English to Old Norse)

English	Old Norse
un-friendship	óvináttu
unknown	ókunnig
unless	nema
unlike	ólíkligt
unpopularity	óvinsældin, óvinsældir
un-quiet	ókyrrt
un-stocked	óbirgr
until	til
unworthy	óvirt
up	upp
uprooted	upptefldir
us	okkr, oss
used-to	vanr
useful	gagni

V, v

English	Old Norse
valuables	fémætt
value	virðir
Vatn (Water) (place)	Vatni
very-few	allfáir
Vidfari (name)	Víðfari
Vidimyr (place)	Víðimýri
voice	rödd
vouch	vörzlu

W, w

English	Old Norse
wailing	veinan
walking	ganganda
wandered	reikar
wanders	reikar
wares	varning, váru
was	er, Gerist, væri, var, varð, váru
was-awake	vekði
was-named	heitir
way	veg
we	oss, vér
wealth	fé, féit
wealth-with-betokened	fjárviðtökunni
wealthy	auðga, auðgastr
wealthy-man	auðigr, auðmaðr
weapons	vápn
we-are	erum, vér
weather	veðri
wedding-feast	boði
week	víkr, viku
well	góðrar, sekð, vel
went	færi, Fara, farit, Ferr, fór, fóru, ganga, gekk, gengit, gengr, gerði
were	er, væri, var, váru, várum
west	vestan, vestr
we-think	þykkjumst
what	hvat
when	er, sem
where	er, hvar, sem, Váru
whether	hvárt
which	er, Hvárt, hvert, sem
while	en
whip	sviga
whipped	keyrir
whistled	blístrar
who	er, hver, hverir, Hverjir, Hverr, sem
why	Hví
wife	kona
wildly	óðliga
will	gjarna, mun, Vil, Vilda, vili, vill, vilt
willed	vilja
willingly	gjarna
wills	vill
will-you	viltu
win	uni, unnit
wind	Vindr
window	gluggr
winter	vetr, vetri, Vetrinn
winter-house	vetrhúsa
winter-need	vetrarnauð
winters	vetr
wise	vitr, vitran
wish	vil, Vilda, vildi, vilja, vill
wished	Gunnarr, vildi, vildu, vilja
wishes	vill

Word List (English to Old Norse)

English	Old Norse	*English*	Old Norse
wish-to	viljum	yours	sinn, sinni, þín, þína, þinn, þinnar, þinni, þíns, þínu, þínum, þitt, yðr
wit	viti		
with	durum, með, móti, við, víða, Vit		
with-goings-on	meðferðina	yule	jól
with-laid	viðrbúningr		
without	án		
withstand	standa		
witnesses	vátta, váttar		
woeful	váligra		
wolves-mouth	úlfsmunni		
woman	kona		
women	Konur		
wonder	Kynligt		
wood	við		
woods-outskirts	skógarnef		
word	orð		
words	orð, orða, orðit		
word-sickened	orðsjúkr		
work	verki		
work-men	verkmanna		
workshop	smiðju		
worse	verr, verra, verri		
worst	versta		
worth	verðr, vert, virt		
worthiness	virðing		
worthy	verða, verðr, virðing, virðuligr		
would	mun, mundi, mundu, muni, munir, munt, munu, mynda, myndi, skyldu		
would-be	væri		
wounded	særum, sárir, sárr		
wrong	rangt, röngu		

Y, y

yard	garði
yes	Já
you	í, þér, þik, þinn, þinni, þú, yðr
your	þína, þinn, þinna, þinni, þitt, yðar, yðr, yðrum, ykkarn

The Saga of Hen-Thorir (Old Icelandic)

The Saga of Hen-Thorir (*Old Icelandic*)

Old Icelandic	Literal	English
1	**1**	**1**
Oddur hét maður Önundarson breiðskeggs, Úlfarssonar, Úlfssonar á Fitjum, Skeggjasonar, Þórissonar hlammanda.	Odd named man son-of-Onund Broad-Beard, son-of-Ulf, son-of-Ulf of Fitiar, Skeggja's-Sons, son-of-Thori The-Stamper.	There was a man named Odd, the son of Onund Broad-Beard, son of Ulf, son of Ulf of Fitjar, Skeggja's sons, son of Thori the Stamper.
Hann bjó á Breiðabólstað í Reykjardal í Borgarfirði.	He lived at Breidabolstad in Reykjardal in Borgafjord.	He lived at Breidabolstad in Reykjardal in Borgafjord.
Hann átti þá konu er Jórunn hét.	He had then a-wife was Jorun named.	He had a wife then who was named Jorun.
Hún var vitur kona og vel látin.	She was wise woman and well spoken-of.	She was a wise woman and well spoken of.
Þau áttu fjögur börn, sonu tvo vel mannaða og dætur tvær.	They had four children, sons two well manly and daughters two.	They had four children, two sons who were manly, and two daughters.
Annar son þeirra hét Þóroddur en annar Þorvaldur.	One sons theirs named Thorodd and another Thorvald.	One son of theirs was named Thorodd, and another Thorvald.
Þuríður hét dóttir Odds en önnur Jófríður.	Thurid named daughter Odd's and the-other Jofrid.	Odd's daughter was named Thurid, and the other Jofrid.
Hann var kallaður Tungu-Oddur.	He was called Tungu-Odd.	He was called Tungu Odd.
Engi var hann kallaður jafnaðarmaður.	Not was he called an-even-man.	He was not called a fair man.
Torfi hét maður og var Valbrandsson, Valþjófssonar, Örlygssonar frá Esjubergi.	Torfi named man and was son-of-Valbrand, son-of-Valthjof, son-of-Orlyg from Esyuberg.	There was a man named Torfi, the son of Valbrand, son of Valthjof, son of Orlyg from Esyuberg.
Hann átti Þuríði Tungu-Oddsdóttur.	He married Thurid Daughter-of-Tungu-Odd.	He married Thurid, the daughter of Tungu Odd.
Þau bjuggu á öðrum Breiðabólstað.	They lived at other Breidabolstad.	They lived at another farm in Breidabolstad.

The Saga of Hen-Thorir (Old Icelandic)

Old Icelandic	Literal	English
Arngrímur hét maður Helgason, Högnasonar er út kom með Hrómundi.	Arngrim named man son-of-Helgi, son-of-Hogni who out came with Hromund.	There was a man named Arngrim, the son of Helfi, son of Hogni, who came out (to Iceland) with Hromund.
Hann bjó í Norðurtungu.	He lived at North-Tongue.	He lived at North Tongue.
Hann var kallaður Arngrímur goði.	He was called Arngrim the-chieftain.	He was called Arngrim the chieftain priest.
Helgi hét son hans.	Helgi named a-son his.	He had a son named Helgi.
Blund-Ketill hét maður, son Geirs hins auðga úr Geirshlíð, Ketilssonar blunds er Blundsvatn er við kennt.	Blund-Ketill named man, son-of Geir's the wealthy from Geir's-Slope, son-of-Ketil Blund who Blundsvatn is with known.	There was a man named Blund-Ketill, the son of Geir the wealthy, from Geir's Slope, the son of Ketil Blund, for which Blundsvatn is known.
Hann bjó í Örnólfsdal.	He lived in Ornolfsdal.	He lived in Ornolfsdal.
Það var nokkuru ofar en nú stendur bærinn.	That was somewhat above which now are-standing the-farm.	That was a little way above where the farm now stands.
Var þar mart bæja upp í frá.	Were there many homes up by from.	There were many homes above there.
Hersteinn hét son hans.	Herstein named son his.	His son was named Herstein.
Blund-Ketill var manna auðgastur og best að sér í fornum sið.	Blund-Ketill was a-man wealthy and the-best of him of the-older traditions.	Blund-Ketill was a wealthy man and kept the best of the old traditions.
Hann átti þrjá tigu leigulanda.	He had three ten tenant-farms.	He had thirty tenant farms.
Hann var hinn vinsælasti maður í héraðinu.	He was the most-popular man in the-district.	He was the most popular man in the district.
Þorkell trefill hét maður.	Thorkel Trefill named man.	There was a man named Thorkel Trefill.
Hann var Rauða-Bjarnarson.	He was son-of-Rauda-Bjarni.	He was the son of Rauda Bjarni.
Hann bjó í Svignaskarði fyrir utan Norðurá.	He lived in Svignaskard before beyond North-River.	He lived in Svignaskard by the North River.

The Saga of Hen-Thorir (Old Icelandic)

Old Icelandic	Literal	English
Helgi var bróðir Þorkels er bjó í Hvammi í Norðurárdal.	Helgi was brother Thorkel's who lived in Hvamm in North-River-Valley.	Thorkel's brother was Helgi, who lived at Hvamm in the North River Valley.
Annar var Gunnvaldur, faðir Þorkels er átti Helgu dóttur Þorgeirs á Víðimýri.	Another was Gunnvald, father Thorkel's was married Helgi daughter Thorgeir of Vidimyr.	Another was Gunnvald, Thorkel's father, who married Helga, daughter of Thorgeir at Vidmyr.
Þorkell trefill var vitur maður og vel vinsæll, stórauðigur að fé.	Thorkel Trefill was wise man and well popular, rich in wealth.	Thorkel Trefil was a wise man and very popular, and rich in wealth.
Þórir hét maður.	Thorir named man.	There was a man named Thorir.
Hann var snauður að fé og eigi mjög vinsæll af alþýðu manna.	He was poor in wealth and not much friends of the-people men.	He was poor in wealth, and had not much in the way of friends of the people.
Hann lagði það í vanda sinn að hann fór með sumarkaup sitt héraða í milli og seldi það í öðru er hann keypti í öðru og græddist honum brátt fé af kaupum sínum.	He became that in custom his that he travelled with summer-market the districts in among and selling that in another what he bought in another and gained him soon wealth of trading his.	He made it his custom to travel to the summer markets in among the districts selling what he bought from one in another, and he soon gained wealth from his trading.
Og eitt sinn er Þórir fór sunnan um heiði hafði hann með sér hænsn í för norður um land og seldi þau með öðrum kaupskap og því var hann kallaður Hænsna-Þórir.	And once then when Thorir travelled the-south about the-heath had he with himself hens on journey north about the-land and sold then with other goods and therefore was he called Hen-Thorir.	And once when Thorir travelled south about the heath he had hens with him on his journey north about the land, and then sold them with other goods, and he was therefore called Hen-Thorir.
Nú græðir Þórir svo mikið að hann kaupir sér land er að Vatni heitir upp frá Norðurtungu.	Now accumulated Thorir so much that he bought himself land that at Vatn (Water) was-named up from North-Tongue.	Now Thorir accumulated so much that he bought himself land that was named Vatn, up from North Tongue.
Og fá vetur hafði hann búið áður hann gerðist svo mikill auðmaður að hann átti undir vel hverjum manni stórfé.	And a-few winters had he dwelled before he became so much wealthy-man that he had under well everyone people great-fee.	And when he had dwelled there a few winters he became such a wealthy man that he had many people that owed him great wealth.
En þó að honum græddist fé mikið þá héldust þó óvinsældir hans því að varla var til ópokkasælli maður en Hænsna-Þórir var.	But though that he gathered wealth much then rather though unpopularity his because that rarely was to disliked man than Hen-Thorir was.	But though he gathered much wealth, his unpopularity rather remained, because rarely was a man so disliked than Hen Thorir was.

The Saga of Hen-Thorir (Old Icelandic)

Old Icelandic	Literal	English
## 2	## 2	## 2
Einn dag gerir Þórir heiman ferð sína og ríður í Norðurtungu og hitti Arngrím goða og bauð honum barnfóstur:	One day did Thorir from-home travel his and rode to North-Tongue and met Arngrim the-chieftain and invited him foster-child:	One day Thorir travelled from his home and rode to North Tongue and met Arngrim the chieftain priest and offered to foster one of his children.
"Vil eg taka við Helga syni þínum og geyma sem eg kann en eg vil hafa vináttu þína í mót og fylgi til þess að eg nái réttu af mönnum".	"Will I take with Helgi son yours and keep as I know but I wish to-have friendship yours in towards and following to this that I can-get rights from men".	"I will take your son Helgi and keep him as well as I know, but I wish to have your friendship going forward and your following so that I can get my rights from people".
Arngrímur svarar:	Arngrim answered:	Arngrim answered:
"Svo líst mér sem lítill höfuðburður muni mér að þessu barnfóstri".	"So appears to-me that little head-bearing would to-me of this child-fostering".	"So it appears to me that little shall I bear my head for this child-fostering".
Þórir svarar:	Thorir answered:	Thorir answered:
"Eg vil gefa sveininum hálft fé mitt heldur en eg nái eigi barnfóstrinu en þú skalt rétta hluta minn og vera skyldur til við hvern sem eg á um".	"I wish to-give the-boy half-of wealth mine rather than I get not child-fostering but you shall rights lot mine and being should to with each as I am about".	I wish to give the boy hald of my wealth, rather than foster him, but you shall help me with my rights, with each that I am about to deal with".
Arngrímur svarar:	Arngrim answered:	Arngrim answered:
"Það ætla eg mála sannast að neita eigi því er svo er vel boðið".	"That intend I the-matter surely to refuse not because is so well as offered".	"I intend not to refuse the matter because it is so well offered".
Fór þá Helgi heim með Þóri og heitir þar nú síðan bærinn að Helgavatni.	Travelled then Helgi home with Thori and named there now since the-farm that Helgivatn.	Helgi then travelled home with Thori and there has since been named Helgivatn.
Arngrímur veitti Þóri umsjá og þykir þegar ódælla við hann og nær hann nú réttu máli af hverjum manni.	Arngrim gave Thori protection and seemed from-there uneasy with him and brought he now rights the-matter of each man.	Arngrim gave Thori protection and he seemed from then on uneasy, and he now brought rights in the matters of each man.

The Saga of Hen-Thorir (Old Icelandic)

Old Icelandic	Literal	English
Græðist honum nú stórmikið fé og gerist hinn mesti auðmaður.	Gathered he now great wealth and became the most wealthy-man.	He now gathered great wealth and became the most wealthy man.
Hélst honum enn óvinsældin.	Held he in unpopularity.	His unpopularity held.
Það var eitt sumar að skip kom af hafi í Borgarfjörð og lögðu þeir eigi inn í ósinn en lögðu utarlega á höfnina.	It was one summer that a-ship came of harbour in Borgarfjord and laid there not in at inlet but laid out-lying of the-harbour.	It was one summer that a ship came to the harbour in Borgafjord, and did not lay in an inlet but outside the harbour.
Örn hét stýrimaður.	Orn named the-steersman.	The steersman was named Orn.
Hann var vinsæll maður og hinn besti kaupdrengur.	He was popular man and the best merchant.	He was a popular man and the best merchant.
Oddur frétti skipkomuna.	Odd heard the-ship-arrival.	Odd heard of the ship's arrival.
Hann var vanur í fyrra lagi í kaupstefnur að koma og leggja lag á varning manna því að hann hafði héraðsstjórn.	He was used-to in before laying in trading-post to come and grant lay in wares people therefore that he had district-administration.	He was accustomed to come to the trading post and have grant of the wares of people because he was the administrator of the district.
Þótti engum dælt fyrr að kaupa en vissi hvað hann vildi að gera.	Thought none dealt before that purchase but to-know what he wished to be-done.	No one thought to deal or purchase until they knew what he wished to be done.
Nú hittir hann kaupmenn og fréttir eftir hversu þeir ætla sína ferð eða hve skjótar sölur þeir vildu hafa og sagði þann vanda að hann legði lag á varning manna.	Now met he trading-men and news after how-so they intended their voyage or how soon sell they wished have and said then custom that he leave grant to wares people.	Now he met the trading men and asked them their business, and how soon they wished to sell their goods, saying that it was his custom to grant wares to people.
Örn svarar:	Orn answered:	Orn answered:
"Sjálfir ætlum vér að ráða vorri eigu fyrir þér því þú átt engan pening með vorum varnaði og muntu ráða að sinni eigi meira en þú mælir".	"Ourselves intend we that rule provisions our-own before you because you own none money with our keeping and should-you rule to yours not more than you speak".	"We intend to decide upon our provisions ourselves without you, because you have no money with us to rule, and you shall rule over no more than the words you speak.
Oddur svarar:	Odd answered:	Odd answered:
"Það grunar mig að það gegni þér verr en mér og svo skal og vera.	"That suspect me that it suits you worse than me and so shall and being.	"I suspect that it will suit you worse than me, but so it shall be.

The Saga of Hen-Thorir (Old Icelandic)

Old Icelandic	Literal	English
Er því að lýsa að vér bönnum öllum mönnum kaup við yður að eiga og svo flutningar allar svo að eg skal fé af þeim taka sem yður veita nokkura björg.	Is therefore that proclaim that we-are banning all men buying from you that own and so moving all so that I shall wealth of them take who you grant any help.	I therefore proclaim that we are banning all men from buying from you, and so I shall take fines from any who help you.
En eg veit að þér flytjist eigi úr höfninni fyrir misgöngin".	Then I know that you move not out-from the-port before tide-change".	Then I know that you cannot move out from the port until the tide changes".
Örn svarar:	Orn answered:	Orn answered:
"Ráða máttu ummælum þínum.	"Decide as-might about-the-matter yours.	"Decide as you might about your matter.
Eigi látum vér kúgast að heldur".	Not allow we to-be-oppressed to either".	We will not allow ourselves to be oppressed either.
Oddur ríður nú heim en Austmenn liggja þar í höfninni og gefur þeim eigi í brottu.	Odd rode now home and The-Easterners remained there in the-port and gave they not to away.	Odd now rode home and the Norwegians remained there in the port and could not get away.

3

Annan dag eftir reið Hersteinn Blund-Ketillsson út á Nes.	Next day after rode Herstein son-of-Blund-Ketill out to The-Headland.	The next day after Herstein son of Blund-Ketill rode out to the headland.
Hann fann Austmenn er hann reið utan.	He found The-Easterners as he rode out.	As he rode out he found the Norwegians.
Kannast hann við stýrimann og varð vel að skapi.	Knew he with the-steersman and became well of mood.	He knew the steersman and became good in his mood.
Örn sagði Hersteini hversu mikinn ójafnað Oddur bauð þeim,	Orn told Herstein how-so greatly un-equally Odd bid them,	Orn told Herstein how unequally Odd had dealt with them,
"og þykjumst vér eigi vita hversu vér skulum með fara voru máli".	"and we-think we not knowing how-so we shall with go our the-matter".	"and we think that we do not know how we shall go forward with the matter".

The Saga of Hen-Thorir (Old Icelandic)

Old Icelandic	Literal	English
Þeir talast við um daginn og að kveldi ríður Hersteinn heim og segir föður sínum frá farmönnum og hvar nú er komið þeirra máli.	They talked together about the-day and to evening rode Herstein home and said father his from travelling-men and where now are come they the-matter.	They talked together about the day and towards the evening Herstein rode home and told his father about the travelling men and where they had come to this matter.
Blund-Ketill svarar:	Blund-Ketill answered:	Blund-Ketill answered:
"Við kennist eg mann þenna að þinni frásögn að því að eg var með föður hans þá eg var barn og hefi eg eigi nýtara dreng fundið en hans föður og er það illa að hans kosti er þröngt.	"With knowing I man this that you from-said that because that I was with father his then I was child and have I not more-helpful fellow found than his father and that it ill that he cost that presses.	"I know this man from what you have said, and I was with his father when I was a child, and I have not found a more helpful fellow than his father, and it is bad that this pressing matter is costly.
Og það mundi faðir hans ætla að eg mundi nokkuð líta á hans mál ef hann þyrfti þess við.	And that would father his intend that I should some company to him matter if he needs this with.	And his father would intend that I should accompany him in this matter if he needs it.
Og nú á morgun snemma skaltu ríða út í Höfn og bjóða honum hingað með svo marga menn sem hann vill.	And now at morning early shall-you ride out to The-harbour and invite him here with so many men as he will.	And now early in the morning you shall ride out to the harbour and invite him here with as many men as he wishes.
En ef hann vill annað heldur þá skal flytja hann hvert er hann vill, suður eða norður, og skal eg leggja á allan hug sem eg hefi föng á honum við að hjálpa".	But if he will another rather then shall carry he which that he will, south or north, and shall I grant to all mind as I have got to him with to help".	But if he wishes rather another way, then shall we carry him as he wishes, north or south, and I shall grant to him all my mind to help him".
Hersteinn kvað það gott ráð og drengilegt	Herstein spoke that good decision and manly	Herstein said that it was a good and manly decision.
"er þó er meiri von að þar fyrir höfum vér óvingan annarra".	"is though is more expected that there before have we difficulty others".	"It is though more expected that before this we shall have difficulty wih others".
Blund-Ketill svarar:	Blund-Ketill answered:	Blund-Ketill answered:
"Þar sem vér berum eigi verra mál til en Oddur þá kann vera að oss falli það létt".	"There as we bear not worse matter to than Odd then know being that us falls it light".	"Since we don't have a worse case than Oddr, it may be that we take it easy".
Nú líður nóttin	Now passed the-night.	Now the night passed.

The Saga of Hen-Thorir (Old Icelandic)

Old Icelandic	Literal	English
en þegar um morguninn snemma lætur Blund-Ketill safna hrossum úr haga og er þá búin ferðin og rekur Hersteinn hundrað hrossa í móti kaupmönnum og þurfti einkis á bú að biðja.	then from-there about morning early had Blund-Ketill gathered horses from pasture and was then ready to-travel and drove Herstein a-hundred horses to meet the-trading-men and needed nothing of prepartions to ask-for.	then from there about early morning Blund-Ketill had gathered horses from pasture and was then ready to travel, and Herstein drove a hundred horses to meet the trading men, and they needed nothing in the way of provisions to ask for.
Hann kemur út þangað og sagði Erni tillag föður síns.	He came out from-there and told Orn proposal father his.	He came out from there and told Orn about his father's proposal.
Örn kvaðst gjarna þenna kost þiggja vilja en kvaðst þó hyggja að þeir feðgar mundu fá óvináttu annarra manna fyrir þetta.	Orn spoke gladly then choose accept willed then said though think that they father-and-son would get un-friendship other men from that.	Orn said that he would gladly wish to accept, then said though that father and son would bet enmity from other men for that.
Hersteinn kvað þá eigi verða farið að því.	Herstein spoke then not become going-away from because-of.	Herstein said that they would not become put off because of it.
Örn mælti:	Orn spoke:	Orn spoke:
"Þá skulu hásetar mínir flytja sig í önnur héruð og er þó ærið í ábyrgð þó að vér séum eigi allir í einu héraði".	"Then shall sailors mine carry themselves to other districts and is then necessary in risk though that we see not all in one district".	"Then shall my sailors carry themselves to other districts, and there is a need to avoid the risk that we are not all seen together in one district".
Hersteinn flytur nú Örn heim með sér og varning hans og skilst eigi fyrr við en allir kaupmenn eru í brottu og búið um skip og öllu til skila komið.	Herstein brought now Orn home with himself and wares his and parted not before with that all trading-men they-were to away and prepared about the-ship and all to return come.	Herstein now brought Orn home with him and his wares, and did not part until all the traders were away from there, and the ship laid up, and everything prepared to return.
Blund-Ketill tekur afar vel við Erni.	Blund-Ketill took great well with Orn.	Blund-Ketill received Orn well.
Sat hann þar í góðum fagnaði.	Sat he there in good celebration.	He stayed there in good celebration.
Komu nú tíðindi þessi fyrir Odd hvað Blund-Ketill hefir ráðs tekið og tala menn nú um að hann hafi sýnt sig í mótgangi við hann.	Came now the-news this before Odd what Blund-Ketill had plan taken and told men now about that he had seemed himself in meeting-going with he.	Now this news came to Odd, what Blund-Ketill had planned, and people were now saying that he had shown himself in opposition to him.
Oddur svarar:	Odd answered:	Odd answered:

The Saga of Hen-Thorir (Old Icelandic)

Old Icelandic	Literal	English
"Kalla má það svo en þar er sá maður er bæði er vinsæll og kappsamur.	"Call may that so then there is seen man is both in friendship and zealous.	"You can call it that, but there is a man who is both popular and ambitious.
Þó vil eg enn vera láta svo búið".	Though wish I then being allowed so settled".	However, for the time being I want to be alone".
Og er nú enn kyrrt.	And was now but peace.	And for now things were peaceful.

4

Sumar þetta var lítill grasvöxtur og eigi góður fyrir því að lítt þornaði og varð alllítil heybjörg manna.	Summer that was little hay-crop and not good before because that little dried and became all-little haystacks people.	That summer there was little grass growth and not a good one, because it did not dry out much, and there was very little hay.
Blund-Ketill mælti um haustið við landseta sína og segir að hann vildi heyleigur hafa á öllum löndum sínum:	Blund-Ketill spoke about autumn with tenants his and said that he willed hay-allowance have to all the-lands his:	Blund-Ketill went to his lands in the autumn and said that he wants to have a hay lease on all his lands:
"Eigum vér mart fé ganganda en hey fást lítil.	"Own we many cattle going but hay getting little.	"We have a lot of cattle, but we've got little hay.
Eg vil og ráða fyrir hversu miklu slátrað er í haust á hverju búi allra minna landseta og mun þá vel hlýða".	I will also decide for how great slaughter is in autumn for each farm all my tenants and should then well obeyed".	I also want to decide how much slaughter there is this autumn on every farm of all my landholders, and I will instruct them".
Nú líður sumar og kemur vetur og er snemma nauðamikill norður um Hlíðina en viðbúningur lítill.	Now passed the-summer and came winter and was early need-much north about The-Slope and with-laid little.	Now the summer was over, and winter was coming, and there was an early need north of Hlíðin, but there was little preparation.
Fellur mönnum þungt.	Fell men difficulty.	Men fell into difficulty.
Fer svo fram um jól.	Went so from about yule.	And so it went until about until Yule.
Og er þorri kemur þá ekur hart að mönnum og eru margir þá upp tefldir.	And was drought came then drives roughly to men and they-were many then up drawn.	And when the drought came, it drove people hard, and many were then uprooted.

The Saga of Hen-Thorir (Old Icelandic)

Old Icelandic	Literal	English
Og að kveldi eins dags kemur landseti Blund-Ketills og segir sig vera í heyþroti og krefur úrlausna.	And to the-evening one day came a-tenant Blund-Ketill and said him being in hay-need and needed solution.	And in the evening one day, a tenant of Blund-Ketill's came and said that he was in trouble and demanded a solution.
Bóndi svarar:	The-farmer answered:	The farmer answered:
"Hverju gegnir það?	"How goes that?	"How is this?
Eg þóttist svo til ætla að hausti að eg hugði að vel mundi hlýða".	I thought so to supposed to autumn that I thought that well would obeyed".	I thought so that I supposed the autumn would be well observed".
Sjá svarar að færra var slátrað en hann sagði.	See answer that fewer were slaughtered than he said.	He answered that he had slaughtered fewer that he said.
Blund-Ketill sagði:	Blund-Ketill said:	Blund-Ketill said:
"Við skulum eiga kaup saman.	"We shall have a-deal together.	"We shall have a deal together.
Eg mun leysa þig úr vandræði þessu um sinn en þú seg þetta engum manni því að eg vil eigi venja menn upp á mig, allra helst síðan þér hafið þó eigi haft mín tillög".	I shall redeem you out-of trouble this about yours but you say this none to-people because that I wish not accustomed men up to me, all rather than you have though not had my suggestions".	I shall help you out of this trouble of yours, but say nothing of this to people because I do not wish to be accustomed to men approaching me, especially since you have not done as I suggested".
Sá fór heim og sagði sínum vin að Blund-Ketill sé afbragð annarra manna í sínum viðskiptum og kvað hann sig úr vandræði leyst hafa.	So went home and told his friend that Blund-Ketill being outstanding others man for his dealings and spoke he his about trouble release had.	So he went home and told his friend that Blund-Ketill was an outstanding man for all his dealings, and about how he had released him from his troubles.
En sá sagði sínum vin og verður það svo víst um allt héraðið.	Then so said-to his friend and became it so known about all the-district.	Then he told his friend, and so it became known about the whole district.
Líður stund og kemur gói.	Passed awhile and came Gói (month, February).	A while passed and then came the month of Gói (February).
Þá koma tveir landsetar hans og segja sig í heyþroti.	Then came two tenants his and said to-him of hay-need.	Then two tenants of his came and said to him that they had need of hay.
Blund-Ketill svarar:	Blund-Ketill answered:	Blund-Ketill answered:

The Saga of Hen-Thorir (Old Icelandic)

Old Icelandic	Literal	English
"Illa hafið þér gert að þér hafið af brugðið mínum ráðum því að það er þann veg þó að vér höfum hey mikil þá höfum vér og fé því fleira.	"Ill have you done that you have of broken my instructions because that it is then the-way though that we have hay much then have we also cattle therefore more.	"You have done wrong, that you have rejected my advice, because it is this way, although we have a lot of hay, we also have more cattle.
Nú ef eg miðla yður þá hefi eg ekki til míns fjár.	Now if I share to-you then have I not to my cattle.	Now if I share it with you, then I will have none for my own cattle.
Er nú hér um að kjósa".	Is now here about to choose".	This is now the choice here".
Þeir ala á málið og tjá vesöld sína.	They bore about the-matter and expressed misery theirs.	They continued expressing their misery in this matter.
En honum þótti hörmulegt að heyra á þeirra veinan og lét reka heim fjóra tigu hrossa og hundrað og lét drepa fjóra tigu hrossa þau er verst voru en gaf landsetum sínum það fóður sem hrossunum var ætlað áður.	Then he thought tragic that heard of their wailing and had driven home four tens horses and a-hundred and had killed forty tens horses they which the-worst were and gave the-tenants his that fodder which the-horses were intended before.	Then he thought it tragic to hear their wailing, and had forty horses and a hundred driven home, slaughtered the forty that were the worst, and gave his tenants the fodder that was intended for those horses.
Fara þeir heim fegnir.	Went they home celebrating.	They went home celebrating.
Veturinn gerist því verri sem meir leið á og verður örkola fyrir mörgum.	Winter became then worse as more passed of and became a-burn-out for many.	The winter became worse the more it passed, and hopes turned to ashed for many.

5

Old Icelandic	Literal	English
Nú kemur einmánuður og koma tveir landsetar Blund-Ketills.	Now came one-month and came two tenants Blund-Ketill's.	Now the next month came in, and two of Blund-Ketill's tenants came.
Þeir áttu sér hóti helst nokkurs kosti í fémunum en þó voru þeir nú í heyproti og biðja hann úrlausna.	They had themselves a-good-deal rather some benefit in goods then though wares theirs now in hay-need and asked he a-solution.	They had themselves a good deal of benefit of goods and wares, but they were now in need of hay, and they asked for a solution.
Hann svarar þá og kveðst eigi til hafa enda lést hann eigi vilja drepa fleira fé.	He answered then and said not to have end let he not wish to-kill more cattle.	He then answered and said he didn't have any, since he didn't want to kill any more cattle.
Þeir fréttu ef hann viti nokkura þá menn er hey hefðu til sölu.	They asked if he knew someone then men that hay had to sell.	They asked if he knew any men who had hay for sale.

The Saga of Hen-Thorir (Old Icelandic)

Old Icelandic	Literal	English
Hann kveðst eigi víst vita.	He said not knowing certainly.	He said that he did not know for certain.
Þeir sækja fast eftir og segja nú að fé þeirra muni deyja ef þeir fá enga hjálp af honum.	They sought fast after and said now that cattle theirs would die if they got none help of him.	They pressed hard and now said that their cattle will die if they don't get help from him.
Hann sagði það af sjálfdáðum orðið "en sagt er mér að Hænsna-Þórir muni hafa hey til sölu".	He said it of self-judgement words "but told am I that Hen-Thorir should have hay to sell".	He said they had done it of their own judgement, "but I am told that Hen-Thorir should have hay to sell".
Þeir svöruðu:	They answered:	They answered:
"Af honum munum vér eigi fá nema þú farir með oss og mun hann þá þegar selja ef þú gengur í vörslu fyrir oss um kaupin".	"Of him should we not get unless you travel with us and should he then from-there sell if you went to vouch for us about the-purchase".	"We will not get anything from him unless you go with us, and he will sell immediately if you take care of the purchase for us".
Hann svarar:	He answered:	He answered:
"Það má eg gera að fara með yður en það er sannlegt að þeir selji sem til hafa".	"That may I be-done that go with you and it is right that they sell who to have".	"I can do that and go with you, for it is right that those who have it should sell it".
Þeir fara snemma um morguninn og var á norðan strykur sá og heldur kaldur.	They travelled early about morning and were over north windy so and rather cold.	They left early in the morning, and it was windy over the north and rather cold.
Þórir bóndi var úti staddur í það mund, sér mennina fara að garði, gengur inn síðan og rekur aftur hurð og lætur fyrir loku, fer til dagverðar.	Thorir the-farmer was outside standing at the time, saw men travelling to the-farmyard, went in then and drove after the-door and had before locked, went to breakfast.	Farmer Thorir was outside at the time, saw the men coming to the garden, then went inside and pushed the door back and closed it, going to breakfast.
Nú er drepið á dyr.	Now was knock on the-door.	Now there was a knock on the door.
Sveinninn Helgi tekur til orða:	The-boy Helgi took to words:	The boy Helgi spoke:
"Gakktu út fóstri minn því að menn munu vilja hitta þig".	"Go-you out foster mine because that men would wish to-meet you".	"Go out, foster, because people will wish to meet you".

The Saga of Hen-Thorir (Old Icelandic)

Old Icelandic	Literal	English
Þórir kveðst mundu matast fyrst en sveinninn hleypur undan borðum og gengur til hurðar og heilsar þeim vel er komnir voru.	Thorir spoke should eat first but the-boy ran from the-table and went to the-doors and greeted them well as welcome they-were.	Thorir said that they would eat first, but the boy ran from the tables and went to the door and greeted those who had arrived.
Blund-Ketill spurði hvort Þórir væri heima.	Blund-Ketill asked whether Thorir was home.	Blund-Ketill asked whether Thorir was home.
Hann sagði svo væri.	He said so was.	He said it was so.
"Bið þú hann útgöngu",	"Ask you he to-come-out",	"Ask him to come out",
sagði hann.	said he.	he said.
Sveinninn gekk inn og sagði að Blund-Ketill var kominn úti og vildi hitta hann.	The-boy went the and said that Blund-Ketill was come out and wished to-meet he.	The boy did so and said that Blund-Ketill had come out and wanted to see him.
Þórir svaraði:	Thorir answered:	Thorir answered:
"Af hverju mun Blund-Ketill draga nasirnar?	"If how should Blund-Ketill dragging his-nose?	"Of what should Blund-Ketill be so nosy about?
Kynlegt ef hann fer að góðu.	Wonder if he goes to good.	It would be a wonder if he is up to any good.
Ekki erindi á eg við hann".	Not errand all I against he".	I have no errand with him".
Sveinninn fer og sagði þeim að Þórir vildi eigi út ganga.	The-boy went and told them that Thorir wished not out to-go.	The boy went and told them that Thorir did not wish to go out.
"Já",	"Yes",	"Yes",
sagði Blund-Ketill, "þá skulum vér inn ganga".	said Blund-Ketill, "then should we in going".	said Blund-Ketill, "then we shall come in".
Þeir ganga til stofu og var þeim heilsað en Þórir þagði.	They went to the-main-room and were them greeted then Thorir silent.	They went into the main room and were greeted, but Thorir was silent.
"Svo er varið",	"So is the-situation",	"So this is the situation",
sagði Blund-Ketill, "að vér viljum kaupa hey að þér Þórir".	said Blund-Ketill, "that we wish-to buy hay from you Thorir".	said Blund-Ketill, "that we wish to buy hay from you, Thorir".
Þórir svarar:	Thorir answered:	Thorir answered:

The Saga of Hen-Thorir (Old Icelandic)

Old Icelandic	Literal	English
"Eigi er mér þitt fé betra en mitt".	"Not is to-me your wealth better than mine".	"I don't think your wealth is better than mine".
Blund-Ketill mælti:	Blund-Ketill spoke:	Blund-Ketill spoke:
"Ýmist veitir það".	"Or provide it".	"It provides various things".
Þórir svarar:	Thorir answered:	Thorir answered:
"Hví ertu í heybroti, auðigur maður?"	"Why are-you in hay-need, wealthy-man man?"	"Why are you in need of hay, wealthy man?"
Blund-Ketill segir:	Blund-Ketill said:	Blund-Ketill said:
"Eigi er eg greiðlega í heybroti og fala eg fyrir landseta mína er þurfa þykjast úrlausna.	"Not am I quite in hay-need and bargain I for tenants mine that need to-see solution.	"I am not in need of may myself, but I bargain for my tenants that need a solution.
Vildi eg gjarna fá þeim ef til væri".	Wish I gladly get them if to were".	I would gladly get them some if it were possible".
"Það muntu eiga allra heimilast að veita öðrum þitt en eigi mitt".	"That should not all right to give others yours but not mine".	"That should you have all right to give others what is yours, but not what is mine".
Blund-Ketill svarar:	Blund-Ketill answered:	Blund-Ketill answered:
"Eigi skulum vér gjafar að biðja.	"Not shall we gifts to ask-for.	"We are not asking for gifts.
Láttu Odd og Arngrím gera verð fyrir þína hönd en þar á ofan vil eg gefa þér gjafir".	Let Odd and Arngrim make the-price for your hand and there of above wish I to-give you gifts".	Let Odd and Arngrim make the price on your hand, and thereabove I wish to give you gifts".
Þórir kveðst eigi hey til hafa að selja	Thorir said not hay to have to sell	Thorir said that he did not have hay to sell.
"enda vil eg eigi selja".	"and wish I not to-sell".	"and I do not wish to sell".
Þá gengur Blund-Ketill út og þeir félagar og sveinninn með þeim.	Then went Blund-Ketill out and those followers and the-boy with them.	Then Blund-Ketill went outside with his followers, and the boy went with them.
Þá tekur Blund-Ketill til orða:	Then took Blund-Ketill to words:	Then Blund-Ketill took to words:
"Hvort er heldur að fóstri þinn hefir engi hey til sölu eða vill hann eigi selja?"	"Which is-it rather that foster yours has not hay to sell or wishes he not sell?"	"Which is it? That your foster father does not have hay to sell, or does not wish to sell?"

The Saga of Hen-Thorir (Old Icelandic)

Old Icelandic	Literal	English
Sveinninn svarar:	The-boy answered:	The boy answered:
"Hefir hann víst ef hann vill".	"Has he certainly if he wishes".	"He certainly has, if he wishes".
Blund-Ketill mælti:	Blund-Ketill spoke:	Blund-Ketill spoke:
"Fylgdu oss þangað til sem heyin eru".	"Follow us there to where haystacks they-are".	"Lead us to where the haystacks are".
Hann gerir svo.	He did so.	He did so.
Nú gerir Blund-Ketill til fjár Þóris og hugðist svo að, þó að algjafta væri til alþingis, að þó mundi af ganga fimm stakkar.	Now did Blund-Ketill to cattle Thori's and thought so that, though to hay-feed was to the-assembly, that though would of going five stacks.	Now Blund-Ketill to Thorir's cattle, and thought that he had enough hay to feed until the next assembly, and that left five stacks.
Og eftir þetta ganga þeir inn.	And after that went they in.	And after that they went in.
Blund-Ketill mælti:	Blund-Ketill spoke:	Blund-Ketill spoke:
"Svo hyggst mér um heykost þinn að góður fengur mun af ganga þó að fé þínu öllu sé inni gefið til alþingis og vil eg það kaupa".	"So seems to-me about hay-supply yours that good getting should of go though to cattle yours all as in given until the-assembly and wish I that to-buy".	"So it seems to me that your hay supply will be good for all your cattle until the assembly, and the remainder I wish to buy".
Þórir svarar:	Thorir answered:	Thorir answered:
"Hvað skal eg þá hafa annan vetur ef þá er slíkur vetur eða verri?"	"What shall I then have next winter if then was such winters or worse?"	"Then what shall I have for another winter, if it is such a winter as this one or worse?"
Blund-Ketill svarar:	Blund-Ketill answered:	Blund-Ketill answered:
"Gera mun eg þér þann kost að fá þér jafnmikinn kost í heyjum í sumar og þó að engu verri og færa í garða þína".	"Make should I to-you this choice that pay to-you equally-great cost of hay in the-summer and then of nothing worse and brought to farmyard yours".	"I will give you the opportunity to get an equal amount of hay this summer, and if nothing worse, also move it to your gardens".
Þórir svarar:	Thorir answered:	Thorir answered:
"Ef þér hafið nú yður eigi heybjörg hvað munuð þér þá heldur hafa í sumar?	"If you have now yours not haystacks what shall you then rather have in summer?	"If you don't have a haystack now, what will you have this summer?

The Saga of Hen-Thorir (Old Icelandic)

Old Icelandic	Literal	English
En veit eg að er sá ríkismunur okkar að þú munt taka mega hey af mér ef þú vilt".	But know I that is so powerful ours that you might take be-able-to hay from me if you wish".	But I know that that is our state different, that you will take a lot of hay from me if you want".
Blund-Ketill svarar:	Blund-Ketill answered:	Blund-Ketill answered:
"Eigi er þann veg upp að taka.	"Not is then the-way up to take.	"That's not the way to go.
Það veistu að silfur gengur í allar skuldir hér á landi og gef eg þér það við".	That know-you that silver went in all debts here in the-land and give I to-you that with".	You know that silver goes into all debts in this country, and I'll give you that".
Þórir svarar:	Thorir answered:	Thorir answered:
"Eigi vil eg silfur þitt".	"Not wish I silver yours".	"I don't want your silver".
"Þá taktu þvílíka vöru sem þeir gera til handa þér, Oddur og Arngrímur".	"Then take-you as-you-like goods as they make to hand to-you, Odd and Arngrim".	"Then you take the goods they make for you, Oddr and Arngrímr".
"Fátt er hér verkmanna",	"Few are here work-men",	"There are few workers here",
segir Þórir, "en eg nenni lítt ferðum og vil eg eigi vasast í slíku".	said Thorir, "but I bother little travel and wish I not entangle-with as such".	said Thorir, "but I don't want to travel, and I don't want to get stuck in such a thing".
Blund-Ketill svarar:	Blund-Ketill answered:	Blund-Ketill answered:
"Þá skal eg láta færa þér heim".	"Then shall I have brought to-your home".	"Then I shall have it brought to your home".
Þórir mælti:	Thorir spoke:	Thorir spoke:
"Eigi hefi eg húsakost til þess að örvænt sé að eigi spillist".	"Not have I house-choice to this to surely be that not get-spoiled".	"I do not have the house room for it, so it is sure to be spoilt".
Blund-Ketill svarar:	Blund-Ketill answered:	Blund-Ketill answered:
"Eg skal fá til húðir og búa um svo að vel sé".	"I shall get to hides and prepare around so that well being".	"I'll get hides and prepare around, so that it will be good".
Þórir svarar:	Thorir answered:	Thorir answered:
"Eigi vil eg spark annarra manna í húsum mínum".	"Not will I trampling other men in house mine".	"I don't want other people trampling in my house".
Blund-Ketill svarar:	Blund-Ketill answered:	Blund-Ketill answered:

The Saga of Hen-Thorir (Old Icelandic)

Old Icelandic	Literal	English
"Þá skal vera hjá oss í vetur og mun eg varðveita".	"Then shall being by us in winter and shall I safeguard".	"Then it will stay with us this winter, and I will preserve it".
"Veit eg gjálgrun þína",	"Know I idle-talk yours",	"I know your idle alk",
segir Þórir, "og vil eg engu kaupa við þig".	said Thorir, "and will I none purchase with you".	said Thorir, "and I don't want to buy anything from you".
Blund-Ketill mælti:	Blund-Ketill spoke:	Blund-Ketill spoke:
"Þá mun fara verr og munum vér allt að einu hafa heyið þó að þú bannir en leggja verð í staðinn og njóta þess að vér erum fleiri".	"Then would going worse and should we all that same have hay though that you banned and granted worth in there and enjoy this that we are more".	"Then it will go worse, because we mean to have the hay all the same, even though you forbid it, and take advantage of the fact that we are more in number".
Þá þagnar Þórir og gerir eigi gott í skapi.	Then silent Thorir and did not good in mood.	Then Thorir was silent and not in a good mood.
Blund-Ketill lætur taka reip og binda heyið.	Blund-Ketill had take ropes and bound the-hay.	Blund-Ketill had the ropes taken and bound the hay.
Eftir það hefja þeir upp klyfjar og bera í brott heyið en ætla vel til alls fjár.	After that heaved they up the-load and carried to away the-hay, and intended well to all cattle.	After that they heaved up the load and carried away the hay, then made provision for all the cattle.

6

Old Icelandic	Literal	English
Nú skal segja frá hvað Þórir hafðist að.	Now shall say from what Thorir had to.	Now shall be told what Thorir did.
Hann býr heiman ferð sína og Helgi fóstri hans með honum.	He farm home travelled-from his and Helgi foster his with him.	He travelled home to his farm, and Helgi, his foster-son with him.
Þeir ríða í Norðurtungu og var þar tekið við þeim afar vel.	They rode to North-Tongue and were there received with them greatly well.	They rode to North-Tongue and were received well there.
Spurði Arngrímur tíðinda.	Asked Arngrim the-news.	Arngrim asked for the news.
Þórir svarar:	Thorir answered:	Thorir answered:
"Ekki hefi eg nú nýlegra spurt en ránið".	"Not have I now newer learned than the-robbery".	"I have not learned of anything newer than the robbery".

The Saga of Hen-Thorir (Old Icelandic)

Old Icelandic	Literal	English
"Hvað var ránið?"	"What was robbery?"	"What robbery was this?"
sagði Arngrímur.	said Arngrim.	said Arngrim.
Þórir svarar:	Thorir answered:	Thorir answered:
"Blund-Ketill hefir rænt mig öllum heyjum svo að eigi ætla eg forkast eftir nautum í köldu veðri".	"Blund-Ketill has robbed me all hay so that not suppose I fodder after cattle in cold weather".	"Blund-Ketill has robbed me of all my hay, so I cannot count on any fodder for the cattle in cold weather".
"Er svo Helgi?"	"Is so Helgi?"	"Is that so Helgi?"
segir Arngrímur.	said Arngrim.	said Arngrim.
"Engu gegnir það",	"Not so-going is-that",	"That is not how it went",
segir Helgi, "fór Blund-Ketill vel með sínu máli".	said Helgi, "went Blund-Ketill well with his the-matter".	said Helgi, "Blund-Ketill behaved well in the matter".
Sagði Helgi þá hversu farið hafði með þeim.	Said Helgi then how-so went had with them.	Helgi said how it had gone.
Þá sagði Arngrímur:	Then said Arngrim:	Then Arngrim said:
"Það var líkara.	"That was likely.	"That sounds more likely.
Betur er það hey komið að hann hefir en hitt er fúnar fyrir þér".	Better is it hay comes that he has than find it rots before you".	It is better use for the hay that he has it, than find it rots before you".
Þórir svarar:	Thorir answered:	Thorir answered:
"Illu heilli bauð eg þér barnfóstur.	"Ill fairly offered I to-you child-foster.	"It is unfortunate that I offered to foster you.
Skal oss aldrei það illbýli gert að oss sé hér tilgangur að heldur og að vor hlutur sé réttur og eru slíkt firn mikil".	Shall we never it ill-harm done to us being here point to rather and to our lot is right and they-are such abomination great".	May we never be harmed that we have a purpose here and that our part is right and such things are a great abomination".
Arngrímur svarar:	Arngrim answered:	Arngrim answered:
"Það var þegar ófyrirsynju því að eg ætla þar vondum manni að duga sem þú ert".	"It was already unexpected because that I suppose there trouble man to be-helping as you are".	"It was already unexpected because I suppose there will be trouble for such poor help as yours".

The Saga of Hen-Thorir (Old Icelandic)

Old Icelandic	Literal	English
Þórir svarar:	Thorir answered:	Thorir answered:
"Eigi er eg orðsjúkur maður en illa uni eg að þú launar svo mína gerð eða það þó að menn ræni mig því að eigi er þetta síður frá þér tekið".	"Not am I word-sickened man but ill win I that you are-repaid so mine made or that then as men steal me because that not is that side from to-you taken".	"I am not a man of words, but I hate how you repay me for my actions or that, even though people rob me, because is this not also taken away from you".
Og skildust við svo búið.	And separated with so prepared.	And on that they parted.
Ríður Þórir á braut og koma á Breiðabólstað og heilsar Oddur honum vel og spyr tíðinda.	Rode Thorir to away and came to Breidabolstad and greeted Odd him well and asked the-news.	Thorir rode away and came to Breidabolstad and greeted Odd well and asked what news there was.
"Ekki hefi eg nýlegra frétt en ránið".	"Not have I newer news than the-robbery".	"I have not any news newer than the robbery".
"Hvað ráni var það?"	"What robbery was that?"	"What robbery was that?"
sagði Oddur.	said Odd.	said Odd.
Þórir svarar:	Thorir answered:	Thorir answered:
"Blund-Ketill tók hey mín öll svo að eg er nú með öllu óbirgur.	"Blund-Ketill took hay mine all so that I am now with all un-stocked.	"Blund-Ketill took all my hay so that I am now out of stock.
Vildi eg gjarna hafa þína ásjá en þetta mál kemur og til þín, þar sem þú ert forráðsmaður héraðsins, að rétta það sem rangt er gert og máttu það á minnast að hann gerðist þinn fjandmaður".	Wish I gladly to-have yours assistance in that matter came and to yours, there as you are manager district, to right that which wrong is done and may it to remember that he became your fiend-man".	I would gladly wish to have your assistance in this matterm and it concerns you too, as you are the head of the district, to right that which is wrong, and you may remember that he has become your enemy".
Oddur spurði:	Odd asked:	Odd asked:
"Er svo Helgi?"	"Is-that so Helgi?"	"Is that so Helgi?"
Hann sagði að Þórir affærði stórmjög, greinir nú allt hversu fór.	He said that Thorir taken-away a-great-much, article now all how-so went.	He said that Thorir had taken away a great deal, and now told him how so it went.
Oddur svarar:	Odd answered:	Odd answered:

The Saga of Hen-Thorir (Old Icelandic)

Old Icelandic	Literal	English
"Eigi vil eg mér af skipta.	"Not wish I more of this-exchange.	"I do not wish to have any part of this exchange.
Mundi eg svo hafa gert ef eg þyrfti".	Should I so have done if I needed".	I should have done the same, had I the need".
Þórir svarar:	Thorir answered:	Thorir answered:
"Satt er það er mælt er, að spyrja er best til válegra þegna og án er illt um gengi nema heiman hafi".	"Truly said that is said is, that to-learn is best to woeful thanes and without is ill about going except from-home having".	"It's true is what is said, it is best to learn of bad things from woeful people, and bad things do not go about unless they are from home".
Ríður Þórir í brott við svo búið og Helgi með honum og fer heim og unir illa við.	Rode Thorir to away with so settled and Helgi with him and travelling home and satisfied ill with.	This this, Thorir rode away with Helgi, and travelled home unsatisfied with the situation.

7

Þorvaldur son Tungu-Odds hafði út komið um sumarið fyrir norðan land og þar vistaðist hann um veturinn.	Thorvald son-of Tungu-Odd's had out came about summer for the-north lands and there guested he about the-winter.	Thorvald son of Tungu had travelled abroad in the summer to the north lnds, and was a guest there about the winter.
Hann fór norðan er leið að sumri á fund föður síns og gisti um nótt í Norðurtungu í góðum beina.	He travelled north as passed the summer to meet father his and guest about the-night in North-Tongue in good assistance.	He travelled north when summer had passed and met his father, and guested for the night in North Tongue with a good welcome.
Sá maður var þar fyrir á gistingu er Víðfari hét.	So a-man was there before in guesting was Vidfari named.	There was a man already there as a guest named Vidfari.
Hann var reikanarmaður.	He was a-roaming-man.	He was a roaming man.
Hljóp hann á milli landshorna.	Ran he in among lands-corners.	He ran among the corners of the land.
Hann var frændi Þóris náinn og ápekkur honum í skapsmunum.	He was a-kinsman Thori's near and similar him in disposition.	He was a kinsman of Thori's and near to him in disposition.
Þetta sama kveld tekur Víðfari föt sín og stökkur á brott og léttir eigi fyrr en hann kemur til Þóris.	That same evening took Vidfari bed-clothing his and heels to away and remained not before that he came to Thori's.	That same evening, Vídfari took his bed clothes and took to his heels away, and did not stop until he came to Thori's.

The Saga of Hen-Thorir (Old Icelandic)

Old Icelandic	Literal	English
Hann tekur við honum báðum höndum:	He took with him both hands:	He received him well with both hands.
"Veit eg og að nokkuð gott mun mér leiða af þinni komu".	"Knew I also that some good would to-me lead of your coming".	"I know that some good comes my way when you do".
Hann svarar:	He answered:	He answered:
"Gerast mætti það því að nú er Þorvaldur Oddsson kominn í Norðurtungu og er þar nú á gistingu".	"Be may it because that now is Thorvald Oddson come to North-Tongue and is there now a guest".	"It may be, for Thorvald Oddson has come to North Tontue and is a guest there now".
Þórir svarar:	Thorir answered:	Thorir answered:
"Það vissi eg að sjá að mér mundi nokkuð gott að höndum koma því að mér varð allgott við er eg sá þig".	"That knew I that see that to-me would some good of hands came because that to-me became all-good with that I saw you".	"I knew to see that something good would happen to me, because I felt good when I saw you".
Nú líður nóttin af hendi og þegar um morguninn ríður Þórir og þeir fóstrar í Norðurtungu.	Now passed the-night of hand and from-there about morning rode Thorir and their foster in North-Tongue.	Now the night in hand passed, and from there early in the morning Thorir and his foster rode to North Tongue.
Er þar fjöldi manna kominn og var sveininum gefið seturúm en Þórir reikar á gólfinu.	Was there many people come and was the-boy given a-seat while Thorir wandered about the-floor.	There were many people who had come there and the boy was found a seat, while Thorir paced around the floor.
Það getur Þorvaldur að líta er hann situr á pallinum og þeir Arngrímur og töluðu sín á milli.	It may Thorvald to company when he sat on the-seat and there Arngrim also talked him in among.	Thorvaldr could see that when he was sitting on the bench that he and Arngrím were talking to each other.
"Hver er sjá maður er reikar um gólfið?"	"Who is see man that wanders about the-floor?"	"Who is that man I see that wanders around the floor?"
segir Þorvaldur.	said Thorvald.	said Thorvald.
Arngrímur svarar:	Arngrim answered:	Arngrim answered:
"Hann er barnfóstri minn".	"He is child's-foster mine".	"He is my son's foster-father",
"Já",	"Yes",	"Yes",

The Saga of Hen-Thorir (Old Icelandic)

Old Icelandic	Literal	English
segir Þorvaldur, "hví skal honum eigi rúm gefast?"	said Thorvald, "why shall he not room be-given?"	said Thorvald, "why shall he not be given room?"
Arngrímur kvað hann eigi varða.	Arngrim spoke he not a-concern.	Arngrim spokr that it was not a concern for him.
"Eigi skal svo vera",	"Not shall so being",	"It shall not be so",
sagði Þorvaldur og lætur kalla hann til sín og gefur honum rúm að sitja hjá sér.	said Thorvald and had called he to his and gave him room to sit beside him.	said Thorvald, and had him called to him and gave him room to sit beside him.
Spyrjast síðan almæltra tíðinda.	Asked then all-matters tidings.	He then asked him what was the news.
Hann svarar Þórir:	He answered Thorir:	He answered Thorir:
"Raun var þetta er Blund-Ketill rændi mig".	"Torment was that when Blund-Ketill robbed me".	"It was a torment when Blund-Ketill robbed me".
Þorvaldur spurði:	Thorvald asked:	Thorvald asked:
"Er sæst á?"	"Is seen about?"	"Has this been seen about?"
"Fjarri fer um það",	"Far went about it",	"Far from it",
segir Þórir.	said Thorir.	said Thorir.
"Hví gegnir það Arngrímur",	"How goes it Arngrim",	"How goes it Arngrim",
sagði Þorvaldur, "að þér höfðingjar látið þá skömm fram fara?"	said Thorvald, "that you chieftains let then shame from go?"	said Thorvald, "that you chieftains let such shameful things go on?"
Arngrímur svarar:	Arngrim answered:	Arngrim answered:
"Lýgur hann mestan hlut frá og er alllítið til haft".	"Lies he mostly part from and is all-little to have".	"Most of what he says is lies, and there is little to it".
"Var það þó satt að hann hafði heyið?"	"Was it though true that he had the-hay?"	"Was it though true that he took the hay?"
segir Þorvaldur.	said Thorvald.	said Thorvald.
"Hafði hann víst",	"Had he certainly",	"He certainly had",
segir Arngrímur.	said Arngrim.	said Arngrim.

The Saga of Hen-Thorir (Old Icelandic)

Old Icelandic	Literal	English
"Bær er hver að ráða sínu",	"Dwelling is who to rule his",	"Everyone rules his dwelling",
sagði Þorvaldur, "og kemur honum fyrir lítið vinfengi við þig ef hann skal þó undir fótum troðinn".	said Thorvald, "and came him for little friendship with you if he shall then under feet trodden".	said Thorvald "and he gains little benefit from being your friend if he shall then be trodden underfoot".
Þórir mælti:	Thorir spoke:	Thorir spoke:
"Allvel líst mér á þig Þorvaldur og svo segir mér hugur um að þú munir nokkuð leiðrétta mitt mál".	"All-well behold me to you Thorvald and so said my thoughts about that you would some have-right mine matter".	"All right, I like you, Thorvaldr, and so my heart tells me that you will correct my case somewhat".
Þorvaldur mælti:	Thorvald spoke:	Thorvald spoke:
"Eg hefi lítið traust undir mér".	"I have little trust under me".	"I have little confidence in myself".
Þórir mælti:	Thorir spoke:	Thorir spoke:
"Eg vil gefa þér fé mitt hálft til þess að þú réttir málið og hafir annaðhvort sektir eða sjálfdæmi svo að óvinir mínir sitji eigi yfir mínu".	"I will give you wealth mine half-of to this that you right the-matter and have either-way penalty or self-judgement so that enemies mine sit not over mine".	"I want to give you half of my money so that you do the right thing and have some guilt or self-control, so that my enemies do not sit over me".
Arngrímur mælti:	Arngrim spoke:	Arngrim spoke:
"Ger eigi þetta Þorvaldur því að eigi er góðum dreng að duga þar sem hann er en þú átt við þann um er bæði er vitur og vel að sér og að öllu vinsæll".	"Do not that Thorvald because that not is good fellow that helping there as he as but you have with then about is both is wise and well that his and to all befriended".	"Don't do this, Thorvald, because a good boy is not enough where he is, but you are talking about the one who is both wise and well-behaved and generally popular".
"Sé eg",	"See I",	"I see",
segir Þorvaldur, "að þér leikur öfund á ef eg tek við fé hans og anntu mér þess eigi".	said Thorvald, "that to-you like envy about if I take with wealth his and care to-me this not".	said Thorvaldr, "that you will be jealous if I take his money, and I don't care".
Þórir mælti:	Thorir said:	Thorir said:

The Saga of Hen-Thorir (Old Icelandic)

Old Icelandic	Literal	English
"Svo er að að hyggja Þorvaldur að fé mitt mun reynast frítt og aðrir menn vita að mér er eigi fé goldið víða fyrir mitt eigin".	"So is it that considered Thorvald that wealth mine will turn-out free and other men know that to-me is not wealth paid with before mine own".	"It's a good thing to think, Thorvaldr, that my money will turn out to be free, and other people know that I don't have much money for my own".
Arngrímur mælti:	Arngrim said:	Arngrim said:
"Letja vil eg þig enn Þorvaldur að þú takir við máli þessu en þú munt gera sem þér líkar.	"Discourage will I you but Thorvald that you take with the-matter this but you must do as to-you like.	"I still want to discourage you, Thorvald, to accept this matter, but you will do what you like.
Uggir mig að mikið hljótist af".	Dread me that much to-get of".	I sense that there is much dread in it".
Þorvaldur svarar:	Thorvald answered:	Thorvald answered:
"Eigi mun eg neita fjárviðtökunni".	"Not will I refuse wealth-with-betokened".	"I will not refuse the receipt of funds".
Nú handsalar Þórir honum fé sitt hálft og þar með málið á hendur Blund-Katli.	Now hands-over Thorir to-him wealth his half-of and there with the-matter in hand Blund-Ketill.	Now Thorir paid him half of his money, and with that the matter of Blund-Ketill is in his hands.
Arngrímur mælti þá enn:	Arngrim spoke then but:	Arngrim then spoke:
"Hversu ætlar þú með að fara máli þessu Þorvaldur?"	"How-so intend you with to go the-matter this Thorvald?"	"How do you intend to fo on with the matter, Thorvald?"
"Eg mun fara fyrst á fund föður míns og hyggja þaðan að ráðum".	"I shall travel first to meet father mine and consider from-there to counsel".	"I shall travel first to meet my father and consider counsel from there".
Þórir mælti:	Thorir spoke:	Thorir spoke:
"Eigi hugnar mér það.	"Not to-mind mine that.	"I do not have a mind for that".
Vil eg eigi hinkur.	Will I not hang-back.	I wll not hang back.
Hefi eg mikið til unnið og vil eg þegar á morgun láta fara og stefna Blund-Katli".	Have I much to win and will I from-there in the-morning have sent and direct Blund-Ketill".	I have achieved a lot, and I want to leave already in the morning and summon for Blund-Ketill".
Þorvaldur svarar:	Thorvald answered:	Thorvald answered:

The Saga of Hen-Thorir (Old Icelandic)

Old Icelandic	Literal	English
"Þetta mun vera reyndar að þú munt vera engi gæfumaður og illt mun af þér hljótast.	"That will being seen that you would being not lucky-man and ill will of you to-get.	"It will be seen that you are not a lucky man, and you will get ill will.
En svo mun nú vera verða".	But so will now being become".	But so will it now be what it is to become".
Og binda þeir Þórir að hittast í ákveðnum stað um morguninn.	And bound they Thorir to meet in meeting place about morning.	And he and Thorir agreed to meet at a meeting place in the morning.

8

Þegar snemma um morguninn ríður Þorvaldur og Arngrímur með honum með þrjá tigu manna.	From-there soon about morning rode Thorvald and Arngrim with him with three tens people.	From there early in the morning Thorvald and Arngrim rode with thirty people.
Hitta þeir Þóri og var hann við þriðja mann.	Met they Thori and was he with third man.	They met Thorir who was one of three men.
Þar var Helgi Arngrímsson og Víðfari frændi Þóris.	There was Helgi son-of-Arngrim and Vidfari kinsman Thori.	Helgi son of Arngrim and Thorir's kinsman Vidfari.
Þorvaldur mælti:	Thorvald spoke:	Thorvald spoke:
"Hví ertu svo fámennur Þórir?"	"Why are-you so few-men Thorir?"	"Why are you so few men, Thorir?"
Hann svarar:	He answered:	He answered:
"Eg vissi að þig mundi eigi lið skorta".	"I knew that you should not company be-short-of".	"I knew you would not be short of company".
Þeir ríða nú upp eftir Hlíðinni.	They rode now up after The-slope.	They now rode up ober The Slope.
Mannferðin var sén af bæjunum og hleypir hver af sínum bæ.	Men-travelling was seen from the-towns and ran who of his dwelling.	Men travelling were seen from the towns and everyone ran from their dwelling.
Þykist sá best hafa er fyrst kemur til Blund-Ketils og er þar mart manna fyrir.	Thought saw best have who first came to Blund Ketil and that there many people for.	He thought it best who first came to Blund-Ketill before with the news of many people.

The Saga of Hen-Thorir (Old Icelandic)

Old Icelandic	Literal	English
Þeir Þorvaldur ríða að garði og stíga þar af hestum sínum og ganga heim að bænum.	They Thorvald rode to yard and leapt there of horses theirs and going home to the-farm.	Thorvald and his men rode up to the yard and leapt off their horses and walked to the house of the farm.
Þegar Blund-Ketill sér þetta gengur hann móti þeim og býður þeim þar að þiggja allan greiða.	From-there Blund-Ketill saw that went he to-meet them and bids them there to receive all assistance.	As soon as Blund-Ketill saw that, he went to meet them, and invited them to take with his hospitality.
Þorvaldur mælti:	Thorvald spoke:	Thorvald spoke:
"Annað er erindi hingað en eta mat.	"Other is errand here than eating food.	"Our errand is other than eating food.
Eg vil vita hverju þú vilt svara fyrir mál það er þú tókst upp hey Þóris".	I will know how you will answer for matter that is you took up hay Thori".	I wish to know how you will answer for the matter of taking Thori's hay".
Blund-Ketill svarar:	Blund-Ketill answered:	Blund-Ketill answered:
"Slíku þér sem honum.	"Such to-you as him.	"The same to you as to him.
Ger einn fyrir svo mikið sem þér líkar og þó skal eg gefa þér gjafir ofan á, því betri og meiri sem þú ert meira verður en Þórir, og svo mikinn skal eg þinn sóma gera að það sé allra manna mál að þú sért vel sæmdur af".	Make one for so much as to-you like and though shall I give to-you gifts above about, accordingly better and greater as you are more worth than Thorir, and so much shall I your honour do to that see all people matter to you are well honoured of".	Make one as much as you like, and I shall give you gifts on top of that, accordingly better and greater they are in worth than Thorir, and so much shall I do your honour that all the people will see in this matter that you are well honoured".
Þorvaldur þagnar og þótti vel boðið.	Thorvald silenced and thought well offered.	Thorvald was silent, and thought it was a good offer.
Þórir svarar þá:	Thorir answered then:	Then Thorir answered.
"Eigi er þetta að þiggja og þarf eigi að hugsa um það.	"Not are that to accept and need not to consider about that.	"That is not acceptable, and there is no need to consider it.
Löngu átti eg þenna kost og kalla eg mér lið eigi veitt þó að slíkt sé og til lítils kom mér að gefa þér fé mitt".	Long had I then choice and call I to-me company not given though to such being and to little come to-me to give to-you wealth mine".	For a long time I had this advantage, and I call myself a company not granted, even though such a thing is and to little it came to me to give you my money".
Þá mælti Þorvaldur:	Then spoke Thorvald:	Then Thorvald spoke:

The Saga of Hen-Thorir (Old Icelandic)

Old Icelandic	Literal	English
"Hvað viltu þá gera fyrir lögmálsstaðinn?"	"What will-you then do for law-matter-standing?"	"What do you wish to do for the legal standing of this matter?"
Blund-Ketill mælti:	Blund-Ketill spoke:	Blund-Ketill spoke:
"Eigi annað en þú gerir og einn skapir slíkt er þú vilt".	"Not other but you do and one mind such that you will".	"None other than you as you are minded to do, and make it such however you want".
Þá svarar Þorvaldur:	Then answered Thorvald:	Then Thorvald Answered:
"Svo líst mér sem engi sé annar á ger en að stefna".	"So seems to-me as nothing being other-than to do but to agreement".	"So it seems to me that there is nothing else to do but to the agreement".
Hann stefnir þá Blund-Katli um rán og nefnir sér votta og hefir þau orð og umkvæði sem hann fékk frekust haft.	He summoned then Blund-Ketill about robbery and named his witnesses and had them word and about-speaking as he got most-often have.	He then summoned Blund-Ketil for the robbery and named his witnesses, and had the most frequent words and phrases he could find.
Nú snýr Blund-Ketill heim að húsum og mætir Austmanninum Erni er hann gekk að varnaði sínum.	Now turned Blund-Ketill home to the-house and met The-Eastern-Men Erne that he got to wares his.	Now Blund-Ketill returned home and met Erni the Easterner, as he went to his defense.
Örn spurði:	Orn asked:	Orn asked:
"Ertu sár bóndi er þú ert svo rauður sem blóð?"	"Are-you wounded the-farmer that you are so red as blood?"	"Are you hurt, farmer, are you as red as blood?"
Hann svarar:	He answered:	He answered:
"Eigi er eg sár en eigi er þetta betra.	"Not am I wounded but not is that better.	"I am not hurt, but this is not better.
Þau orð eru töluð við mig sem aldrei hafa áður töluð verið.	They words they-were told with me as never have before told been.	Words are spoken to me that have never been spoken before,
Eg er kallaður þjófur og ránsmaður".	I am called thief and robber-man".	I am called a thief and a robber".
Örn tekur boga sinn og lætur koma ör á streng og kemur þá út í því er þeir stigu á bak.	Orn took bow his and had came an-arrow on the-string and came then out as because were they stepping out back.	Orn took his bow and put an arrow on the string and brought them when they stepped back outside.

The Saga of Hen-Thorir (Old Icelandic)

Old Icelandic	Literal	English
Hann skaut og varð maður fyrir og lætur sígast niður af hestinum og var það Helgi son Arngríms goða.	He shot and became man for and had sank down of horse and was that Helgi son Arngrim the-chieftain.	He shot and a man was hit by it and he sank from the horse, and it was Helgi son of Arngrím the chieftain.
Þeir hlaupa að honum.	They ran at him.	They ran at him.
Þórir otar sér fram milli manna og hratt mönnum frá sér og biður gefa sér rúm	Thorir pushed his from among people and quickly men from his and bid to-give his room	Thorir pushed forward between them, and people quickly moved away from him to give him room.
"því að mér mun mest um	"because to to-me should most about	"For this is of the most concern to me.
Hann laut að Helga niður og var hann þá dauður.	He leant to Helgi down and was he then dead.	He leant down to Helgi and then he was dead.
Þórir mælti:	Thorir spoke:	Thorir spoke:
"Er lítill mátturinn fóstri minn?"	"Is little power foster mine?"	"Do you have so little power, my foster-son?"
Þórir réttist þá frá honum og mælti:	Thorir straightened-up then from him and spoke:	Thor then straightened up from him and spoke:
"Talaði sveinninn við mig.	"Said the-boy with me.	"The boy spoke with me.
Sagði hann tvisvar hið sama, þetta hérna:"	Spoke he twice then the-same, that here:"	He spoke the same thing twice, and it was this:"
Brenni, brenni	"Burn, burn	"Burn, burn
Blund-Ketill inni.	Blund-Ketill in".	Blund-Ketill in".
Arngrímur svarar þá:	Arngrim answered then:	Then Arngrim answered:
"Nú fór sem mig varði að oft hlýtur illt af illum og grunaði mig að mikið illt mundi af þér hljótast Þórir og eigi veit eg hvað sveinninn hefir sagt þó að þú fleiprir eitthvert.	"Now goes as me expected to often must ill of evil and mistrust me to much ill should of to-you to-get Thorir and not know I what the-boy has said though to you babble something.	"Now it occurred to me that evil often comes from evil, and I suspected that a lot of evil would come from you, Thorir, and I don't know what the boy had said, even though you're babbling something.
En þó er eigi ólíklegt að slíkt verði gert.	But though is not unlike to such became done.	but it is not unlikely that such a thing will be done.
Hófst þetta mál illa.	Began that matter ill.	The matter began badly.

The Saga of Hen-Thorir (Old Icelandic)

Old Icelandic	Literal	English
Kann og vera að svo lúkist".	Knows and being to so end".	And I know it will end so".
Þórir svarar:	Thorir answered:	Thorir answered:
"Eiga þykir mér þú nokkuð nauðsynlegra en ávíta mig".	"Not thought I you some need-like but to-rebuke me".	"I did not think you would have some need to rebuke me".
Þeir Arngrímur ríða nú brott undir skógarnef eitt og stíga af hestum og eru nú þar til þess að náttar.	They Arngrim ride now away under woods-outskirts one and leapt of horses and they-were now there to this to nightfall.	Arngrim and his men now rode away along the outskirts of the woods, and leapt off their horses, and there they were until nightfall.
En Blund-Ketill þakkar mönnum vel sitt liðsinni og bað hvern mann ríða heimleiðis sem best gegndi.	But Blund-Ketill thanked men well his assistance and bid each man ride home-ways as best might.	But Blund-Ketill thanked the men well for their assistance and bid each man to ride homeward best he might.

9

Svo er sagt að þegar er náttaði ríða þeir Þorvaldur að bænum í Örnólfsdal.	So is said to from-there that nightfall ride they Thorvald to estate in Ornolfsdal.	So it is said that from there when it was nightfall Thorvald and his men rode to the estate in Ornolfsdal.
Voru þar þá allir menn í svefni.	Where there then all men in sleep.	All of the men there were asleep.
Þeir draga viðarköst að bænum og slá í eldi.	There dragged brushwood to the-farmhouse and struck to fire.	They dragged brushwood up to the house and struck a fire.
Vakna þeir Blund-Ketill eigi fyrr en húsin loguðu yfir þeim.	Awoke they Blund-Ketill not before but house burned over them.	Blund-Ketill and his men awoke but not before the house was burning over them.
Blund-Ketill spurði hverjir þar kveiktu svo heitan eld.	Blund-Ketill asked who there kindled so threatening fire.	Blund-Ketill asked who had kindled so threatening a fire.
Þórir sagði hverjir voru.	Thorir said who were.	Thorir said who they were.
Blund-Ketill frétti ef nokkuð skyldi ná sáttum.	Blund-Ketill inquired if some should near fulfilled.	Blund-Ketill asked if there was any chance of an agreement.
Þórir sagði að engi er kostur annar en brenna.	Thorir said to none is choice other but burn.	Thorir said that there was no other choice than to burn.

The Saga of Hen-Thorir (Old Icelandic)

Old Icelandic	Literal	English
Þeir skiljast nú eigi fyrr við en hvert mannsbarn er þar inni brunnið.	They departed now not before with but each born-man was there in burnt.	They now departed but not before each man-born inside was burned.
Hersteinn son Blund-Ketills hafði farið um kveldið til fóstra síns er Þorbjörn hét og var kallaður stígandi.	Herstein son Blund-Ketill's had gone about evening to foster-father his was Thorbjorn named and was called Strider.	Hersteinn, son of Blund-Ketill, had gone that evening to his foster-father, whose name was Thorbjorn and who was called Strider.
Það er mælt að Þorbjörn væri eigi allur jafnan þar sem hann var sénn.	That was said to Thorbjorn was not all equally there as he was seen.	It is said that Thorbjorn was not quite the same as he appeared to be.
Hersteinn vaknar um morguninn og spurði hvort fóstri hans vekti.	Herstein awoke about morning and asked whether foster-father his was-awake.	Hersteinn awoke around morning and asked whether his foster-father was awake.
Hann kveðst vaka	He said awake	He said that he was awake.
"eða hvað viltu?"	"or what will-you?"	"and what do you want?"
"Mig dreymdi að mér þótti sem faðir minn gengi hér inn og loguðu um hann klæðin öll og allur þótti mér sem hann væri eldur einn".	"Me dreamed that to-me seemed as father mine went here the and burned about he clothes all and all seemed to-me as he was fire one".	"I dreamt, that it seemed to me that my father walked in here, and all the clothes around him burned, and it seemed to me that he was all on fire".
Þeir standa upp og ganga út og sjá skjótt logann.	They stood up and went out and saw quickly the-fire.	They stood up and went outside, and quickly saw the fire.
Þeir taka vopn sín og fara hvatlega og voru þá allir menn á brottu er þeir komu þar.	They take weapons theirs and went quickly and were then all men to away when they came there.	Then they took their weapons and went quickly, and when they got there, all the men were gone.
Hersteinn mælti:	Herstein spoke:	Hersteinn spoke:
"Hér eru orðin hörmuleg tíðindi eða hvað er nú til ráða?"	"Here they-are become harm-like tidings and what is now to decide?"	"Here has become harmful news, and what is to be done now?"
Þorbjörn svarar:	Thorbjorn answered:	Thorbjorn answered:
"Nú skal neyta þess boðs er Tungu-Oddur hefir oft mælt að eg skyldi til hans koma ef eg þyrfti nokkurs við".	"Now shall make-use this offer that Tungu-Odd has often spoken to I should to his came if I needed someone with".	"Now I shall make use of this offer that Tungu-Odd has often spoken about, that I should come to him if I had need of someone".

The Saga of Hen-Thorir (Old Icelandic)

Old Icelandic	Literal	English
Hersteinn svarar:	Herstein answered:	Herstein answered:
"Eigi þykir mér það vænlegt".	"Not seemed to-me that hopeful".	"That does not seem to me to be that hopeful".
En þó fara þeir og koma á Breiðabólstað og kalla út Odd.	But though went they and came to Breidabolstad and called out Odd.	But though they went and came to Breidabolstad and called Odd outside.
Hann gengur út og tekur við þeim vel og spurði tíðinda.	He went out and took with them well and asked the-news.	He went out and received them well and asked what the news was.
Þeir sögðu slík sem orðin voru.	They said such as became were.	They said what had happened.
Hann lætur illa yfir.	He had ill over.	He felt bad over it.
Þorbjörn karl tekur þá til orða:	Thorbjorn a-man took then to words:	The man Thorbjorn took to words:
"Á þá leið er Oddur bóndi", sagði hann, "að þú hefir heitið mér ásjá þinni og vil eg nú til þess taka að þú leggir til nokkur góð ráð og komir til".	"So then the-way is Odd the-farmer", said he, "to you has pledged to-me assistance yours and will I now to this take to you place to some good counsel and come to".	"So it is this way, farmer Odd", he said, "you pledged your assistance to me, and I now wish to have some good advice to come".
Oddur kvaðst svo gera mundu.	Odd spoke so do would.	Odd spoke and said that he would do.
Ríða þeir nú í Örnólfsdal og koma þar fyrir dag.	Rode they now to Ornolfsdal and came there for the-day.	They now rode to Ornolfsdal and got there before mid-day.
Voru þá fallin húsin og fölskaður mjög eldurinn.	Were then fallen the-houses and pale-burnt much the-fire.	The houses were then fallen and the fire had burnt much.
Nú ríður Oddur að húsi einu því er eigi var allt brunnið.	Now rode Odd to house one because was not was all burned.	Now Odd rode to one house because it was not all burned.
Hann seilist til birkirafts eins og kippir brott úr húsinu, ríður síðan andsælis um húsin með loganda brandinn og mælti:	He reached to birch-rafter one and drew away from the-house, rode then anti-sun-wise about the-house with flaming brand and spoke:	He reached for one of the birch rafters and then rode anti-sun-wise around the house with the flaming brand and spoke:
"Hér nem eg mér land fyrir því að hér sé eg nú eigi byggðan bólstað.	"Here take I to-me land for because to here see I now not settled building.	"Here I take the land for myself, for because I see now no settled building.

The Saga of Hen-Thorir (Old Icelandic)

Old Icelandic	Literal	English
Heyri það vottar þeir er hjá eru".	Hear that witnesses they that nearby they-are".	There the witnesses hear that are nearby".
Hann keyrir síðan hestinn og ríður í brott.	He whipped then horse and rode to away.	He then spurred his horse and rode away.
Hersteinn mælti:	Herstein spoke:	Herstein spoke:
"Hvað er nú til ráða?	"What is now to decide?	"What is the decision to be now?"
Eigi reyndust þessi vel".	Not turned-out this well".	This has not turned out well".
Þorbjörn mælti:	Thorbjorn spoke:	Thorbjorn spoke:
"Þegi þú ef þú mátt hvað sem í gerist".	"Silence you if you might what as in befalls".	"Be silent if you can, whatever happens".
Hersteinn svarar og kvaðst það eina talað hafa er eigi var við of.	Herstein answered and said that only spoken have was not was with of.	Hersteinn answered and said that they had only spoken, which was not too much.
Útibúr var óbrunnið, það sem varningur Austmanns var inni og mikið fé annað.	Out-house was unburnt, that as goods Easterners was inside and much wealth other.	The storeroom was unburnt, the Easterner's goods were inside and a lot of other wealth.
Í þessu hverfur Þorbjörn karl.	In this turned Thorbjorn the-man.	At this moment, the man Thorbjorn vanished.
Nú lítur Hersteinn heim til bæjarins og sér útibúrið opið og út borið féið en engan sér hann manninn.	Now looked Herstein home to dwellings and his out-house open and out carried wealth but none his he people.	Now Hersteinn looked towards the dwellings and saw that his storeroom was open, and the goods being carried out, but none of his people.
Þar eru bundnar klyfjar.	There they-were bound loaded.	Then they bounded up the loads.
Þar næst heyrir hann hark mikið í túnið, sér nú að heim eru rekin hross öll þau er faðir hans hafði átt, sauðir og naut úr fjósi og allt ganganda fé.	There nearest heard he noise much in the-fields, his now to home they-were driven horses all they were father his had had, sheep and bulls about the-barn and all walking cattle.	Then he heard a great noise in the fields, and now all the horses that his father had were being driven home, sheep and bulls from the barn, and all livestock.
Síðan eru klyfjar upp hafðar og því næst öllu á ferð snúið og allt fémætt á brott fært.	After they-were loaded up had and accordingly near all to travelled away and all valuables to away taken.	After they had loaded up, straightaway they all travelled away, and all valuables were taken away.

The Saga of Hen-Thorir (Old Icelandic)

Old Icelandic	Literal	English
Hersteinn víkur nú eftir og sér að Þorbjörn karl rekur féið.	Herstein turned now after and saw, that Thorbjorn the housekeeper driving the-cattle.	Herstein now turned and went after them, and saw that the man Thorbjorn was driving the cattle.
Þeir snúa leið sinni ofan eftir héraði í Stafholtstungur og svo út yfir Norðurá.	They turned the-ways theirs over after the-district in Stafholtstungur and so out over Norðurá.	They moved on their way over through the district in Stafholtstunga and then out over Nordura.

10

Old Icelandic	Literal	English
Sauðamaður Þorkels trefils úr Svignaskarði gekk þenna morgun að fé sínu.	Shepherd Thorkel Trefil about Svignaskardi went that morning to cattle his.	The shepherd of Thorkel Trefil of Svignaskard went that morning to his cattle.
Hann sér hvar þeir fara og reka alls kyns fénað.	He saw where they fared and drove all kinds-of cattle.	He saw where they travelled and drove all their kins' cattle.
Hann segir þetta Þorkatli en hann svarar:	He said that Thorkel but he answered:	He told Thorkel, and he answered:
"Veit eg hverju gegna mun.	"Know I how going should.	"I know how it should go forward.
Það munu vera Þverhlíðingar vinir mínir.	That will be Þverhlíðingar friends mine.	That will be my friends of Therarhlid.
Þeir hafa vetrarnauð mikla og munu þeir reka hingað fé sitt.	They have winter-need much and shall they drive here cattle his.	They have much need this winter and we shall drive his cattle here.
Skal þeim það heimilt.	Shall them that allow.	they shall be allowed to.
Eg hefi hey ærin.	I have hay a-year.	I have hay for a year.
Eru hér og nógar jarðir útifé".	They-were here and enough earth grazing".	There are also enough lands here for grazing.
Hann gekk út er þeir komu í tún og fagnar þeim og býður allan greiða slíkan sem þeir vilja þegið hafa.	He went out as they came to the-plot and gave them and invited all assistance such as they wished receive have.	He went out when they came to the field, and welcomed them and offered them all the favours they wanted.
Varla náðu þeir að stíga af baki, svo var bóndi beinn við þá.	Hardly reached they to dismount of horseback, so was the-farmer hospitable with then.	They barely managed to get off the back of their horses, than the farmer was right at them.
Þorbjörn mælti:	Thorbjorn spoke:	Thorbjorn spoke:

The Saga of Hen-Thorir (Old Icelandic)

Old Icelandic	Literal	English
"Mikið er nú um beina þinn og væri mikið undir að þú efndir þetta allt vel er þú hefir heitið okkur".	"Much is now about assistance yours and was much under to you fulfilment that all well that you has pledged us".	"There is much that now depends on your assistance, and it would be well undertaken, if you did all this well, what you promised us".
"Veit eg erindi þitt að féið mun hér skulu eftir vera og skortir hér eigi jörð nóga og góða".	"Know I errand yours, that cattle will here should after being, and shortage here not the-earth enough and good".	"I know your errand, that the cattle will be here after, and there is no shortage of good enough earth".
Þorbjörn mælti:	Thorbjorn spoke:	Thorbjorn spoke:
"Þiggja munum við það".	"Accept shall with that".	"I shall accept that".
Þá víkur hann Þorkatli hjá húsunum og mælti:	Then took he Thorkel aside the-house and spoke:	Then he took Thorkel beside the house and spoke:
"Tíðindi mikil eru að segja".	"Tidings great there-are to say".	"There are great tidings to tell".
Þorkell spurði hver þau væru.	Thorkel asked what they were.	Thorkell asked what they were.
"Blund-Ketill bóndi var brenndur inni í nótt",	"Blund-Ketill the-farmer was burned in about the-night",	"Blund-Ketil the farmer was burned during the night",
sagði Þorbjörn.	said Thorbjorn.	said Thorbjorn.
"Hverjir gerðu það níðingsverk?"	"Who did that low-deed?"	"Who did that low-deed?"
sagði Þorkell.	said Thorkel.	said Thorkel.
Þorbjörn sagði þá allt sem farið hafði	Thorbjorn said then all as gone had	Thorbjorn told him all that had happened.
"og þarf Hersteinn nú þinna heillaráða".	"and needed Hersteinn now your good-advice".	"and now Herstein needs your good advice".
Þorkell mælti:	Thorkel spoke:	Thorkel spoke:
"Eigi þætti mér ráðið hvort eg mundi svo skjótt á boð brugðist hafa ef eg hefði þetta vitað fyrr.	"Not seems to-me advised if I should so quickly to offer accustomed have if I had that known before.	"It does not seem to me well advised that I should have been so quick with my offer, if I had known that before.
En mínum ráðum vil eg nú láta fram fara og förum nú til matar fyrst".	But my advice will I now allow from going and let-us-go now to feed first".	But my counsel I will now go along with, and let us go now and eat first".

The Saga of Hen-Thorir (Old Icelandic)

Old Icelandic	Literal	English
Þeir játuðu því.	They affirmed accordingly.	They affirmed accordingly.
Þorkell trefill var þá mjög fámálugur og nokkuð hugsi.	Thorkel Trefill was then much of-few-words and somewhat thoughtful.	Thorkel Trefil was then very much of few words and somewhat thoughtful.
Og er þeir voru mettir lætur hann taka hesta þeirra.	And when they were full-of-food had he brought horses theirs.	And when they were full of food he had their horses brought.
Síðan taka þeir vopn sín og stíga á bak.	Then took they weapons theirs and mounted on back.	Then they took their weapons and mounted on the backs.
Ríður Þorkell fyrir þann dag og mælti áður að vel skyldi geyma fjárins í haganum en gefa vel því sem inni var.	Rode Thorkel before that day and spoke before that well should retain cattle in the-pastures and given well accordingly as inside was.	Thorkel rode in front that day and said before that the cattle in the pastures should be as well kept as those inside.
Þeir ríða nú út á Skógarströnd á Gunnarsstaði.	They rode now out to Skogarstrand in Gunnarsstadirr.	They now rode out to Skogarstrand in Gunnarsstadir.
Það er innarlega á ströndinni.	That which lying-in of the-strand.	Tha was lying far in from the strand.
Þar bjó sá maður er Gunnar hét og var Hlífarson, mikill maður og sterkur og hinn mesti garpur.	There lived so a-man who Gunnar named and was son-of-Hlifar, big man and strong and the most brave-strong.	There lived a man named Gunnar the son of Hlifar, a big strong man and the most brave.
Hann átti systur Þórðar gellis er Helga hét.	He married sister-of Thord Gellir who Helgi named.	He married the sister of Thord Gellir who was named Helgi.
Gunnar átti tvær dætur.	Gunnar had two daughters.	Gunnar had two daughters.
Hét önnur Jófríður en önnur Þuríður.	Named one Jofrid and another Thurid.	One named Jofrid and another Thurid.
Þeir koma þar síð dags, stíga af baki fyrir ofan hús.	They came there late day, dismounted of horseback for above the-house.	They arrived there late in the day, dismounted from horseback above the house.
Vindur var á norðan og heldur kalt.	Wind was in the-north and rather cold.	The wind was in the north and rather cold.

The Saga of Hen-Thorir (Old Icelandic)

Old Icelandic	Literal	English
Þorkell gengur að durum og klappar en húskarl gengur til hurðar og heilsar vel þeim sem kominn var og spyr hver hann væri.	Thorkel went to the-door and knocked but the-housekeeper went to the-door-beam and greeted well them as come was and asked who he was.	Thorkel went to the door and knocked, but the housekeepet went to the door beam and greeted them well, and asked who he was.
Þorkell kvað hann eigi vita mundu að gerr þó hann segði honum	Thorkel spoke he not knowing would if done though he said him	Thorkel said that he would not know, even if he told him.
"og bið Gunnar út ganga".	"and bid Gunnar out going".	"and ask Gunnar to come out".
Hann kvað Gunnar kominn í rekkju.	He spoke Gunnar come to bed.	He said that Gunnar had gone to bed.
Hann biður hann segja að maður vill hitta hann.	He asked him to-say to man wishes to-meet him.	He asked him to say that a man wishes to meet him.
Húskarl gerir svo, gengur inn og segir Gunnari að maður vill hitta hann.	The-housekeeper did so, went in and told Gunnar that a-man wished to-meet him.	The housekeeper did so, went in and told Gunnar that a man wished to meet him.
Gunnar spurði hver hann væri.	Gunnar asked who he was.	Gunnar asked who he was.
Húskarl kvaðst það eigi vita	The-housekeeper said that not knowing	The housekeeper said that he did not know.
"en mikill er hann vexti".	"but great-big was he grown".	"but he was great and large grown".
Gunnar mælti:	Gunnar spoke:	Gunnar spoke:
"Far þú og seg honum að hann sé hér í nótt".	"Go you and say to-him that he bed here about the-night".	"Go and say to him that he should bed here for the night".
Húskarl fer og gerir sem Gunnar bauð en Þorkell kvaðst eigi vilja þiggja boð af þrælum heldur að bónda sjálfum.	The-housekeeper went and did as Gunnar bid but Thorkel spoke not wished to-accept the-invitation of a-thrall rather to the-farmer himself.	The housekeeper went and did as Gunnar asked, but Thorkel said that he did not wish to accept the invitation of a thrall rather than from the farmer himself.
Húskarl segir að það væri sannlegra	The-housekeeper said that it was true-like	The housekeeper said that it might well be so.
"en eigi hefir Gunnar vana til þess að standa upp um nætur.	"but not has Gunnar custom to this to stand up about the-night.	"but Gunnar is not accustomed to getting up in the night.
Gerðu annaðhvort",	Do either-way",	Do one thing or the other",

The Saga of Hen-Thorir (Old Icelandic)

Old Icelandic	Literal	English
sagði húskarl, "að þú far á brott eða gakk inn og ver hér í nótt".	said the-housekeeper, "that you go to away or come in and be here in the-night".	said the housekeeper, "that you go away or come in and be here for the night".
"Gerðu annaðhvort",	"Do either-way",	Do one thing or the other",
segir Þorkell, "að þú rek erindi duganda eða eg legg sverðshjöltin á nasir þér".	said Thorkel, "that you drive errand sufficiently or I lay sword's-hilt on nose to-you".	said Thorkel, "that you fulfil my errand sufficiently or I lay my sword's hilt to your nose".
Húskarl hleypur inn og rekur aftur hurðina.	The-housekeeper ran in and drove after the-door-beam.	The housekeeper ran in and drove the door bean behind.
Gunnar spurði hví hann færi svo óðlega.	Gunnar asked why he went so wildly.	Gunnar asked why he went so wildly.
Hann sagðist eigi vildu tala fleira við hinn komna mann	He said not wished to-talk more with the come man	He said that he did not wish to talk anymore with the man who had come.
"því að hann er mjög hastorður".	"because to him was much harsh-spoken".	"because that he was much too harshly spoken".
Gunnar reis þá upp og gekk út í túnið.	Gunnar rose then up and went out into the-enclosure.	Gunnar then got up and went out into the enclosure.
Hann var í skyrtu og línbrókum, möttul yfir sér og svarta skó á fótum, sverð í hendi.	He was in shirt and linen-breeches, mantle over him and black shoes on feet, sword in hand.	He was in a shirt and linen breeches, with a cloak over him, and black shoes on his fee, and a sword in hand.
Hann fagnar vel Þorkatli og biður hann inn ganga.	He greeted well Thorkel and bid he inside going.	He greeted Thorkel well and invited him to go inside.
Hann segir að þeir voru fleiri saman.	He said that they were more together.	He said that there were still more of them together.
Gunnar gengur út í túnið en Þorkell þrífur í hurðarhringinn og rekur aftur hurðina.	Gunnar went out into the-enclosure but Thorkel deftly to the-door-ring and drove behind the-door-beam.	Gunnar went out into the enclosure but Thorkel quickly went to the door ring and pulled the door to.
Þeir ganga þá á bak húsunum.	They went then to the-back of-the-house.	They then went to the back of the house.
Gunnar heilsar þeim.	Gunnar greeted them.	Gunnar greeted them.
Þorkell sagði:	Thorkel said:	Thorkel said:

The Saga of Hen-Thorir (Old Icelandic)

Old Icelandic	Literal	English
"Setjumst vér niður því að vér eigum mart að tala við þig Gunnar".	"Let-us-sit we down because that we have many to say with you Gunnar".	"Let us sit down, because we have much to discuss with you Gunnar".
Þeir gera svo, setjast niður á tvær hendur honum og svo nær að þeir sátu á skikkjunni er Gunnar hafði yfir sér.	They did so, sitting down on two hands his and so close that they sat on cloak that Gunnar had over himself.	They did so, sitting on the left hand and the right hand of him, and so close that they sat on the cloak that Gunnar had over himself.
Þorkell mælti þá:	Thorkel spoke then:	Thorkel spoke then:
"Svo er háttað Gunnar bóndi að hér er sá maður í ferð með mér er Hersteinn heitir, son Blund-Ketills.	"So is the-way Gunnar the-farmer to here is so a-man in travelled with to-me is Herstein named, son-of Blund-Ketill's.	"This is the way it is, farmer Gunnar, there is a man travelling with me that is named Herstein, the son of Blund-Ketil.
Er eigi því erindi að leyna að hann vill biðja dóttur þinnar Þuríðar.	Is not therefore errand to hide that he will invite daughter yours Thorid.	There is no point in hiding the fact that he wishes to ask for the hand of your daughter Thurid.
Hefi eg og fyrir þessa sök með honum farið að eg vildi eigi að þú vísaðir manninum frá því að mér sýnist happaráð hið mesta.	Have I and for this reason with him travelling to I wish not to you turn-away the-man from because to to-me seems happy-decision the most.	I have travelled with him for this reason, that you do not turn this man away, because to me it seems to be the most happy decision.
Þykir mér og miklu varða að eigi sé óvirt þetta mál og mín tillög eða seint svarað".	Seemed to-me and much concern that not see unworthy that matter and mine proposal or coldly answered".	It is a matter of deep concern to me, and also my matter, that the proposal is not seen as unworthy or answered coldly".
Gunnar mælti:	Gunnar spoke:	Gunnar spoke:
"Eigi er eg einhlítur um svör þessa máls og vil eg ráðast um við móður hennar og svo við dóttur mína og einkum við Þórð gelli frænda hennar.	"Not am I sufficient about answer this matter and will I arrange about with mother hers and so with daughter mine and especially with Thord Gellir kinsman hers.	"I am not sufficient to answer this matter, and I will arrange with her mother and with my daughter and especially with Thord Gellir her kinsman.
En góðar einar fréttir höfum vér til þessa manns og svo til föður hans og er þetta ásjámál".	But good Einar news have we to this man and so to father his and is that matter-consideration".	But we have heard good things of this man and also of his father, and this is a matter of consideration".
Þá svarar Trefill:	Then answered Trefill:	Then Trefill answered:

The Saga of Hen-Thorir (Old Icelandic)

Old Icelandic	Literal	English
"Svo skaltu til ætla að vér munum eigi lengi vonbiðlar vera konunnar og þykjumst vér eigi minnur sjá fyrir þinni sæmd en vorri.	"So shall-you to suppose that we shall not longer hope-abide being the-woman and think we not less seems for your honour than ours.	"So should you suppose that we shall not longer be abiding in hope of the woman, and we think this is no less an honour to you than to us.
Þykir mér og kynlegt um svo vitran mann sem þú ert að þú virðir slíka hluti fyrir þér svo vel sem boðið er.	Seems to-me also strange about so wise man as you are that you value such part for to-you so well as invitation is.	It also seems to me strange, since you are such a wise man and you respect such things for yourself, as well as they are offered.
Höfum vér og svo að eins heiman gert ferð vora að eigi mun til einskis ætluð.	Have we also so to one's home made journey further that not should to nothing intend.	We have also made such a long journey from home, that it should not be for nothing.
Og mun eg Hersteinn veita þér slíkt lið sem þú vilt að þetta fari fram ef hann kann eigi að sjá hvað honum sómir".	And should I Herstein grant to-you such assistance as you wish to that goes from if he can not to see what him honourable".	And Herstein, I shall grant you such assistance as you wish in order for this to go forward, if he cannot see what is honourable to him".
Gunnar svarar:	Gunnar answered:	Gunnar answered:
"Það fæ eg eigi skilið hví þér látið svo brátt að þessu eða haldið við heitan sjálfa því að mér líst þetta mjög jafnræði en einskis ills örvænti eg fyrir yður og mun eg það ráð upp taka að rétta fram höndina".	"That get I not understand why you let so soon that this or holding with threatening myself because that to-me appears that much equally and nothing ill desperation I from you and should I that decision up take that rights from hand",	"What I don't understand is why you wish it to happen so soon, or hold with threatening me, because to me it appears very much equal, but in vain do I despair of you, and I should take the decision to extend my hand".
Og svo gerir hann en Hersteinn nefnir sér votta og fastnar sér konu.	And so did he then Herstein named his witnesses and betrothed himself the-woman.	And so he did, then Herstein named his witnesses and betrothed himself to the woman.
Eftir þetta standa þeir upp og ganga inn.	After that stood they up and went in.	After that they stood up and went in.
Er þeim veittur beini góður.	Were they given benefit good.	They were well looked after.
Nú spyr Gunnar tíðinda.	Now asked Gunnar news.	Now Gunnar asked the news.
Þorkell segir að þeir hafi nú eigi annað nýlegar frétt en brennu Blund-Ketills.	Thorkel said that they had now not other newer news than the-burning Blund-Ketill's.	Thorkell said that they had no newer news than the burning of Blund-Ketill.

The Saga of Hen-Thorir (Old Icelandic)

Old Icelandic	Literal	English
Gunnar spurði hver því olli.	Gunnar asked who therefore caused.	Gunnar asked, who therefore caused it.
Þorkell segir að Þorvaldur Oddsson var upphafsmaður að og Arngrímur goði.	Thorkel said that Thorvald son-of-Odd was the-instigators to and Arngrim chieftain.	Thorkel said that Thorvald son of Odd was the instigator and also Arngrim the chieftain.
Gunnar svaraði fá, lastaði lítt enda lofaði eigi.	Gunnar answered gave, blame little and praised not.	Gunnar gave his answer, blamed little and praised not.

11

Old Icelandic	Literal	English
Þegar um morguninn í ár er Gunnar á fótum og gengur að Þorkatli og bað þá klæðast.	From-there about morning in early was Gunnar on feet and went to Thorkel and asked then to-dress.	Early in the morning, Gunnar was on his feet and went to Thorkel and asked him to get dressed.
Þeir gera svo, ganga síðan til snæðings.	They did so, going then to eating.	They did so, and then went to eat.
Eru þá og búnir hestar þeirra og stíga þeir á bak.	They-were then and prepared horses theirs and mounted they on back.	Then their horses were ready, and they mounted on the back.
Ríður Gunnar fyrir inn með firðinum.	Rode Gunnar before the along fjord.	Gunnar rode in front along the fjord.
Þá voru íslög mikil.	Then was ice-bound much.	Then it was very much ice-bound.
Eigi létta þeir fyrr en þeir koma í Hvamm til Þórðar gellis og fagnar hann þeim vel og spurði tíðinda.	Not let-up they before but they came to Hvamm to Thord Gellir and took he them well and asked the-news.	They did not let up before they came to Hvamm to Thord Gellir and he received them well and asked the news.
Þeir sögðu slíkt er þeim líkaði.	They told so was they liked.	They told him so as they liked.
Gunnar heimtir Þórð á mál og segir að þar er í för Hersteinn son Blund-Ketills og Þorkell trefill,	Gunnar got Thord to the-matter and said that there was with going Herstein son Blund-Ketill's and Thorkel Trefill,	Gunnar got on to the matter with Thord and said what was happening with Hersteinn son of Blund-Ketill and Thorkel Trefill,
"er það erindi þeirra að Hersteinn mælir til mægða við mig en til samfara við Þuríði dóttur mína eða hversu ráðlegt líst þér það?	"are that errand theirs to Herstein discussing to marriage with me but to together-travelling with Thurid daughter mine or how-so advise appears to-you that?	"Is it their business that Hersteinn is recommending me as a father-in-law, but for marriage with my daughter Thurid, or how advisable do you think it is?

The Saga of Hen-Thorir (Old Icelandic)

Old Icelandic	Literal	English
Maður er vænn og gervilegur.	Man is handsome and accomplished.	The man is handsome and accomplished.
Hann skortir og eigi fé því faðir hans hefir það mælt að hann mundi af hendi láta búið en Hersteinn tæki við".	He shortage and not wealth because father his has that said that he would of hand let place but Herstein take with".	He is not short of wealth because of his father has said that he would leave the estate, then Herstein would take over".
Þórður svarar:	Thord answered:	Thord answered:
"Vel er mér við Blund-Ketill því að einn tíma er við Tungu-Oddur deildum á alþingi um þrælsgjöld er dæmdust á hendur honum og fór eg að heimta í foraðsillu veðri og vér þrír saman og komum um nótt til Blund-Ketills og var oss þar allvel fagnað og þar vorum vér viku.	"Well am to-me with Blund-Ketill because that one time that with Tungu-Odd shared at the-assembly about servant-fees were judged to hand him and went I to insist in abominable weather and we three together and came about night to Blund-Ketill's and were us there all-well celebrating and there were we a-week.	"I am fine with Blund-Ketill, because of that time when Tungu-Odd and I were arguing at the assembly about servant fees, and it was judged to his hand, and I went to insist in bad weather, and the three of us came in the night to Blund-Ketill's and we were well received there and stayed for a week.
Hann skipti við oss hestum en gaf mér góð stóðhross.	He exchanged with us horses but gave to-me good stallions.	He exchanged horses with us, but gave me good stallions.
Slíkt reyndi eg af honum en þó líst mér svo á að eigi muni því misráðið þó að eigi sé þessu keypt".	Such experience I of him but though appears to-me so as to not should because mis-advised though to not see this bought".	That was my experience of him, but though it appears to me that it would not be mis-advised not to conclude this matter".
"Svo máttu til ætla",	"So might to suppose",	"So might you suppose",
sagði Gunnar, "að eigi mun hún föstnuð öðrum manni þó henni bjóðist því að mér líst sjá maður vasklegur og vel boðinn og mikil hætta í hversu til tekst ef þessum manni er frá vísað".	said Gunnar, "to not should her betrothe other man though her offered because to to-me appears see the-man bold and well invited and great danger in how-so to take if this people for from turn-away".	said Gunnar, "that she should not be betrothed to any other man though she is offered, because it appears to me that he is a bold man with a good offer, and there is great danger from these people if they are turned away".
Eftir það gengur Gunnar til fundar við dóttur sína því að hún var með Þórði á fóstri og fréttir hana eftir hversu henni var um gefið.	After that went Gunnar to meet with daughter his because to she was with Thord in fostering and news hers after how-so to-her was about given.	After that Gunnar went to meet with his daughter because she was being fostered with Thord, and the news after her, and how she was given to the idea.

The Saga of Hen-Thorir (Old Icelandic)

Old Icelandic	Literal	English
Hún svarar að eigi er henni svo mikil manngirnd í hug að henni þætti eigi jafngott að sitja heima	She answered that not was she so greatly men-desiring in thought to her seemed not equal-good to settle at-home	She replied that she didn't have so much love for people, and in her mind that she would just as well sit at home,
"því að eg á kost góðrar forsjá þar sem Þórður er frændi minn.	"because to I in provided-for well custody there as Thord who kinsman mine.	"because I have the advantage of good guardianship, where Thord is my kinsman.
En ykkarn vilja mun eg gera um þetta og annað".	But your wish should I do about this and other-things".	But according to your will, I will do about this and other things".
Nú elur Gunnar á málið við Þórð og segir að honum líst þetta ráð allsæmilegt.	Now came Gunnar to the-matter with Thord and said to him appeared that counsel decent.	Now Gunnar came to the matter with Thord and said to him that it appeared to be good counsel.
Þórður svarar:	Thord answered:	Thord answered:
"Hví skaltu eigi gefa honum dóttur þína ef þér líkar?"	"Why shall-you not give him daughter yours if to-you like?"	"Then why not give him your daughter if you like?"
Gunnar svarar:	Gunnar answered:	Gunnar answered:
"Því að eins gef eg hana að það sé jafnvel þinn vilji sem minn".	"Because to one give I her to that being equal-good your will as mine".	"Because I will give her if your will is as good as mine".
Þórður kvað beggja þeirra ráð þetta vera skyldu.	Thord said both theirs counsel that being would.	Thord said that both of them agreed that this was a duty.
"Eg vil",	"I will",	"I will",
sagði Gunnar, "að þú Þórður fastnir Hersteini konuna".	said Gunnar, "to you Thord betrothe Herstein a-wife".	said Gunnar, "that you, Thord, betrothe Herstein a wife".
Þórður svarar:	Thord answered:	Thord answered:
"Sjálfur skaltu það gera að fastna dóttur þína".	"Self shall-you that do to betrothe daughter yours".	"You yourself shall betrothe your own daughter".
Gunnar svarar:	Gunnar answered:	Gunnar answered:
"Mér þykir meiri virðing í að þú fastnir hana því að það samir betur".	"To-me seems more worthy to that you betrothe her because to that same better".	"It seems to me more worthy that you to betrothe her because it will be better".
Þórður lét nú þetta leiðast og fóru nú festar fram.	Thord let now that lay and went now fixed from.	Now Thord let it lie and it was fixed upon.

The Saga of Hen-Thorir (Old Icelandic)

Old Icelandic	Literal	English
Þá mælti Gunnar:	Then spoke Gunnar:	Then Gunnar spoke:
"Bið eg enn að þú látir hér vera boðið í Hvammi og mun þá gert verða með mestri sæmd".	"Ask I but to you let here being the-wedding in Hvamm and should then done worthy with the-most honour".	"But I ask, that you let the wedding me here in Hvamm, and then it should be done worthily with the most honour".
Þórður bað hann því og ráða ef honum þætti svo betur.	Thord bid him accordingly and advised if he seemed so better.	Thord agreed with him accordingly and was advised that it seemed better.
Gunnar segir:	Gunnar said:	Gunnar said:
"Svo munum vér til ætla að vér látum þegar vera á viku fresti".	"So should we to intend to we let from-there being one week from-now".	"So we should intend to it, that we have from there being one week from now".
Eftir það stíga þeir á bak og snúa á ferð og víkur Þórður á götu með þeim og spurði enn ef nokkuð væri nýtt að segja.	After that mounted their on back and turned to travelled and week Thord and the-path with them and asked but if any was new to say.	After that they mounted on horseback and turned on their way, and Thord turned to the path with them and asked again if there was any news.
Gunnar svarar:	Gunnar answered:	Gunnar answered:
"Ekki höfum vér nú nýlegar frétt en brennu Blund-Ketills bónda".	"Not have we now new news but the-burning Blund-Ketill the-farmer".	"We do not have any news newer than the burning of Blund-Ketill the farmer".
Þórður spurði hversu það varð	Thord asked how-so that became	Thord asked how it had happened.
en Gunnar sagði allan atburðinn um brennuna og hver henni olli og svo hverjir það gerðu.	but Gunnar said all at-carried about the-burning and who he that-caused and so who that did.	Then Gunnar told the whole story about the fire and who caused it and who did it.
Þórður mælti:	Thord spoke:	Thord spoke:
"Eigi mundi þessu gjaforði svo skjótt ráðið hafa verið ef eg hefði þetta vitað og þykist þér nú allmjög hafa komist fyrir mig í viti og beittan brögðum í þessu.	"Not should this reserved so quickly advised had been if I have that known and seems to-you now all-much have come for me in wit and cunning strategy in this.	"This would not have been possible with such a quick decision if I had known about it, and now you're pretty sure you've outsmarted me and used cunning strategy in this.
En þó þykir mér eigi víst að þér séuð yður einhlítir að þessu máli".	But though seems to-me not certain to you see-you your sufficient to this the-matter".	But even so, I don't think you are of one mind on this matter".

The Saga of Hen-Thorir (Old Icelandic)

Old Icelandic	Literal	English
Gunnar mælti:	Gunnar spoke:	Gunnar spoke:
"Þar er gott til trausts að ætla sem þú ert enda er þér nú skylt að veita mági þínum en vér erum skyldir að veita þér því að margir heyrðu að þú fastnaðir konuna og þetta var allt við þitt ráð gert.	"There is good to trust to suppose as you are concluded are you now should to grant son-in-law yours but we are obliged to grant to-you because to many heard that you betrothed the-woman and that was all with your consent done.	"There is good for trust to believe in you, since you are now obliged to provide for your son-in-law, and we are obliged to provide for you, because many people heard that you caught the woman and this was all arranged by you,
Og er nú vel að þér reynið eitt sinn hver yðvar drjúgastur er höfðingjanna því að þér hafið lengi úlfs munni af etist".	And as now well to to-you test one they who your greatly are chieftain because to to-you have long wolves mouth of eating".	and now it is good that you try for once which of you is the best of the chieftains, because you have had a wolf's mouth for eating for a long time".

12

Nú skiljast þeir og er Þórður hinn reiðasti og þykir honum þeir hafa gabbað sig.	Now parted they and was Thord the most-angry and seemed him they have fooled him.	Now they parted and Thord was angry as could be, and it seemed that they had fooled him.
En þeir ríða nú fyrst á Gunnarsstaði og þykjast allvel leikið hafa að þeir höfðu komið Þórði í málið með sér og voru nú allkátir.	But they rode now first to Gunnarsstadir and considered all-well played have that they had come Thord to the-matter with his and were now merry.	But they now rode first to Gunnarsstadir and thought that they had played their hand very well in bringing Thord into the matter and they were now merry.
Eigi ríða þeir nú suður að sinni en bjóða mönnum til boðs og sækja í Hvammi að ákveðnum tíma.	Not rode they now south to they but invited men to the-wedding and sought to Hvamm to certain time.	They did not ride to the south, but they invited men to the wedding and returned to Hvamm at the appointed time.
Hafði Þórður þar mart fyrirboðsmanna og skipar mönnum í sæti um kveldið.	Had Thord there many invited-people and ordered people in seated about evening.	Thord had many invited people there and ordered them to their seats in the evening.
Sat hann sjálfur á annan bekk og Gunnar mágur hans og hans menn en Þorkell trefill hjá brúðguma á annan bekk og þeirra boðsmenn.	Sat he himself on opposite bench and Gunnar son-in-law his and his men and Thorkel Trefill beside bridegroom on opposite bench and theirs invited-people.	He himself sat on the second bench, and his brother-in-law Gunnar and his men, while Thorkell Trefill with the groom on the second bench and their attendants.
Brúðir skipuðu pall.	The-bride appointed platform.	The bride was on the appointed platform.

The Saga of Hen-Thorir (Old Icelandic)

Old Icelandic	Literal	English
Og svo sem borð voru sett og allir menn í sæti komnir þá stökk Hersteinn brúðgumi fram yfir borðið og gengur þar að sem einn steinn stóð.	And so when the-tables were set and all people in seats came then sprang Herstein the-bridegroom from over the-tables and went there to as one stone stood.	And when the tables were set and all the people came to their seats, Herstein the bridegroom strode over the tables and went to where a stone stood.
Hann steig öðrum fæti upp á steininn og mælti:	He stepped other foot up on the-stone and spoke:	He stepped one foot up on the stone and spoke:
"Þess strengi eg heit",	"This binding I pledge",	"This binding I pledge",
sagði hann, "að áður alþingi er úti í sumar skal eg hafa fullsektað Arngrím goða eða sjálfdæmi ella".	said he, "that before the-assembly is out this summer shall I have fully-outlawed Arngrim the-chieftain or self-judgement otherwise".	he said, "that before the assembly is finished this summer, I shall have Arngrim the chieftain fully outlawed, or the right to make my own judgement".
Síðan stígur hann í sæti sitt.	Then climbed he in seat his.	Then he climbed to his seat.
Gunnar stökk þá fram og mælti:	Gunnar sprang then from and spoke:	Gunnar then sprang up and spoke:
"Þess strengi eg heit",	"This binding I pledge",	"This binding I pledge",
sagði hann, "að áður alþingi er úti í sumar skal eg hafa sótt til útlegðar Þorvald Oddsson eða hafa sjálfdæmi ella".	said he, "that before the-assembly is out this summer shall I have sought to outlawry Thorvald son-of-Odd or have self-judgement otherwise".	he said, "that before the assembly is finished this summer I shall have sought outlawry for Thorvald son of Odd, or have self-judgement".
Upp stígur hann undir borð og mælti til Þórðar:	Up climbed he under the-table and spoke to Thord:	He climbed back under the table and spoke to Thord:
"Hví situr þú Þórður og mælir eigi um?	"Why sit you Thord and speak not about?	"Why do you sit Thord and no speak out?
Vitum vér að slíkt er þér í hug sem oss".	Know we that such is to-you in thought as us".	We know that you have the same thought as us".
Þórður svarar:	Thord answered:	Thord answered:
"Kyrrt mun það að sinni".	"Still should it to mind".	"It should be still in mind".
Gunnar svarar:	Gunnar answered:	Gunnar answered:

The Saga of Hen-Thorir (Old Icelandic)

Old Icelandic	Literal	English
"Ef þú vilt að vér tölum fyrir þig þá er það til reiðu.	"If you wish that we talk for you then is that to readily.	"If you wish that we talk for you, then that can readily be done".
En vitum vér að þú ætlar þér Tungu-Odd".	But know we what you intend to-you Tungu-Odd".	But we know what you intend for Tungu-Odd".
Þórður mælti:	Thord spoke:	Thord spoke:
"Þér skuluð ráða yðrum ummælum en eg mun því ráða hvað eg tala.	"To-you should decide your about-speech but I should therefore decide what I say.	"You should settle your announcements, and I will decide what I say.
Endið þetta vel sem þér hafið um mælt".	End that well which you have about to-say".	End it well, what you have said about".
Eigi var til nýlundu fleira að boðinu en þó fór það allskörulega fram og er það braut fór hver sem fyrir lá.	Not was to news more than the-wedding but though went that all-clear from and was that away went each as before laying.	There was no more news of the wedding, except that it went well from then on, and when it was over, each went as they had been before.
Og líður veturinn af hendi.	And passed the-winter of hand.	And the winter passed on.
Og er vorar safna þeir að sér mönnum og fara suður til Borgarfjarðar og koma í Norðurtungu og stefna Arngrími til þings í Þingnes og Hænsna-Þóri.	And when spring raised they to his men and went south to Borgafjord and came to North-Tongue and summoned Arngrim to the-assembly in Assembly-Headland and Hen-Thorir.	And when spring came, they gathered their men and went south to Borgarfjord and came to North-Tongue and summoned Arngrim to the assembly at Thingnes along with Hen-Thorir.
Nú skilst Hersteinn frá liðinu með þrem tigum manna þangað sem hann sagði hinn síðasta náttstað verið hafa Þorvalds Oddssonar, því að hann var þá farinn af vist sinni.	Now parted Herstein from the-company with three tens men from-there as he said the last night-quarters been have Thorvald's son-of-Odd, because that he was then travelling of hospitality his.	Now Herstein separated from the company with thirty men to where he said that the last night's lodgings had been Thorvald Oddsson's, because he had then left his place.
Nú er ókyrrt í héraðinu og mikil umræða og samandráttur liðs af hvorratveggja hendi.	Now is un-quiet in the-district and much about-discussion and gathering company of each-way arms.	Now there was unquiet in the district and much discussion about and gathering of companies to arms on either side.

The Saga of Hen-Thorir (Old Icelandic)

Old Icelandic	Literal	English
# 13	# 13	# 13
Það varð til tíðinda að Hænsna-Þórir hvarf brott úr héraðinu við tólfta mann þegar hann spurði hverjir í málið voru komnir og fréttist alls eigi til hans.	That was to the-news to Hen-Thorir disappeared away from the-district with twelve men from-there he learned each in the-matter were come and enquired all not to his.	It was news that Hen-Thorir disappeared away from the district with twelve men, as soon as he learned who were coming to the case, and no one could find out anything about him.
Oddur safnar nú liði um dalina, Reykjardal hvorntveggja og Skorradal, og um allar sveitir fyrir sunnan Hvítá og þó hafði hann mart úr öðrum sveitum.	Odd gathered now company about the-valleys, Reykjardal either-way and Skorradal, and about all areas for the-south Hvita and though had he many about other countryside.	Now Odd gathered a company from either side of the valleys, Reyjardal and Skorradal, and all about the areas south of Hvita and also many others in the countryside.
Arngrímur goði safnaði mönnum um Þverárhlíð og Norðurárdal að sumum hluta.	Arngrim chieftain collected men about Þverarhlíd and Norduradal to some parts.	Arngrim the chieftain gathered men around some parts of Thverarhlid and Norduradal.
Þorkell trefill safnaði mönnum hið neðra um Mýrar og Stafholtstungur og suma Norðurdæla hefir hann með sér því að Helgi bróðir hans bjó í Hvammi og hefir hann hann með sér.	Thorkel Trefill gathered men then lower about Myrar and Stafholtstunga and some Norðurdæla had he with him because that Helgi brother his lived in Hvamm and had he he with him.	Thorkel Trefill then gathered men around lower Myrar and Stafholtstunga and had some in Norduradal with him because his brother Helgi lived in Hvamm and he was with him.
Nú safnar Þórður gellir liði vestan og hefir eigi mart lið.	Now gathered Thord Gellir company west and had not many company.	Now Thord Gellir gathered a company in the west, but not a large company.
Hittast nú þessir allir er í voru málinu og hafa alls tvö hundruð manna, ríða nú ofan fyrir utan Norðurá og yfir á að Eyjavaði fyrir ofan Stafholt og ætla yfir Hvítá þar sem heitir Þrælastraumur.	Met now these all are in were this-case and had all two hundred men, rode now over for outside Norðura and over about to Eyjavaði for above Stafholt and intended over White-water there as named Þrælastraumur.	Now all who were involved in this case met, and had two hundred men in all, and they rode over outside Nordura and over to Eyjavadi above Stafholt, intending to cross over Hvita at a place named Thraelastraum.
Þá sjá þeir mannaferð mikla fyrir sunnan ána.	Then saw they journey-of-men great ahead from-the-south river.	They they saw the journey of a great body of men from the south river.
Er þar Tungu-Oddur og nær fjögur hundruð manna.	Were there Tungu-Odd and nearly four hundreds people.	Tungu-Odd was there with nearly four hundred people.

The Saga of Hen-Thorir (Old Icelandic)

Old Icelandic	Literal	English
Gæða nú ferðina og vilja fyrr koma til vaðsins.	Increased now travelling and willed for to-come to wading-water.	They increased their travelling and wished to come to the water first.
Hittast nú við ána og hlaupa þeir Oddur af baki og verja vaðið en þeim Þórði gengur ógreitt framreiðin og vildu gjarna komast á þingið.	To-reach now with river and leapt they Odd off horseback and guarded the-ford that they Thord went obstructed riding-on and wished willingly to-come to the-assembly.	They now met at the river, and Odd's men leapt from horseback and guarded the ford so that Thord and his men were obstructed from riding on, though they wished to come to the assembly.
Slær nú í bardaga og verða þegar áverkar.	Struck now in battle and became from-there injuries.	Now there was a battle, and injuries came from it.
Féllu fjórir menn af Þórði.	Fell many men of Thord.	Many of Thord's men fell.
Þar féll Þórólfur refur bróðir Álfs úr Dölum, virðulegur maður, og hverfa nú frá við svo búið.	There fell Thorolf Refur brother-of Alf of Dölum, worthy man, and turned-back now from with so done.	There fel Thorolf Refur, the brother of Alf of Dolum, a worthy man, and when this was done they turned back.
Einn maður féll af Oddi en þrír urðu mjög sárir.	One man fell of Odd's but three became much wounded.	One of Odd's men fell, and three became much wounded.
Þórður snýr nú málinu til alþingis.	Thord turned now this-case to the-assembly.	Thord turned this case over to the national assembly.
Þeir ríða nú heim vestur og þykir mönnum mjög hallast hafa metorð vestanmanna.	They rode now home west and seemed men much slanted had reputation the-western-men.	Now they rode west to home, and the men from the west seemed to have had their reputation slanted.
Nú ríður Oddur á þingið.	Now rode Odd to the-assembly.	Now Odd rode to the assembly.
Hann sendi heim þræla sína með hross.	He sent home servants his with horses.	He sent his servants home with horses.
Jórunn kona hans spurði tíðinda er þeir komu heim.	Jorunn wife his asked the-news when they came home.	Jorunn his wife asked for news when they came home.
Þeir kváðust engi segja kunna önnur en þau að sá maður var einn kominn vestan úr Breiðafirði að svara kunni Tungu-Oddi "og var hans hljómur og rödd sem griðungur gelldi".	They said nothing to-say could other-than that they to saw man was one come west about Breidafjord to answer could Tungu-Odd "and was his sound and voice as a-bull bellowing".	They said that there was nothing that they could say other than that they saw a man who had come from the west around Breidafjord who could answer Tungu-Odd "and his sound and voice was like that of a bull bellowing".

The Saga of Hen-Thorir (Old Icelandic)

Old Icelandic	Literal	English
Hún kvað það engi tíðindi þótt honum væri svarað sem öðrum manni en kvað þó það hafa gerst að tíðindum að eigi væri líklegra til.	She said that no news thought he was answered as other men but spoke though that have done to news to not was likely to.	She said that this was not news even though he was answered as other men, but said that this news was not very likely.
"Var þar og bardagi",	"Was there also a-battle",	"There was also a battle",
sögðu þeir, "og féllu fimm menn alls en margir urðu sárir".	said they, "and fell five men in-all but many became wounded".	they said, "and five men fell in all but many became wounded".
En áður gátu þeir þess að engu.	But before got they this to nothing.	But before they got nothing of this.
Nú líður þingið og verður þar eigi til tíðinda.	Now passed the-assembly and became there not to the-news.	Now the assembly passed and there came no news.
En er þeir mágar koma heim vestur skipta þeir bústöðum.	But when they father-and-son came home west, exchanged they residences,	But when the father and son came home to the west, they exchanged residences.
Fer Gunnar í Örnólfsdal en Hersteinn tekur Gunnarsstaði.	Went Gunnar to Ornolfsdal but Herstein took Gunnarsstað.	Gunnar went to Ornolfsdal, but Herstein took Gunnarsstadir.
Eftir þetta lætur Gunnar færa til sín vestan við þann allan sem Örn austmaður hafði átt og flytja heim í Örnólfsdal.	After that had Gunnar brought to him west wood that all which Orn the-eastern-man had owned and carried home to Ornolfsdal.	After that Gunnar had all of the wood which Orn the Easterner had owned brought to him and carried home to Ornolfsdal.
Tekur hann til síðan og húsar upp bæinn í annað sinn því að Gunnar var allra manna hagastur.	Took he to then and house-built up dwellings about another he because that Gunnar was all man the-best.	He then took building up the dwellings about him, because Gunnar was the best of all men.
Hann var og um allt atgervismaður og manna best vígur og hinn vaskasti í öllu.	He was and about all dynamic-man and people the-best spear-man and the boldest of all.	He was dynamic in all ways, and was the best with a spear, and the boldest of all.

14

Nú líða stundir fram allt til þess að menn ríða til þings.	Now passed awhile from all to this that men rode to the-assembly.	Now a while passed from all this until the men rode to the assembly.
Er nú mikill viðbúnaður í héruðunum.	Was now much preparation among the-districts.	There was now much preparation among the districts.

The Saga of Hen-Thorir (Old Icelandic)

Old Icelandic	Literal	English
Ríða nú hvorirtveggju ákafa fjölmennir.	Rode now each-side eager crowd.	There now rode an eager crowd on either side.
Og er þeir Þórður gellir koma á Gunnarsstaði er Hersteinn sjúkur og má eigi fara til þings.	And when they Thord Gellir came to Gunnarsstað was Herstein sick and may not travel to the-assembly.	And when Thord Gellir and his men came to Gunnarsstadir, Herstein was sick and unable to travel to the assembly.
Selur hann nú öðrum í hendur sakirnar.	Sold he now other in hand the-sake.	He handed over his part in the lawsuits.
Eftir voru hjá honum þrír tigir manna.	After were beside him three tens men.	Thirty men stayed behind beside him.
Nú ríður Þórður til þings.	Now rode Thord to the-assembly.	Now Thord rode to the assembly.
Hann safnar að sér vinum sínum og frændum og kemur snemma til þings.	He gathered to his friends his and kinsmen and came soon to the-assembly.	He gathered his friends and kinsmen and soon came to the assembly.
En þingið var þá undir Ármannsfelli.	But the-assembly was then from Armannsfell.	But the assembly was then held from Armannsfell.
Og svo sem flokkar koma hefir Þórður liðsdrátt mikinn.	And so as groups came had Thord assembling-troops great.	And as the groups arrived, Thord had a great assembling of troops.
Nú er sén ferð Tungu-Odds.	Now when seen travelling Tungu-Odd's.	Now when Tungu-Odd's company was seen travelling.
Ríður Þórður þá í mót honum og vill eigi að hann nái þinghelginni.	Riding Thord then in meeting him and willed not that he got-to the-assembly-sanctuary.	Then Thord rode to meet him and wished that he did not get to the sanctuary of the assembly.
Oddur ríður með þremur hundruðum manna.	Odd rode with three hundred men.	Odd rode with three hundred men.
Þeir Þórður verja þingið og slær þá þegar í bardaga.	They Thord blocked the-assembly and struck then from-there in battle.	Thord and his men blocked the assembly and then struck them in battle.
Tekst brátt mannfall en allmargir urðu sárir.	Took soon men-fallen and all-many became wounded.	Soon men were taken and fell, and many became wounded.
Þar féllu sex menn af Oddi því Þórður var miklu fjölmennari.	There fell six men of Odd because Thord was great following-men.	Six of Odd's men fell there, because Thord had a great following of men.

The Saga of Hen-Thorir (Old Icelandic)

Old Icelandic	Literal	English
Þetta sjá góðgjarnir menn að þau vandræði mundu af standa ef þingheimurinn berðist að seint mundi bætur bíða.	That saw benevolent men that they difficulty would of withstand if the-asembly fought to late should reconciliation bid.	Benevolent men then saw that there would be difficulty to withstand if the assembly fought, so they asked for a reconciliation.
Er þá gengið í milli og verða skildir og snúið málum til sættar og var Oddur ofurliði borinn og varð undan að láta fyrir því að bæði var að hann þótti þyngra málahlut eiga að flytja enda varð hann aflvani fyrir liðs sakir.	Was then went to between and became shields and turned matters to settle and was Odd outnumbered bore and became give-way to allow for because to both was to he seemed heavy case-load had to carry conclude became he overpowered for the-company sake.	Then they came to an agreement, then the shields were turned, and things were settled, and Odd was overmatched and had to give in, because both of them thought he had a more difficult case to deal with, and he became overpowered for the sake of the company against him.
Var þá það mælt að Oddur mundi tjalda á brottu úr þinghelgi en ganga til dóma og að nauðsynjum sínum, fara með sig spaklega, sýna enga þrjósku né hans menn.	Was then that spoke to Odd should tent in away about the-assembly but going to the-court and to necessities his, went with himself heavily, show no belligerance not his men.	It was then declared that Odd should set his tent away from the assembly, but go about his business in the court, this went heavily with him, and he was to show no belligerence nor were any of his men.
Sitja menn nú yfir málum og leita að sætta þá	Sat men now over the-matter and let to settle then	Men now sat over the matter and had to settle it then.
og horfir Oddi þunglega fyrir það mest að mikið ofurefli var í móti.	and looked Odd heavily for that most to much overwhelming was in meeting.	and Oddi regretted the fact that there was a lot of overreaction in the meeting.

15

En nú skal segja nokkuð af Hersteini, að honum létti brátt sóttarinnar er þeir riðu til þingsins.	But now shall say some of Herstein, to him left soon sickness when they rode to the-assembly.	But new shall be told something of Herstein, that he was soon be relieved of his illness, when they rode to the parliament.
Fer hann þá í Örnólfsdal.	Went he then to Ornolfsdal.	He then went to Ornolfsdal.
Það var einn morgun snemma að hann var í smiðju því að hann var manna hagastur á járn.	That was one morning soon that he was in workshop because that he was people the-best at iron.	It was early one morning, that he was in the workshop, because he was the best of all people at smithing.
Þá kemur þar bóndi einn sá er Örnólfur hét og sagði svo:	Then came there the-farmer one saw was Ornolf named and said so:	Then a farmer came there, whose name was Ornolfr, and said so:

The Saga of Hen-Thorir (Old Icelandic)

Old Icelandic	Literal	English
"Sjúk er kýr mín",	"Sick is cow mine",	"My cow is sick",
sagði hann, "og bið eg þig Hersteinn að þú farir og sjáir hana.	said he, "and ask I you Herstein that you travel and see her.	he said, "and I ask you, Herstein, that you travel and see her.
Þykir oss nú gott að þú ert aftur kominn og höfum vér þá nokkuð svo iðgjöld föður þíns er oss varð að mestu gagni".	Seemed us now good that you are returned come and have we then some so recompensed father yours that us became to most useful".	It seems good to us that you are back, and we have some of your father's compensation, which was of great use to us".
Hersteinn svarar:	Herstein answered:	Herstein answered:
"Eigi hirði eg um kú þína og kann eg eigi að sjá hvað henni er til meins".	"Not shepherd I about cow yours and can I not to see what her is to harm".	I am not a shepherd for your cow, and I can not see, what is her harm".
Bóndi svarar:	The-farmer answered:	The farmer answered:
"Mikill er þó munur að faðir þinn gaf mér kúna en þú vilt eigi sjá hana".	"Much is though difference that father your given to-me the-cow but you will not see her".	"There is much difference, than the cow your father gave me, but you will not see her".
Hersteinn svarar:	Herstein answered:	Herstein answered:
"Eg gef þér aðra kú ef þessi deyr".	"I give to-you another cow if this-one dies".	"I will give you another cow if this one dies".
Bóndi svarar:	The-farmer answered:	The farmer answered:
"Það vil eg fyrst þiggja að þú sjáir þessa".	"That will I first receive to you see this-one".	"The first that I wish to receive is that you see this one".
Hersteinn sprettur þá upp og verður hermt við og gengur út og bóndinn með honum, snúa síðan í veg til skógar.	Herstein sprang then up and became angry with and went out and the-farmer with him, turned then the way to the-woods.	Herstein then sprang up and became angry at this, and walked out of the smith and the farmer went with him, turned away and went to the woods.
Liggur þar ein sneiðigata og skógurinn á tvær hendur.	Lying there along the-path and forests on two hands.	Lying there along the path there were forests on either side.
Og er Hersteinn fer klifgötuna nemur hann staðar.	And when Herstein went cliff-path took he to-stand.	And when Herstein went to the cliff-path, he came to a stand.

The Saga of Hen-Thorir (Old Icelandic)

Old Icelandic	Literal	English
Hann var allra manna skyggnastur.	He was of-all people keen-eyed.	He was the keenest eyed of all people.
Hann mælti þá:	He spoke then:	He then spoke:
"Kom þar fram skjöldur í skóginum?"	"Come there from the-shield in the-woods?"	"Come there from behind the shield in the woods?"
Bóndi þagði.	The-farmer silent.	The farmer remained silent.
Hersteinn mælti:	Herstein spoke:	Herstein spoke:
"Hefir þú svikið mig hundurinn þinn?	"Have you betrayed me mongrel you?	"Have you betrayed me, you mongrel?
Nú ef þú ert í nokkurum særum að leyna þá leggst þú niður í götuna og tala eigi orð.	Now if you are in somewhat wounded to hiding then lay you down on the-path and speak not words.	Now if you have some wounds to hide, then you lie down on the path and don't speak a word,
En ef þú gerir eigi þetta þá mun eg drepa þig".	But if you do not that then shall I kill you".	and if you do not, then I shall kill you".
Bóndinn leggst þá niður en Hersteinn snýr heim og kallar á menn sína.	The-farmer laid then down then Herstein turned home and called to men his.	The farmer then laid down, then Herstein turned home and called to his men.
Þeir taka vopn sín og fara þegar í skóginn og finna Örnólf í götunni.	They took weapons theirs and went from-there to the-woods and found Ornolf on the-path.	They took their weapons and immediately went to the forest and found Ornolf on the path.
Þeir biðja hann fara með sér þangað sem mælt var að þeir skyldu finnast.	They bid him to-go with them from-there as said was to they should meet.	They asked him to go with them from there, where it was said, that they should meet.
Nú fara þeir þar til er þeir koma í eitt rjóður.	Now went they there to where they came to a clearing.	Now they went to where they came to a clearing.
Þá mælti Hersteinn til Örnólfs:	Then spoke Herstein to Ornolf:	Then Herstein spoke to Ornolf:
"Eigi vil eg skylda þig til að tala en far nú sem fyrir þig var lagið".	"Not will I should you to to speak but go now as for you were laying".	"I don't want to oblige you to talk, but go now as was arranged for you".
Bóndi hleypur þá upp á hól einn og blístrar hátt.	The-farmer leapt then up on the-hill one and whistled loudly.	The farmer then ran up the hill alone and whistled loudly.

The Saga of Hen-Thorir (Old Icelandic)

Old Icelandic	Literal	English
Síðan hlaupa þar fram tólf menn og var þar Hænsna-Þórir fyrir flokki.	Then ran there from twelve men and was there Hen-Thorir before the-flock.	Then twelve men ran forward there, and Hen-Thorir was there in front of the group,
En þeir Hersteinn taka þessa menn höndum og drepa.	But they Herstein took these men in-hand and death.	but then Herstein and his men took these man in hand and killed them.
Höggur Hersteinn sjálfur höfuð af Þóri og hefir með sér, ríða nú síðan suður til þings og segja þar þessi tíðindi.	Struck Herstein himself head of Thorir and had with him, rode now then south to the-assembly and say there these tidings.	It was Herstein himself who struck the head off Thorir and took it with him, they now rode to the assembly and told them of this news.
Verður Hersteinn ágætur mjög af þessu verki og fær af virðing mikla sem von var að.	Became Herstein honoured much of this work and accomplishment of worthiness great as expected was to.	Herstein became very much honoured for his work, and accomplishment of great worthiness, as was expected.
Nú er setið yfir málum manna og verða þær málalyktir að Arngrímur goði verður sekur fullri sekt og allir þeir er að brennunni voru nema Þorvaldur Oddsson.	Now was settled over the-matter people and became there concluded to Arngrim the-chieftain became outlawed fully well and all they who at the-burning were taken Thorvald son-of-Odd.	Now the cases of the men were being discussed, and they concluded that Arngrím the chieftain would be fully outlawed and all those who were at the burning, except Thorvald Oddson,
Hann skyldi vera utan þrjá vetur og eiga þá útkvæmt.	He should being outside three winters and have then out-freed.	he should go out of the land for three winters and then be free.
Gefið var fé fyrir hann og svo til farningar öðrum mönnum.	Given was money for him and so to the-faring other men.	Money was given for him and to the faring of other men.
Þorvaldur fór utan um sumarið og var leiddur upp á Skotlandi og þjáður þar.	Thorvald went abroad about summer and was led up to Scotland and enthralled there.	Thorvald went abroad about summer and was led up to Scotland and was enslaved there.
Nú eftir þetta var slitið þinginu og þykir mönnum Þórður vel og skörulega hafa fylgt þessum málum.	Now after that was settled the-assembly and thought men Thord well and boldly have followed this matter.	Now after that the assembly was settled, and men thought that Thord had followed the matter boldly and well.
Arngrímur goði fór og utan um sumarið og er það eigi ákveðið hversu mikið fé goldið var.	Arngrim the-chieftain went and abroad about summer and was that not un-spoken how-so much wealth paid was.	Arngrim the chieftain went abroad about summer, and it was not spoken about how much wealth was paid over.
Lýkur á þá leið þessum málum.	Ended so then passed this matter.	And so the matter passed and was ended.

The Saga of Hen-Thorir (Old Icelandic)

Old Icelandic	Literal	English
Ríða menn síðan heim af þingi en þeir fara utan sem mælt var er sekir voru.	Rode men then home from the-assembly and those journeying out as spoken were who outlawed were.	Men then rode home from the assembly, and those journeying out, who were outlawed.
16	**16**	**16**
Gunnar Hlífarson situr nú í Örnólfsdal og hefir húsað vel.	Gunnar son-of-Hlifar sat now at Ornolfsdal and had housed well.	Gunnar son of Hlifar settled now at Ornolfsdal and house himself well.
Hann hafði selför og var jafnan mannfátt heima.	He had cattle-keeping and was even lack-of-people at-home.	He had cattle keeping, and there were few people at home.
Jófríður dóttir Gunnars átti sér tjald úti því að henni þótti það ódauflegra.	Jofrid daughter Gunnar's had herself a-tent outside because to her thought that less-dreary.	Jofrid, Gunnar's daughter, had herself a tent outside, because she found this less dull.
Einn dag ber svo til að Þóroddur son Tungu-Odds ríður í Þverárhlíð.	One day befell so to that Thorodd son-of Tungu-Odd rode to Þverárhlíð.	One day it happened, that Thorodd, son of Tungu-Odd, rode to Thverarhlid.
Hann kemur í Örnólfsdal um farinn veg og gengur inn í tjaldið til Jófríðar.	He came to Ornolfsdal about travelling way and went in to tent to Jofrid.	He came to Ornolfsdal while travelling on his way and went in to Jofrid's tent.
Hún heilsar honum vel.	She greeted him well.	She greeted him well.
Hann sest niður hjá henni og taka þau tal sín á milli og í því kemur sveinn frá selinu og biður Jófríði taka ofan klyfjar með sér.	He sat down beside her and took they talking theirs in between and so because came a-boy from mountain-pasture and asked Jofrid take off pack-loads with him.	He sat down beside her, and they took to talking together, when there came a boy from the mountain pasture, who asked Jofrid to help unpack the horses with him.
Þóroddur fer til og tekur ofan klyfjarnar en sveinninn fer síðan í brott og kemur til sels.	Thorodd went to and took above pack-loads but the-boy went then to away and came to summer-pasture.	Thorodd went with him to unload the packs, but the boy then went away and came to the summer pasture.
Gunnar spyr hví honum yrði nú svo fljótt.	Gunnar asked how he could now so quickly.	Gunnar asked him how he had done it so quickly.
Hann svarar engu.	He answered nothing.	He did not answer.
Gunnar spurði:	Gunnar asked:	Gunnar asked:

The Saga of Hen-Thorir (Old Icelandic)

Old Icelandic	Literal	English
"Sástu nokkuð til tíðinda?"	"Saw-you anything to news?"	"Did you see anything of news?"
"Alls eigi",	"All not",	"Not at all",
kvað sveinninn.	said the-boy.	said the boy.
"Nei",	"No",	"No",
sagði Gunnar, "þannig ertu í bragði sem nokkuð hafi þér fyrir augu borið það sem þér þykir umræðu vert og seg mér ef svo er.	said Gunnar, "that-way are-you you looking as something have you for eyes bear that as to-you seemed about-discussion worth and say to-me if so is.	Gunnar said, "the way you look, is like something your eyes bear, that you seemed worthy of discussion, and tell me if it is.
Eða er nokkuð manna komið til bæjarins?"	Or is some man come to the-estate?"	or did a man come to the estate?"
"Engan sá eg kominn",	"None saw I come",	"I saw none coming",
sagði sveinninn.	said the-boy.	said the boy.
"Þú munt nú segja verða",	"You should now say be",	"You should now say",
sagði Gunnar og tók sviga einn mikinn og ætlar að berja piltinn með.	said Gunnar and took whip one great and intended to beat the-boy with.	said Gunnar, and took a great whip and intended to beat the boy with it.
Eigi fékk hann af honum heldur en áður.	Not got he of him rather than before.	Yet he got nothing out of him rather than before.
Eftir það fékk Gunnar sér hest og hleypur á bak og ríður skyndilega ofan til veturhúsa með hlíðinni.	After that got Gunnar his horse and leapt on back and rode suddenly above to winter-house along the-hillside.	After that Gunnar got his horse and leapt on its back, and rode suddenly up to the winter house along the hillside.
Jófríður getur að líta ferð föður síns og sagði Þóroddi og biður hann ríða brott	Jofrid caught to company travelled father hers and told Thorodd and bid he ride away	Jofrid caught sight of the company of her father's travelling and told Thorodd and bid that he then ride away.
"vildi eg gjarna að eigi hlytist illt af mér".	"wish I will to not result-in ill of me".	"I wish that nothing ill result because of me".
Þóroddur segist munu bráðlega ríða.	Thorodd said would soon ride.	Thorodd said he would ride soon enough.

The Saga of Hen-Thorir (Old Icelandic)

Old Icelandic	Literal	English
Gunnar ber fljótt að og hleypur af baki, gengur þegar inn í tjaldið.	Gunnar bore quickly to and leaping off horseback, went from-there the to the-tent.	Gunnar bore quickly towards and leapt off horseback, and went from there to the tent.
Þóroddur heilsar honum vel en Gunnar tók kveðju hans og spurði síðan hví hann væri þar kominn.	Thorodd greeted him well then Gunnar took greeting his and asked then why he was there come.	Thorodd greeted him well, and Gunnar took his greeting and then asked, why he had come there.
Þóroddur sagði að svo bar til um ferðir hans	Thorodd said that so bore to about journey his	Thorodd said that he was about his journey,
"og vil eg þó eigi gera þetta til fjandskapar við þig.	"and wish I though not do that to hostility with you.	"and I wish though for there not to be hostility with you.
En vita vil eg hverju þú vilt svara mér ef eg bið Jófríðar dóttur þinnar".	But know wish I how you will answer me if I ask-for Jofrid daughter yours".	And I wish to know, how you will answer me, if I ask for the hand of Jofrid, your daughter".
Gunnar svarar:	Gunnar answered:	Gunnar answered:
"Eigi mun eg gifta þér dóttur mína við þessa meðferðina.	"Not should I give to-you daughter mine with these with-goings-on.	"I should not give you my daughter with these goings on.
Hefir nú og í odda staðist með oss um hríð".	Has now and on a-spear-point standing with us about awhile".	And also there has been a spear-point between us for a while".
Síðan reið Þóroddur heim.	Then rode Thorodd home.	Then rode Thorodd home.

17

Það var einn dag að Oddur segir að eigi mundi illa fallið að hafa nokkurar landsnytjar af Örnólfsdal	That was one day that Odd said that not should ill fall to have some-of produce of Ornolfsdal	It was one day that Odd said that it wouldn't be a bad idea to have a few pieces of land from Ornolfsdal,
"þar er aðrir menn hafa sest á eigur mínar að röngu".	"there as other men have sat in ownership mine to wrong".	"there where other people have settled on my property by mistake".
Konur sögðu það til liggja,	Women said that to lay-out,	The women said that this was a good idea.
"gerist fé harðla nytlétt og mun þá miklu betur mjólka ef svo er breytt".	"was cattle hard of-little-milk and should then much better milk if so was changed".	"If cattle becomes hard and of little milk, it will milk much better if this is changed".

The Saga of Hen-Thorir (Old Icelandic)

Old Icelandic	Literal	English
"Þá skal þangað fénu halda",	"Then shall from-there cattle hold",	"Then that's where the cattle should be kept",
sagði Oddur, "því að þar eru hagar góðir".	said Odd, "because that there they-were pasture good".	said Oddr, "because there are good pastures".
Þá sagði Þóroddur:	Then said Thorodd:	Then Thorodd said:
"Eg mun bjóðast til að fylgja fénu og mun þá óágengilegra þykja".	"I should offer to that follow cattle and should then less-likely regarded".	"I will offer to follow the cattle, and it will make it less likely regarded".
Oddur segist það gjarna vilja og fara þeir nú með fénu.	Odd said that gladly wished and went they now with cattle.	Oddr says he would like to, and now they go with the cattle.
Og er þeir eru langt komnir segir Þóroddur að þeir skulu þangað halda fénu að þeir fá versta haga og skermsl eru mest.	And as they they-were long coming said Thorodd to they should from-there hold cattle that they got worst pasture and barren-ground they-were the-most.	And when they had come a long way, Thorodd said that should keep the cattle there, where they got the worst grazing and the most barren ground.
Nú líður nóttin af hendi og reka þeir heim féið um morguninn.	Now passed the-night of hand and drove they home cattle about morning.	Now the night passed, and they drove the cattle home around morning.
Og er konur hafa mjólkað þá kveða þær aldrei jafnilla nýst hafa sem þá og er þessa eigi oftar freistað.	And when women had milking then said then never equal used have as now and was this not more tried.	And when the women did the milking, they said that never had they had to try as hard to milk then, and this was not tried again.
Líða nú svo stundir fram.	Passed now so awhile from.	And so a while passed.
Það var einn morgun snemma að Oddur kemur að máli við Þórodd son sinn:	It was one morning early that Odd came to the-matter with Thorodd son his:	It was early one morning that Odd spoke to Thorod, his son:
"Þú skalt fara ofan í sveit og safna mönnum og vil eg nú reka menn af eignum vorum en Torfi skal fara upp um Hálsa og gera þeim í kunnleika um þenna fund.	"You shall travel over to company and gather men and will I now drive men of owning ours but Torfi shall travel up about Halsa and do them to make-known about this find.	"You shall go down into the countryside and gather men, and now I want to drive men from our property, but Torfi shall go up through Hals and let them know about this meeting.
Vér skulum hittast við Steinsvað".	We shall meet with Steinsvað".	We shall all meet at Steinsvad".

The Saga of Hen-Thorir (Old Icelandic)

Old Icelandic	Literal	English
Þeir gera nú svo, safna liði.	They went now so, raised company.	They did so, and now raised a company.
Fá þeir Þóroddur níu tigi manna, ríða síðan til vaðsins.	Got they Thorodd nine tens people, rode they to the-ford.	Thorodd and his men got ninety men, and rode to the ford.
Þeir Þóroddur koma fyrri til vaðsins.	They Thorodd came before to the-ford.	Thorodd's party was the first to arrive there at the ford.
Hann biður þá ríða fyrir	He asked then ride before	He asked them to ride on,
"en eg vil bíða föður míns".	"that I will abide father mine".	"but I will wait for my father".
Og er þeir koma að garði í Örnólfsdal er Gunnar að gera hlass.	And as they came to the-fence at Ornolfsdal was Gunnar to make heavy-load.	And when they came to the farmyard at Ornolfsdal, Gunnar was loading a cart with a heavy load.
Nú ræðir sveinn um er var með Gunnari:	Now discussed the-boy about that was with Gunnar:	Now the boy that was with Gunnar spoke:
"Menn fara að bænum eigi allfáir saman".	"Men travel to the-estate not very-few together".	"There are men travelling to the estate, and not just a few of them all together".
"Já",	"Yes",	"Yes",
sagði Gunnar, "svo er það"	said Gunnar, "so is it	said Gunnar, "so it is",
og gengur heim til bæjarins og tók boga því að hann skaut allra manna best af honum og er þar helst til jafnað er var Gunnar að Hlíðarenda.	and went home to the-estate and took a-bow because that he shot of-all people the-best of him and was there rather to equal as was Gunnar of Hlidarendi.	and he went home to the farmhouse and took a bow, because he was the best shot of all men, and was equal only to Gunnar of Hlíðarendi.
Hann hafði þá húsað vel bæinn en gluggur var á útihurðinni svo að inn mátti rétta og út höfuð sitt.	He had then a-house well built but window was in the-front-door so to in might straighten and out head his.	He had a well built house, but there was a window in the front door, so that one might straighten out his head.
Hann stóð við hurðina með bogann.	He stood with the-front-door with a-bow.	He stood with the door beam with a bow.
Nú kemur Þóroddur að bænum, gengur að durum við fá menn og spyr ef Gunnar vill nokkura sætt bjóða.	Now came Thorodd to the-house, going to the-door with a-few men and asked if Gunnar wished some settlement invitation.	Now Thorodd came to the house and went to the door with a few men and asked if Gunnar could be invited to make some sort of atonement.

The Saga of Hen-Thorir (Old Icelandic)

Old Icelandic	Literal	English
Hann svarar:	He answered:	He answered:
"Eg veit eigi að eg eigi nokkuð að bæta.	"I know not that I not anything to atone-for.	"I do not know that I have anythng to atone for,
En hitt væntir mig, áður þér fáið mitt vald, að griðkonur mínar muni stungið hafa nokkura þína félaga svefnþorni áður eg hnígi í gras".	But find expect me, before you get of-me power, that handmaidens mine shall pierce have some of-your companions sleep-thorn before I bite the grass".	but expect this of me, that before you overpower me, that my handmaidens shall have pierced some of your companions with sleep-thorn before I bite the grass".
Þóroddur svarar:	Thorodd answered:	Thorodd answered:
"Satt er það að þú ert afbragð flestra manna nú þeirra sem uppi eru.	"True is it that you are outstanding the-most of-people now they as about-standing they-are.	"It's true, that you are the most outstanding of people now, among those who are outstanding,
En þó má koma svo mart lið í móti þér að þú getir eigi við staðið því að faðir minn ríður að garði með mikið lið og ætlar að drepa þig".	But though may come so many company to meet to-you that you get not with stand because that father mine rides to the-path with much company and intends to kill you".	but there may come so many men to meet you, that you will not withstand, because my father is riding the path with a great company and intends to kill you".
Gunnar svarar:	Gunnar answered:	Gunnar answered:
"Vel er það. En það mundi eg vilja að eg hefði mann fyrir mig áður eg hnígi að velli.	"Well is that. "But that should I wish to I have man before me before I slump to fields.	"That is all well, but I wish to take a man with me before I slump into the fields.
En eigi gruna eg það þótt faðir þinn haldi lítt sættirnar".	But not suspect I that thought father yours holds little the-settlement".	And I suspect that your father hold little of the same sentiment".
"Hina leið er",	"Then the-way is",	"Then it is this way",
sagði Þóroddur, "að vér viljum gjarna sættast og rétt nú fram höndina með góðum vilja þínum og gift mér Jófríði dóttur þína".	said Thorodd, "that we will gladly reconcile and right now from hand with good wish yours and marry to-me Jofrid daughter yours".	said Thorodd, "that we wish to gladly reconcile, right now by handshake, and with your good wishes, that I will marry your daughter Jofrid".
Gunnar svarar:	Gunnar answered:	Gunnar answered:
"Eigi kúgar þú dóttur mína af mér.	"Not cower you daughter mine off me.	"I will not be cowed by you to give you my daughter".

The Saga of Hen-Thorir (Old Icelandic)

Old Icelandic	Literal	English
En eigi væri það fjarri jafnaði boðið sakir þín því að þú ert góður drengur".	But not was that far-from equal offer sake yours because that you are good fellow".	But it wouldn't be far off an equal match if you offered, because you are a good fellow".
Þóroddur svarar:	Thorodd answered:	Thorodd answered:
"Eigi mun það svo virt af góðgjörnum mönnum og kann eg mikla þökk fyrir að þú takir þenna kost með þeim máldögum sem því hæfir".	"Not should that so worth of good-doing men and know I great thanks for that you take then proposal with them agreement as because have".	"It will not be so respected by benevolent people, and I would be very grateful if you take this option with the agreement as appropriate".
Og nú við umtölur vina sinna og það annars að honum þótti Þóroddur jafnan vel farið hafa með sínu máli þá verður það af að Gunnar réttir fram höndina og lúka svo þessu máli.	And now with about-talking friends his and that others to him thought Thorodd equal well going have with his the-matter then worthy that of that Gunnar righted from hand and concluded so this the-matter.	And now with the prsuasion of his friends and others, he thought Thorodd equally well going in this matter, and then worthy, that Gunnar extended out his hand, and so the matter was concluded.
Nú í þessu kemur Oddur í tún og snýr Þóroddur þegar í mót föður sínum og spyr hvað hann ætlar.	Now in this came Odd to the-yard and turned Thorodd from-there in meeting father his and asked what he intended.	Now at this Oddr came to the field, and Thorodd immediately turned to face his father and asked what he was up to.
Hann kveðst ætla að brenna bæinn og svo mennina.	He said intended to burn dwellings and so men.	He said that he intended to burn the house, and so men.
Þóroddur svarar:	Thorodd answered:	Thorodd answered:
"Á aðra leið er nú komið málinu og erum við Gunnar nú sáttir"	"About other passes then now coming the-matter and we-are with Gunnar now settled"	"Now things have taken a different turn, and Gunnar and I are now satisfied".
og segir allt hve komið er.	and said all how come is.	and he told him how everything had happened.
"Heyr hér á endemi",	"Hear here of shame",	"Hear here of shame",
segir Oddur,	said Odd,	said Odd,
"væri þér þá verra að eiga konuna þótt Gunnar væri drepinn áður er mestur var vor mótstöðumaður?	"was to-you then worse to have this-woman thought Gunnar was killed before that most was our enemy?	"Would it be worse for you to have the woman, even though Gunnar was killed first, who was our greatest opponent?
Og höfum vér illt að verki að hefja þig".	And have we ill to work to have you".	And we have done ill work in raising you".

The Saga of Hen-Thorir (Old Icelandic)

Old Icelandic	Literal	English
Þóroddur svarar og mælti:	Thorodd answered and spoke:	Thorodd answered and spoke:
"Við mig skaltu nú fyrst berjast ef eigi kemur öðru við".	"With me shall-you now first battle if not comes other with".	"Fight with me first, if nothing else".
Ganga menn nú í milli og sætta þá feðga.	Going men now in among and settled then father-and-son.	People now went between them and reconciled the father and son.
Urðu þær málalyktir að Jófríður er gefin Þóroddi og líkar Oddi stórilla.	Became there conclusions that Jofrid was given-to Thorodd and disliked Odd greatly.	They concluded that Jofrid be given to Thorodd, and Oddi disliked this very much,
Fara nú heim við svo búið.	Went now home with so settled.	they now travelled home with the matter settled.
Eftir það sitja menn að boði og unir Þóroddur allvel sínu ráði.	After that sat men that announced, and satisfied Thorodd all-well his counsel.	After that men sat at the wedding-feast, and Thorodd was very satisfied with his counsel.
Og að vetri afliðnum fer Þóroddur utan því að hann hafði spurt að Þorvaldur bróðir hans var í höftum og vildi leysa hann með fé.	And to winter passed went Thorodd travelled-out because to he had learned that Thorvald brother his was in bondage and wished release him with wealth.	And as winter passed, Thorodd travelled out, because he had learned that Thorvald, his brother, was in bondage, and he wished to release him with wealth.
Hann kemur til Noregs og kom eigi út síðan og hvorgi þeirra bræðra.	He came to Norway and came not out then and neither theirs brothers.	He came to Norway and did not come back, and neither did his brother.
Oddur tók nú að eldast mjög.	Odd took now to old-age much.	Odd now took very much to old age.
Og er hann spurði það að hvorgi sona hans mundi til koma tók hann sótt mikla og er að honum tók að þröngva mælti hann við vini sína að þeir mundu flytja hann upp á Skáneyjarfjall þá er hann væri dauður og kvaðst þaðan vildu sjá yfir Tunguna alla.	And as he learned that, to neither sons his should to come, took he sickness much, and when to him took to heavily, spoke he with friends his, that there would carry he up of Skaney-Fell, then was he was dead, and spoke he from-there wished see over The-Tongue all,	And when he learned that neither of his sons would come back, he took great pains, and when he began to strain, he said to his friends that they would carry him up to Skaneyjarfjall when he was dead, and he said from there he wanted to see over the whole of Tungu,
Og svo var gert.	And so was done.	And so it was done.

The Saga of Hen-Thorir (Old Icelandic)

Old Icelandic	Literal	English
En Jófríður Gunnarsdóttir var síðan gefin Þorsteini Egilssyni að Borg og var hinn mesti kvenskörungur.	But Jofrid Daughter-of-Gunnar was then married Thorstein son-of-Egil of Burg and was the most noblest-women.	But Jofrid, daughter of Gunnar was then married to Thorstein, son of Egil of Burg, and was the noblest of women.
Og lýkur þar Hænsna-Þóris sögu.	And ends there Hen-Thorir saga.	And here ends the saga of Hen-Thorir.

Word List *(Old Icelandic to English)*

Old Icelandic	English

A, a

að	as, at, from, if, in, it, of, than, that, the, to, what
aðra	another, other
aðrir	other
af	from, from, if, of, of, off
afar	great, greatly
afbragð	outstanding
affærði	taken-away
afliðnum	passed
aflvani	overpowered
aftur	after, behind, returned
ala	bore
aldrei	never, never
algjafta	hay-feed
alla	all
allan	all
allar	all
allfáir	very-few
allgott	all-good
allir	all, all
allkátir	merry
alllítið	all-little
alllítil	all-little
allmargir	all-many
allmjög	all-much
allra	all, all, of-all, of-all
alls	all, all, in-all
allsæmilegt	decent
allskörulega	all-clear
allt	all, all
allur	all, all
allvel	all-well, all-well
almæltra	all-matters
alþingi	the-assembly, the-assembly
alþingis	the-assembly
alþýðu	the-people
andsælis	anti-sun-wise
annað	another, other, other-things
annaðhvort	either-way
annan	next, opposite
annar	another, one, other, other-than
annarra	other, others
annars	others
anntu	care
Arngrím	Arngrim (name)
Arngrími	Arngrim (name)
Arngríms	Arngrim (name)
Arngrímsson	Son-of-Arngrim (name)
Arngrímur	Arngrim (name)
atburðinn	at-carried
atgervismaður	dynamic-man
auðga	wealthy
auðgastur	wealthy
auðigur	wealthy-man
auðmaður	wealthy-man, wealthy-man
augu	eyes
austmaður	the-eastern-man
Austmanninum	the-Eastern-Men (name)
Austmanns	Easterners (name)
Austmenn	the-Easterners (name), the-Easterners (name)

Á, á

á	a, about, all, am, and, as, at, for, from, in, of, on, one, out, over, so, to
ábyrgð	risk
áður	before
ágætur	honoured
ákafa	eager
ákveðið	un-spoken
ákveðnum	appointed, meeting
álfs	alf

Word List (Old Icelandic to English)

Old Icelandic	English	Old Icelandic	English
án	without	baki	horseback
ána	river	bannir	banned
ár	early	bar	bore
Ármannsfelli	Armannsfell (place)	bardaga	battle
ásjá	assistance	bardagi	a-battle
ásjámál	matter-consideration	barn	child
áþekkur	similar	barnfóstri	child-fostering, child's-foster
átt	had, have, own, owned	barnfóstrinu	child-fostering
átti	had, married	barnfóstur	child-foster, foster-child
áttu	had	bauð	bid, offered
áverkar	injuries	beggja	both
ávíta	to-rebuke	beina	assistance
		beini	benefit

Æ, æ

		beinn	hospitable
		beittan	cunning
ærið	necessary	bekk	bench
ærin	a-year	ber	befell, bore
ætla	intend, intended, suppose, supposed	bera	carried
		berðist	fought
ætlað	intended	berja	beat
ætlar	intend, intended, intends	berjast	battle
		berum	bear
ætluð	intend	best	best, the-best
ætlum	intend	besti	best
		betra	better

B, b

		betri	better
		betur	better
bað	asked, bid	bið	ask, ask-for, bid
báðum	both	bíða	abide, bid
bæ	dwelling	biðja	asked, ask-for, bid, invite
bæði	both		
bæinn	built, dwellings, the-estate	biður	asked, bid
		binda	bound
bæja	homes	birkirafts	birch-rafter
bæjarins	dwellings, the-estate	bjó	lived
bæjunum	the-towns	bjóða	invitation, invite, invited
bænum	estate, farmhouse, the-estate, the-farm, the-house		
		bjóðast	offer
		bjóðist	offered
bær	dwelling	björg	help
bærinn	the-farm	bjuggu	lived
bæta	atone-for	blístrar	whistled
bætur	reconciliation	blóð	blood
bak	back, the-back	Blund-	Blund (name)

Word List (Old Icelandic to English)

Old Icelandic	English
Blund-Katli	Blund-Ketill (name)
Blund-Ketill	Blund-Ketill (name)
Blund-Ketills	Blund-Ketill (name), Blund-Ketill's (name)
Blund-Ketillsson	Son-of-Blund-Ketill (name)
blunds	Blund (name)
Blundsvatn	Blundsvatn (name)
boð	offer, the-invitation
boði	wedding-feast
boðið	invitation, offer, offered, the-wedding
boðinn	invited
boðinu	the-wedding
boðs	offer, the-wedding
boðsmenn	invited-people
boga	a-bow, bow
bogann	a-bow
bólstað	building
bónda	the-farmer
bóndi	the-farmer
bóndinn	the-farmer
bönnum	banning
borð	the-table, the-tables
borðið	the-tables
borðum	the-table
Borg	Burg (place)
Borgarfirði	Borgafjord (place)
Borgarfjarðar	Borgafjord (place)
Borgarfjörð	Borgafjord (place)
borið	bear, carried
borinn	bore
börn	children
bráðlega	soon
bræðra	brothers
bragði	looking
brandinn	brand
brátt	soon
braut	away
Breiðabólstað	Breidabolstad (place)
Breiðafirði	Breidafjord (place)
breiðskeggs	Broad-Beard (name)
brenna	burn, burning
brenndur	burned
brenni	burn
brennu	the-burning
brennuna	the-burning
brennunni	the-burning
breytt	changed
bróðir	brother, brother-of
brögðum	strategy
brott	away
brottu	away
brúðguma	bridegroom
brúðgumi	the-bridegroom
brúðir	the-bride
brugðið	broken
brugðist	accustomed
brunnið	burned, burnt
bú	prepartions
búa	prepare
búi	farm
búið	done, dwelled, place, prepared, settled
búin	ready
bundnar	bound
búnir	prepared
bústöðum	residences
býður	bids, invited
byggðan	settled
býr	farm

D, d

Old Icelandic	English
dælt	dealt
dæmdust	judged
dætur	daughters
dag	day, the-day
daginn	the-day
dags	day
dagverðar	breakfast
dalina	the-valleys
dauður	dead
deildum	shared
deyja	die
deyr	dies
Dölum	Dölum (place)
dóma	judgement
dóttir	daughter
dóttur	daughter
draga	dragged, dragging

Word List (Old Icelandic to English)

Old Icelandic	English
dreng	fellow
drengilegt	manly
drengur	fellow
drepa	death, kill, killed, to-kill
drepið	knock
drepinn	killed
dreymdi	dreamed
drjúgastur	greatly
duga	be-helping, helping
duganda	sufficiently
durum	the-door
dyr	the-door

E, e

Old Icelandic	English
eða	and, or
ef	if
efndir	fulfilment
eftir	after
eg	I
Egilssyni	Son-of-Egil (name)
eiga	had, have, not, own
eigi	not
eigin	own
eignum	owning
eigu	our-own
eigum	have, own
eigur	ownership
ein	along
eina	only
einar	Einar (name)
einhlítir	sufficient
einhlítur	sufficient
einkis	nothing
einkum	especially
einmánuður	one-month
einn	one
eins	one, one's
einskis	nothing, only
einu	one, same
eitt	a, once, one
eitthvert	something
ekki	not
ekur	drives
eld	fire
eldast	old-age
eldi	fire
eldur	fire
eldurinn	the-fire
ella	otherwise
elur	came
en	and, but, in, than, that, then, which, while
enda	and, conclude, concluded, end
endemi	shame
endið	end
enga	no, none
engan	none
engi	no, none, not, nothing
engu	none, not, nothing
engum	none
enn	but, in, then
er	am, are, as, for, in, is, is-it, is-that, said, that, then, was, well, were, what, when, where, which, who
erindi	errand
Erni	Erne (name), Orn (name)
ert	are
ertu	are-you
eru	there-are, they-are, they-were
erum	are, we-are
Esjubergi	Esyuberg (place)
eta	eating
etist	eating
Eyjavaði	Eyjavaði (place)

F, f

Old Icelandic	English
fá	a-few, gave, get, got, pay
faðir	father
fæ	get
fær	accomplishment
færa	brought

Word List (Old Icelandic to English)

Old Icelandic	English
færi	went
færra	fewer
ført	taken
fæti	foot
fagnað	celebrating
fagnaði	celebration
fagnar	gave, greeted, took
fáið	get
fala	bargain
falli	falls
fallið	fall
fallin	fallen
fámálugur	of-few-words
fámennur	few-men
fann	found
far	go
fara	fared, go, going, journeying, sent, to-go, travel, travelled, travelling, went
fari	goes
farið	going, going-away, gone, travelling, went
farinn	travelling
farir	travel
farmönnum	travelling-men
farningar	the-faring
fast	fast
fást	getting
fastna	betrothe
fastnaðir	betrothed
fastnar	betrothed
fastnir	betrothe
fátt	few
fé	cattle, money, wealth
feðga	father-and-son
feðgar	father-and-son
fegnir	celebrating
féið	cattle, the-cattle, wealth
fékk	got
félaga	companions
félagar	followers
féll	fell
féllu	fell
fellur	fell

Old Icelandic	English
fémætt	valuables
fémunum	goods
fénað	cattle
fengur	getting
fénu	cattle
fer	goes, travelling, went
ferð	journey, travel, travelled, travelled-from, travelling, voyage
ferðin	to-travel
ferðina	travelling
ferðir	journey
ferðum	travel
festar	fixed
fimm	five
finna	found
finnast	meet
firðinum	fjord
firn	abomination
Fitjum	Fitiar (place)
fjandmaður	fiend-man
fjandskapar	hostility
fjár	cattle
fjárins	cattle
fjarri	far, far-from
fjárviðtökunni	wealth-with-betokened
fjögur	four
fjöldi	many
fjölmennari	following-men
fjölmennir	crowd
fjóra	forty, four
fjórir	many
fjósi	the-barn
fleiprir	babble
fleira	more
fleiri	more
flestra	the-most
fljótt	quickly
flokkar	groups
flokki	the-flock
flutningar	moving
flytja	carried, carry
flytjist	move
flytur	brought

Word List (Old Icelandic to English)

Old Icelandic	English
fóður	fodder
föður	father
fölskaður	pale-burnt
föng	got
fór	goes, travelled, went
för	going, journey
foraðsillu	abominable
forkast	fodder
fornum	the-older
forráðsmaður	manager
forsjá	custody
fóru	went
förum	let-us-go
föstnuð	betrothe
fóstra	foster-father
fóstrar	foster
fóstri	foster, foster-father, fostering
föt	bed-clothing
fótum	feet
frá	from
frænda	kinsman
frændi	a-kinsman, kinsman
frændum	kinsmen
fram	from
framreiðin	riding-on
frásögn	from-said
freistað	tempted
frekust	most-often
fresti	from-now
frétt	news
frétti	heard, inquired
fréttir	news
fréttist	enquired
fréttu	asked
frítt	free
fullri	fully
fullsektað	fully-outlawed
fúnar	rots
fund	find, meet
fundar	meet
fundið	found
fylgdu	follow
fylgi	following
fylgja	follow
fylgt	followed

Old Icelandic	English
fyrir	ahead, before, for, from
fyrirboðsmanna	invited-people
fyrr	before, for
fyrra	before
fyrri	before
fyrst	first

G, g

gabbað	fooled
gæða	increased
gæfumaður	lucky-man
gaf	gave, given
gagni	useful
gakk	come
gakktu	go-you
ganga	go, going, to-go, went
ganganda	going, walking
garða	farmyard
garði	the-farmyard, the-fence, the-path, yard
garpur	brave-strong
gátu	got
gef	give
gefa	give, given, to-give
gefast	be-given
gefið	given
gefin	given-to, married
gefur	gave
gegna	going
gegndi	might
gegni	suits
gegnir	goes, so-going
Geirs	Geir's (name)
Geirshlíð	Geir's-Slope (place)
gekk	got, went
gelldi	bellowing
gelli	Gellir (name)
gellir	Gellir (name)
gellis	Gellir (name)
gengi	going, went
gengið	went
gengur	going, went
ger	do, make

Word List (Old Icelandic to English)

Old Icelandic	English
gera	be-done, did, do, make, went
gerast	be
gerð	made
gerðist	became
gerðu	did, do
gerir	did, do
gerist	became, befalls, was
gerr	done
gerst	done
gert	done, made
gervilegur	accomplished
getir	get
getur	caught, may
geyma	keep, retain
gift	marry
gifta	give
gisti	guest
gistingu	guest, guesting
gjafar	gifts
gjafir	gifts
gjaforði	reserved
gjálgrun	idle-talk
gjarna	gladly, will, willingly
gluggur	window
góð	good
goða	the-chieftain
góða	good
góðar	good
góðgjarnir	benevolent
góðgjörnum	good-doing
goði	chieftain, the-chieftain
góðir	good
góðrar	well
góðu	good
góðum	good
góður	good
Gói.	Gói (month, February)
goldið	paid
gólfið	the-floor
gólfinu	the-floor
gott	good
götu	the-path
götuna	the-path
götunni	the-path
græddist	gained, gathered
græðir	accumulated
græðist	gathered
gras	grass
grasvöxtur	hay-crop
greiða	assistance
greiðlega	quite
greinir	article
griðkonur	handmaidens
griðungur	a-bull
gruna	suspect
grunaði	mistrust
grunar	suspect
Gunnar	Gunnar (name)
Gunnari	Gunnar (name)
Gunnars	Gunnar's (name)
Gunnarsdóttir	Daughter-of-Gunnar (name)
Gunnarsstaði	Gunnarsstadir (place)
Gunnvaldur	Gunnvald (name)

H, h

Old Icelandic	English
hæfir	have
hænsn	hens
Hænsna-Þóri	Hen-Thorir (name)
Hænsna-Þórir	Hen-Thorir (name)
Hænsna-Þóris	Hen-Thorir (name)
hætta	danger
hafa	had, have, to-have
hafðar	had
hafði	had
hafðist	had
hafi	had, harbour, have, having
hafið	have
hafir	have
haft	had, have
haga	pasture
haganum	the-pastures
hagar	pasture
hagastur	the-best
halda	hold
haldi	holds
haldið	holding
hálft	half-of

Word List (Old Icelandic to English)

Old Icelandic	English	Old Icelandic	English
hallast	slanted	Helgi	Helgi (name)
Hálsa	Halsa (place)	Helgu	Helgi (name)
hana	her, hers	helst	rather
handa	hand	hélst	held
handsalar	hands-over	hendi	arms, hand
hann	he, him	hendur	hand, hands
hans	he, him, his	hennar	hers
happaráð	happy-decision	henni	he, her, she, to-her
harðla	hard	hér	here
hark	noise	héraða	districts
hart	roughly	héraði	district, the-district
hásetar	sailors	héraðið	the-district
hastorður	harsh-spoken	héraðinu	the-district
hátt	loudly	héraðsins	district
háttað	the-way	héraðsstjórn	district-administration
haust	autumn	hermt	angry
hausti	autumn	hérna	here
haustið	autumn	Hersteini	Herstein (name)
hefði	had, have	Hersteinn	Herstein (name)
hefðu	had	héruð	districts
hefi	have	héruðunum	the-districts
hefir	had, has, have	hest	horse
hefja	heaved, raising	hesta	horses
heiði	the-heath	hestar	horses
heillaráða	good-advice	hestinn	horse
heilli	fairly	hestinum	horse
heilsað	greeted	hestum	horses
heilsar	greeted	hét	named
heim	home	hey	hay
heima	at-home, home	heybjörg	haystacks
heiman	from-home, home	heyið	hay, the-hay
heimilast	right	heyin	haystacks
heimilt	allow	heyjum	hay
heimleiðis	home-ways	heykost	hay-supply
heimta	insist	heyleigur	hay-allowance
heimtir	got	heyr	hear
heit	pledge	heyra	heard
heitan	threatening	heyrðu	heard
heitið	pledged	heyri	hear
heitir	named, was-named	heyrir	heard
heldur	either, rather	heyþroti	hay-need
héldust	rather	hið	the, then
Helga	Helgi (name)	hina	then
Helgason	Son-of-Helgi (name)	hingað	here
Helgavatni	Helgivatn (place)	hinkur	hang-back

Word List (Old Icelandic to English)

Old Icelandic	English
hinn	the
hins	the
hirði	shepherd
hitt	find, it
hitta	met, to-meet
hittast	found, meet, to-reach
hitti	met
hittir	met
hjá	aside, beside, by, nearby
hjálp	help
hjálpa	help
hlammanda	The-Stamper (name)
hlass	heavy-load
hlaupa	leapt, ran
hleypir	ran
hleypur	leaping, leapt, ran
Hlíðarenda	Hlidarendi (place)
Hlíðina	The-Slope (place)
hlíðinni	the-hillside, the-slope
Hlífarson	Son-of-Hlifar (name)
hljómur	sound
hljóp	ran
hljótast	to-get
hljótist	to-get
hlut	part
hluta	lot, parts
hluti	part
hlutur	lot
hlýða	obeyed
hlytist	result-in
hlýtur	must
hnígi	bite, slump
höfðingjanna	chieftain
höfðingjar	chieftains
höfðu	had
höfn	the-harbour
höfnina	the-harbour
höfninni	the-port
hófst	began
höftum	bondage
höfuð	head
höfuðburður	head-bearing
höfum	have
höggur	struck
Högnasonar	Son-of-Hogni (name)

Old Icelandic	English
hól	the-hill
hönd	hand
höndina	hand
höndum	hands, in-hand
honum	he, him, his, to-him
horfir	looked
hörmuleg	harm-like
hörmulegt	tragic
hóti	a-good-deal
hratt	quickly
hríð	awhile
Hrómundi	Hromund (name)
hross	horses
hrossa	horses
hrossum	horses
hrossunum	the-horses
húðir	hides
hug	mind, thought
hugði	thought
hugðist	thought
hugnar	to-mind
hugsa	consider
hugsi	thoughtful
hugur	thoughts
hún	her, she
hundrað	a-hundred
hundruð	hundred, hundreds
hundruðum	hundred
hundurinn	mongrel
hurð	the-door
hurðar	the-door-beam, the-doors
hurðarhringinn	the-door-ring
hurðina	the-door-beam, the-front-door
hús	the-house
húsað	a-house, housed
húsakost	house-choice
húsar	house-built
húsi	house
húsin	house, the-house, the-houses
húsinu	the-house
húskarl	the-housekeeper
húsum	house, the-house

Word List (Old Icelandic to English)

Old Icelandic	English
húsunum	of-the-house, the-house
hvað	what
Hvamm	Hvamm (place)
Hvammi	Hvamm (place)
hvar	where
hvarf	disappeared
hvatlega	quickly
hve	how
hver	each, how, what, who
hverfa	turned-back
hverfur	turned
hverjir	each, who
hverju	each, how, how-so
hverjum	each, everyone
hvern	each
hversu	how, how-so
hvert	each, which
hví	how, why
Hvítá	Hvita (place)
hvorgi	neither
hvorirtveggju	each-side
hvorntveggja	either-side
hvorratveggja	each-way
hvort	if, whether, which
hyggja	consider, considered, think
hyggst	seems

I, i

Old Icelandic	English
iðgjöld	recompensed
illa	ill
illbýli	ill-harm
ills	ill
illt	ill
illu	ill
illum	evil
inn	in, inside, the
innarlega	lying-in
inni	in, inside

Í, í

Old Icelandic	English
í	a, about, among, as, at, by, for, in, into, of, on, so, the, this, to, with, you
íslög	ice-bound

J, j

Old Icelandic	English
já	yes
jafnað	equal
jafnaðarmaður	an-even-man
jafnaði	equal
jafnan	equal, equally, even
jafngott	equal-good
jafnilla	equally
jafnmikinn	equally-great
jafnræði	equally
jafnvel	equal-good
jarðir	earth
járn	iron
játuðu	affirmed
Jófríðar	Jofrid (name)
Jófríði	Jofrid (name)
Jófríður	Jofrid (name)
jól	yule
jörð	the-earth
Jórunn	Jorun (name), Jorunn (name)

K, k

Old Icelandic	English
kaldur	cold
kalla	call, called
kallaður	called
kallar	called
kalt	cold
kann	can, know, knows
kannast	knew
kappsamur	zealous
karl	a-man, the-man
kaup	a-deal, buying
kaupa	buy, purchase, to-buy

Word List (Old Icelandic to English)

Old Icelandic	English
kaupdrengur	merchant
kaupin	the-purchase
kaupir	bought
kaupmenn	trading-men
kaupmönnum	the-trading-men
kaupskap	goods
kaupstefnur	trading-post
kaupum	trading
kemur	came, comes
kennist	knowing
kennt	known
Ketils	Ketil (name)
Ketilssonar	Son-of-Ketil (name)
keypt	bought
keypti	bought
keyrir	whipped
kippir	drew
kjósa	choose
klæðast	to-dress
klæðin	clothes
klappar	knocked
klifgötuna	cliff-path
klyfjar	loaded, pack-loads, the-load
klyfjarnar	pack-loads
köldu	cold
kom	came, come
koma	came, come, to-come
komast	to-come
komið	came, come, comes, coming
kominn	come
komir	come
komist	come
komna	come
komnir	came, come, coming, welcome
komu	came, coming
komum	came
kona	wife, woman
konu	a-wife, the-woman
konuna	a-wife, the-woman, this-woman
konunnar	the-woman
konur	the-women, women
kost	choice, choose, cost, proposal, provided-for
kosti	benefit, cost
kostur	choice
krefur	needed
kú	cow
kúgar	cower
kúgast	to-be-oppressed
kúna	the-cow
kunna	could
kunni	could
kunnleika	make-known
kvað	said, spoke
kvaðst	said, saying, spoke
kváðust	said
kveða	said
kveðju	greeting
kveðst	said, saying, spoke
kveiktu	kindled
kveld	evening
kveldi	evening, the-evening
kveldið	evening
kvenskörungur	noblest-women
kynlegt	strange, wonder
kyns	kinds-of
kýr	cow
kyrrt	peace, still

L, l

Old Icelandic	English
lá	laying
lætur	had
lag	grant, lay
lagði	became
lagi	laying
lagið	laying
land	land, lands, the-land
landi	the-land
landseta	tenants
landsetar	tenants
landseti	a-tenant
landsetum	the-tenants
landshorna	lands-corners
landsnytjar	produce
langt	long

Word List (Old Icelandic to English)

Old Icelandic	English
lastaði	blame
láta	allow, allowed, have, let
látið	laid, let
látin	spoken-of
látir	let
láttu	let
látum	allow, let
launar	are-repaid
laut	leant
legði	leave
legg	lay
leggir	place
leggja	grant, granted
leggst	laid, lay
leið	passed, passes, the-way, the-ways
leiða	lead
leiðast	lay
leiddur	led
leiðrétta	have-right
leigulanda	tenant-farms
leikið	played
leikur	like
leita	let
lengi	long, longer
lést	let
lét	had, let
letja	discourage
létt	light
létta	let-up
létti	left
léttir	remained
leyna	conceal, hiding
leysa	redeem, release
leyst	release
lið	assistance, company
líða	passed
liði	company
liðinu	the-company
liðs	company, the-company
liðsdrátt	assembling-troops
liðsinni	assistance
líður	passed
liggja	lay-out, remained
liggur	lying
líkaði	liked
líkar	disliked, like
líkara	likely
líklegra	likely
línbrókum	linen-breeches
líst	appeared, appears, behold, seems
líta	company
lítið	little
lítil	little
lítill	little
lítils	little
lítt	little
lítur	looked
lofaði	praised
loganda	flaming
logann	the-fire
lögðu	laid
lögmálsstaðinn	law-matter-standing
loguðu	burned
loku	locked
löndum	the-lands
löngu	long
lúka	concluded
lúkist	end
lýgur	lies
lýkur	ended, ends
lýsa	proclaim

M, m

Old Icelandic	English
má	may
maður	a-man, man, the-man
mægða	marriage
mælir	discussing, speak
mælt	said, spoke, spoken
mælti	said, spoke
mætir	met
mætti	may
mágar	father-and-son
mági	son-in-law
mágur	son-in-law
mál	matter, matter, the-matter

186

Word List (Old Icelandic to English)

Old Icelandic	English
mála	the-matter
málahlut	case-load
málalyktir	concluded, conclusions
máldögum	agreement
máli	the-matter
málið	the-matter
málinu	the-matter, this-case, this-case
máls	matter
málum	matter, matters, the-matter
mann	man, man, men
manna	a-man, man, men, of-people, people
mannaða	manly
mannaferð	journey-of-men
mannfall	men-fallen
mannfátt	lack-of-people
mannferðin	men-travelling
manngirnd	men-desiring
manni	man, men, people, to-people
manninn	people
manninum	the-man
manns	man
mannsbarn	born-man
marga	many
margir	many, many
mart	many
mat	food
matar	feed
matast	eat
mátt	might
mátti	might
máttu	as-might, may, might
mátturinn	power
með	along, between, with
meðferðina	with-goings-on
mega	be-able-to
meins	harm
meir	more
meira	more
meiri	greater, more
menn	men
mennina	men

Old Icelandic	English
mér	I, me, mine, more, my, to-me
mest	most, the-most
mesta	most
mestan	mostly
mesti	most
mestri	the-most
mestu	most
mestur	most
metorð	reputation
mettir	full-of-food
miðla	share
mig	me
mikið	much
mikil	great, greatly, much
mikill	big, great-big, much
mikinn	great, greatly, much
mikla	great, much
miklu	great, much
milli	among, between
mín	mine, my
mína	mine
mínar	mine
mínir	mine
minn	mine
minna	my
minnast	remember
minnur	less
míns	mine, my
mínu	mine
mínum	mine, my
misgöngin	tide-change
misráðið	mis-advised
mitt	mine, of-me
mjög	much
mjólka	milk
mjólkað	milked
móður	mother
mönnum	men, people
mörgum	many
morgun	morning, the-morning
morguninn	morning
mót	meeting, towards
mótgangi	meeting-going
móti	meet, meeting, to-meet

Word List (Old Icelandic to English)

Old Icelandic	English	*Old Icelandic*	English
mótstöðumaður	enemy	nemur	took
möttul	mantle	nenni	bother
mun	shall, should, will, would	Nes	The-Headland (place)
		neyta	make-use
mund	time	níðingsverk	low-deed
mundi	should, would	niður	down
mundu	should, would	níu	nine
muni	shall, should, would	njóta	enjoy
munir	would	nóga	enough
munni	mouth	nógar	enough
munt	might, must, should, would	nokkuð	any, anything, some, something, somewhat
muntu	should, should-you	nokkur	some
munu	shall, will, would	nokkura	any, some, someone
munuð	shall	nokkurar	some-of
munum	shall, should	nokkurs	some, someone
munur	difference	nokkuru	somewhat
Mýrar	Myrar (place)	nokkurum	somewhat
		norðan	north, the-north
		norður	north
		Norðurá	Norðura (place), Norðurá (place), North-River (place)

N, n

		Norðurárdal	Norduradal (place), North-River-Valley (place)
ná	near		
náðu	reached		
nær	brought, close, nearly		
næst	near, nearest	Norðurdæla	Norðurdæla (place)
nætur	the-night	Norðurtungu	North-Tongue (place)
nái	can-get, get, got	Noregs	Norway (place)
náinn	near	nótt	night, the-night
nasir	nose	nóttin	the-night
nasirnar	his-nose	nú	now
náttaði	nightfall	nýlegar	new, newer
náttar	nightfall	nýlegra	newer
náttstað	night-quarters	nýlundu	news
nauðamikill	need-much	nýst	new
nauðsynjum	necessities	nýtara	more-helpful
nauðsynlegra	need-like	nytlétt	of-little-milk
naut	bulls	nýtt	new
nautum	cattle		
né	not		

O, o

neðra	lower		
nefnir	named		
nei	no	Odd	Odd (name)
neita	refuse	odda	a-spear-point
nem	take	Oddi	Odd (name)
nema	except, taken, unless		

Word List (Old Icelandic to English)

Old Icelandic	English
Odds	Odd's (name)
Oddsson	Oddson (name), Son-of-Odd (name)
Oddssonar	Son-of-Odd (name)
Oddur	Odd (name)
of	of
ofan	above, off, over
ofar	above
oft	often
oftar	often
ofurefli	overwhelming
ofurliði	outnumbered
og	also, and
okkar	ours
okkur	us
olli	caused, that-caused
opið	open
orð	word, words
orða	words
orðið	words
orðin	became, become
orðsjúkur	word-sickened
oss	us, we
otar	pushed

Ó, ó

Old Icelandic	English
óágengilegra	less-likely
óbirgur	un-stocked
óbrunnið	unburnt
ódælla	uneasy
ódauflegra	less-dreary
óðlega	wildly
ófyrirsynju	unexpected
ógreitt	obstructed
ójafnað	un-equally
ókyrrt	un-quiet
ólíklegt	unlike
ósinn	inlet
óþokkasælli	disliked
óvináttu	un-friendship
óvingan	difficulty
óvinir	enemies
óvinsældin	unpopularity
óvinsældir	unpopularity
óvirt	unworthy

Ö, ö

Old Icelandic	English
öðru	another, anything
öðrum	other, others
öfund	envy
öll	all
öllu	all
öllum	all
önnur	another, one, other, other-than, the-other
Önundarson	Son-of-Onund (name)
ör	an-arrow
örkola	a-burn-out
Örlygssonar	Son-of-Orlyg (name)
Örn	Orn (name)
Örnólf	Ornolf (name)
Örnólfs	Ornolf (name)
Örnólfsdal	Ornolfsdal (place)
Örnólfur	Ornolf (name)
örvænt	surely
örvænti	desperation

P, p

Old Icelandic	English
pall	platform
pallinum	the-seat
pening	money
piltinn	the-boy

R, r

Old Icelandic	English
ráð	advice, consent, counsel, decision
ráða	advised, decide, rule
ráðast	arrange
ráði	counsel
ráðið	advised
ráðlegt	advise
ráðs	plan
ráðum	counsel, instructions
ræðir	discussed

Word List (Old Icelandic to English)

Old Icelandic	English
rændi	robbed
ræni	steal
rænt	robbed
rán	robbery
rangt	wrong
ráni	robbery
ránið	robbery, the-robbery
ránsmaður	robber-man
Rauða-Bjarnarson	Son-of-Rauda-Bjarni (name)
rauður	red
raun	torment
refur	Refur (name)
reið	rode
reiðasti	most-angry
reiðu	readily
reikanarmaður	a-roaming-man
reikar	wandered, wanders
reip	ropes
reis	rose
rek	drive
reka	drive, driven, drove
rekin	driven
rekkju	bed
rekur	driving, drove
rétt	right
rétta	right, rights, straighten, stretch-out
réttir	right, righted
réttist	straightened-up
réttu	rights
réttur	right
Reykjardal	Reykjardal (place)
reynast	turn-out
reyndar	seen
reyndi	experience
reyndust	turned-out
reynið	test
ríða	ride, rode
riðu	rode
ríður	rides, riding, rode
ríkismunur	powerful
rjóður	clearing
rödd	voice
röngu	wrong
rúm	room

S, s

Old Icelandic	English
sá	saw, seen, so
sækja	sought
sæmd	honour
sæmdur	honoured
særum	wounded
sæst	seen
sæti	seat, seated, seats
sætt	settlement
sætta	settle, settled
sættar	settle
sættast	reconcile
sættirnar	the-settlement
safna	gather, gathered, raised
safnaði	collected, gathered
safnar	gathered
sagði	said, said-to, spoke, told, told
sagðist	said
sagt	said, said, told
sakir	sake
sakirnar	the-sake
sama	same, the-same
saman	together
samandráttur	gathering
samfara	together-travelling
samir	same
sannast	surely
sannlegra	true-like
sannlegt	right
sár	wounded
sástu	saw-you
sat	sat
satt	true, truly
sáttir	settled
sáttum	fulfilled
sátu	sat
sauðamaður	shepherd
sauðir	sheep
sé	as, be, bed, being, is, see
seg	say

Word List (Old Icelandic to English)

Old Icelandic	English
segði	said
segir	said, told
segist	said
segja	said, say, to-say
seilist	reached
seint	coldly, late
sekir	outlawed
sekt	well
sektir	penalty
sekur	outlawed
seldi	selling, sold
selför	cattle-keeping
selinu	mountain-pasture
selja	sell, to-sell
selji	sell
sels	summer-pasture
selur	sold
sem	as, that, when, where, which, who
sén	seen
sendi	sent
sénn	seen
sér	herself, him, himself, his, saw, them, themselves
sért	are
sest	sat
setið	settled
setjast	sitting
setjumst	let-us-sit
sett	set
seturúm	a-seat
séuð	see-you
séum	see
sex	six
sið	traditions
síð	late
síðan	after, since, than, then, they
síðasta	last
síður	side
sig	him, himself, his, themselves, to-him
sígast	sank
silfur	silver
sín	him, his, theirs
sína	his, their, theirs
sinn	he, his, then, they, yours
sinna	his
sinni	his, mind, theirs, they, yours
síns	hers, his
sínu	his
sínum	his, theirs
sitja	sat, settle, sit
sitji	sit
sitt	his, the
situr	sat, sit
sjá	look, saw, see, seems
sjáir	see
sjálfa	myself
sjálfdáðum	self-judgement
sjálfdæmi	self-judgement
sjálfir	ourselves
sjálfum	himself
sjálfur	himself, self
sjúk	sick
sjúkur	sick
skal	shall
skalt	shall
skaltu	shall-you
Skáneyjarfjall	Skaney-Fell (place)
skapi	mood
skapir	mind
skapsmunum	disposition
skaut	shot
Skeggjasonar	Skeggja's-Sons (name)
skermsl	barren-ground
skikkjunni	cloak
skila	return
skildir	shields
skildust	separated
skilið	understand
skiljast	departed, parted
skilst	parted
skip	a-ship, the-ship
skipar	ordered
skipkomuna	the-ship-arrival
skipta	exchanged, this-exchange

Word List (Old Icelandic to English)

Old Icelandic	English	Old Icelandic	English
skipti	exchanged	*snemma*	early, soon
skipuðu	appointed	*snúa*	turned
skjöldur	the-shield	*snúið*	away, turned
skjótar	soon	*snýr*	turned, turned-back
skjótt	quickly	*sögðu*	said, told
skó	shoes	*sögu*	saga
skógar	the-woods	*sök*	reason
skógarnef	woods-outskirts	*sölu*	sell
Skógarströnd	Skogarstrand (place)	*sölur*	sell
skóginn	the-woods	*sóma*	honour
skóginum	the-woods	*sómir*	honourable
skógurinn	forests	*son*	a-son, son, son-of, sons
skömm	shame		
Skorradal	Skorradal (place)	*sona*	sons
skorta	be-short-of	*sonu*	sons
skortir	shortage	*sótt*	sickness, sought
skörulega	boldly	*sóttarinnar*	sickness
Skotlandi	Scotland (place)	*spaklega*	profoundly
skuldir	debts	*spark*	trampling
skulu	shall, should	*spillist*	get-spoiled
skuluð	should	*sprettur*	sprang
skulum	shall, should	*spurði*	asked, learned
skyggnastur	keen-eyed	*spurt*	learned
skylda	should	*spyr*	asked
skyldi	should	*spyrja*	to-learn
skyldir	obliged	*spyrjast*	heard
skyldu	should, would	*stað*	place
skyldur	should	*staðar*	to-stand
skylt	should	*staddur*	standing
skyndilega	suddenly	*staðið*	stand
skyrtu	shirt	*staðinn*	there
slá	struck	*staðist*	standing
slær	struck	Stafholt	Stafholt (place)
slátrað	slaughter, slaughtered	Stafholtstungur	Stafholtstungur (place)
slík	such	*stakkar*	stacks
slíka	such	*standa*	stand, stood, withstand
slíkan	such		
slíkt	so, such	*stefna*	agreement, direct, summoned
slíku	such		
slíkur	such	*stefnir*	summoned
slitið	settled	*steig*	stepped
smiðju	workshop	*steininn*	the-stone
snæðings	eating	*steinn*	stone
snauður	poor	Steinsvað	Steinsvað (place)
sneiðigata	the-path	*stendur*	are-standing

Word List (Old Icelandic to English)

Old Icelandic	English
sterkur	strong
stíga	dismount, dismounted, leapt, mounted
stígandi	Strider (name)
stigu	stepping
stígur	climbed
stóð	stood
stóðhross	stallions
stofu	the-main-room
stökk	sprang
stökkur	heels
stórauðigur	rich
stórfé	great-fee
stórilla	greatly
stórmikið	great
stórmjög	a-great-much
streng	the-string
strengi	binding
ströndinni	the-strand
strykur	struck
stund	awhile
stundir	awhile
stungið	pierce
stýrimaður	the-steersman
stýrimann	the-steersman
suður	south
suma	some
sumar	summer, the-summer
sumarið	summer
sumarkaup	summer-market
sumri	summer
sumum	some
sunnan	from-the-south, the-south
svara	answer
svarað	answered
svaraði	answered
svarar	answer, answered
svarta	black
svefni	sleep
svefnþorni	sleep-thorn
sveininum	the-boy
sveinn	a-boy, the-boy
sveinninn	the-boy
sveit	company
sveitir	areas
sveitum	countryside
sverð	sword
sverðshjöltin	sword's-hilt
sviga	whip
Svignaskarði	Svignaskard (place), Svignaskardi (place)
svikið	betrayed
svo	so
svör	answer
svöruðu	answered
sýna	show
syni	son
sýnist	seems
sýnt	seemed
systur	sister-of

T, t

Old Icelandic	English
tæki	take
taka	take, taken, took
takir	take
taktu	take-you
tal	talking
tala	say, speak, told, to-talk
talað	spoken
talaði	said
talast	talked
tefldir	drawn
tek	take
tekið	received, taken
tekst	take, took
tekur	took
tíðinda	news, the-news
tíðindi	news, the-news, tidings
tíðindum	news
tigi	tens
tigir	tens
tigu	ten, tens
tigum	tens
til	to, until
tilgangur	point
tillag	proposal

Word List (Old Icelandic to English)

Old Icelandic	English
tillög	proposal, suggestions
tíma	time
tjá	expressed
tjald	a-tent
tjalda	tent
tjaldið	tent, the-tent
tók	took
tókst	took
tólf	twelve
tólfta	twelve
töluð	told
töluðu	talked
tölum	talk
Torfi	Torfi (name)
traust	trust
trausts	trust
trefill	Trefill (name)
trefils	Trefil (name)
troðinn	trodden
tún	the-plot, the-yard
Tunguna	The-Tongue (place)
Tungu-Odd	Tungu-Odd (name)
Tungu-Oddi	Tungu-Odd (name)
Tungu-Odds	Tungu-Odd (name), Tungu-Odd's (name)
Tungu-Oddsdóttur	Daughter-of-Tungu-Odd (name)
Tungu-Oddur	Tungu-Odd (name)
túnið	enclosure, the-enclosure
tvær	two
tveir	two
tvisvar	twice
tvo	two
tvö	two

Þ, þ

Old Icelandic	English
þá	then
það	is-that, it, that, the
það"	it
þaðan	from-there
þær	there, they
þætti	seemed, seems
þagði	silent
þagnar	silenced, silent
þakkar	thanked
þangað	from-there, there
þann	that, then, this
þannig	that-way
þar	there, there
þarf	need, needed
þau	them, then, they
þegar	already, from-there
þegi	silence
þegið	receive
þegna	thanes
þeim	them, they
þeir	their, theirs, there, they, those
þeirra	their, theirs, they
þenna	that, then, this
þér	to-you, to-your, you
þess	this
þessa	these, this, this-one
þessi	these, this, this-one
þessir	these
þessu	this
þessum	this
þetta	that, then, this
þig	you
þiggja	accept, receive, to-accept
þín	yours
þína	of-your, your, yours
þingheimurinn	the-asembly
þinghelgi	the-assembly
þinghelginni	the-assembly-sanctuary
þingi	the-assembly
þingið	the-assembly
þinginu	the-assembly
Þingnes	Assembly-Headland (place)
þings	the-assembly
þingsins	the-assembly
þinn	you, your, yours
þinna	your
þinnar	yours
þinni	you, your, yours
þíns	yours

Word List (Old Icelandic to English)

Old Icelandic	English
þínu	yours
þínum	yours
þitt	your, yours
þjáður	enthralled
þjófur	thief
þó	then, though
þökk	thanks
Þorbjörn	Thorbjorn (name), Thorbjorn (name)
Þórð	Thord (name), Thord (name)
Þórðar	Thord (name)
Þórði	Thord (name)
Þórður	Thord (name)
Þorgeirs	Thorgeir (name)
Þóri	Thori (name), Thorir (name)
Þórir	Thorir (name)
Þóris	Thori (name), Thori's (name)
Þórissonar	Son-of-Thori (name)
Þorkatli	Thorkel (name), Thorkel (name)
Þorkell	Thorkel (name)
Þorkels	Thorkel (name), Thorkel's (name)
þornaði	dried
Þórodd	Thorodd (name)
Þóroddi	Thorodd (name)
Þóroddur	Thorodd (name)
Þórólfur	Thorolf (name)
þorri	drought
Þorsteini	Thorstein (name)
Þorvald	Thorvald (name)
Þorvalds	Thorvald's (name)
Þorvaldur	Thorvald (name)
þótt	thought
þótti	seemed, thought
þóttist	thought
þræla	servants
Þrælastraumur	Þrælastraumur (place)
þrælsgjöld	servant-fees
þrælum	a-thrall
þrem	three
þremur	three
þriðja	third
þrífur	deftly
þrír	three
þrjá	three
þrjósku	belligerance
þröngt	presses
þröngva	heavily
þú	you
þunglega	heavily
þungt	difficulty
þurfa	need
þurfti	needed
Þuríðar	Thorid (name)
Þuríði	Thurid (name)
Þuríður	Thurid (name)
Þverárhlíð	Þverarhlíd (place), Þverarhlíð (place)
Þverhlíðingar	Þverhlíðingar (place)
því	accordingly, because, because-of, then, therefore
þvílíka	as-you-like
þykir	seemed, seems, thought
þykist	seems, thought
þykja	regarded
þykjast	considered, to-see
þykjumst	think, we-think
þyngra	heavy
þyrfti	needed, needs

U, u

Old Icelandic	English
uggir	dread
um	about, around
umkvæði	about-speaking
ummælum	about-the-matter, announcements
umræða	about-discussion
umræðu	about-discussion
umsjá	protection
umtölur	about-talking
undan	from, give-way
undir	along, from, under, undertaken
uni	win
unir	satisfied

Word List (Old Icelandic to English)

Old Icelandic	English
unnið	win
upp	up
upphafsmaður	the-instigators
uppi	about-standing
urðu	became
utan	abroad, beyond, out, outside, travelled-out
utarlega	out-lying

Ú, ú

Old Icelandic	English
Úlfarssonar	Son-of-Ulf (name)
úlfs	wolves
Úlfssonar	Son-of-Ulf (name)
úr	about, from, of, out-from, out-of
úrlausna	a-solution, solution
út	out
útgöngu	to-come-out
úti	out, outside
útibúr	out-house
útibúrið	out-house
útifé	grazing
útihurðinni	the-front-door
útkvæmt	out-freed
útlegðar	outlawry

V, v

Old Icelandic	English
vaðið	the-ford
vaðsins	the-ford
vænlegt	hopeful
vænn	handsome
væntir	expect
væri	was, were, would-be
væru	were
vaka	awake
vakna	awoke
vaknar	awoke
Valbrandsson	Son-of-Valbrand (name)
vald	power
válegra	woeful
Valþjófssonar	Son-of-Valthjof (name)
vana	custom
vanda	custom
vandræði	difficulty, trouble
vanur	used-to
var	was, were
varð	became, was
varða	a-concern, concern
varði	expected
varðveita	safeguard
varið	the-situation
varla	hardly, rarely
varnaði	keeping, wares
varning	wares
varningur	goods
vasast	entangle-with
vaskasti	boldest
vasklegur	bold
Vatni	Vatn (Water) (place)
veðri	weather
veg	the-way, way
veinan	wailing
veistu	know-you
veit	knew, know
veita	give, grant
veitir	provide
veitt	given
veitti	gave
veittur	given
vekti	was-awake
vel	as, well
velli	fields
venja	accustomed
ver	be
vér	we, we-are
vera	be, being
verð	the-price, worth
verða	be, became, become, worthy
verði	became
verður	became, worth, worthy
verið	been
verja	blocked, guarded
verki	work
verkmanna	work-men
verr	worse

Word List (Old Icelandic to English)

Old Icelandic	English
verra	worse
verri	worse
verst	the-worst
versta	worst
vert	worth
vesöld	misery
vestan	west
vestanmanna	the-western-men
vestur	west
vetrarnauð	winter-need
vetri	winter
vetur	winter, winters
veturhúsa	winter-house
veturinn	the-winter, winter
vexti	grown
við	against, from, together, we, with, wood
víða	with
viðarköst	brushwood
viðbúnaður	preparation
viðbúningur	with-laid
Víðfari	Vidfari (name), Vidfari (name)
Víðimýri	Vidimyr (place)
viðskiptum	dealings
vígur	spear-man
viku	a-week, week
víkur	took, turned, week
vil	will, wish
vildi	willed, wish, wished
vildu	wished, would
vilja	willed, wish, wished
vilji	will
viljum	will, wish-to
vill	will, willed, wished, wishes
vilt	will, wish
viltu	will-you
vin	friend
vina	friends
vináttu	friendship
vindur	wind
vinfengi	friendship
vini	friends
vinir	friends
vinsælasti	most-popular
vinsæll	befriended, friends, friendship, popular
vinum	friends
virðing	worthiness, worthy
virðir	value
virðulegur	worthy
virt	worth
vísað	turn-away
vísaðir	turn-away
vissi	knew, to-know
vist	hospitality
víst	certain, certainly, knowing, known
vistaðist	guested
vita	certainly, know, knowing
vitað	known
viti	knew, wit
vitran	wise
vitum	know
vitur	wise
von	expected
vonbiðlar	hope-abide
vondum	trouble
vopn	weapons
vor	our
vora	further
vorar	spring
vorri	ours, provisions
vörslu	vouch
voru	our, they-were, wares, was, were, where
vöru	goods
vorum	our, ours, were
votta	witnesses
vottar	witnesses

Y, y

Old Icelandic	English
yðrum	your
yður	to-you, you, your, yours
yðvar	your
yfir	over

Word List (Old Icelandic to English)

Old Icelandic	English
ykkarn	your
yrði	could

Ý, ý

| *ýmist* | or |

Word List *(English to Old Icelandic)*

English	Old Icelandic

A, a

English	Old Icelandic
a	á, eitt, í
a-battle	bardagi
abide	bíða
abominable	foraðsillu
abomination	firn
about	á, í, um, úr
about-discussion	umræða, umræðu
about-speaking	umkvæði
about-standing	uppi
about-talking	umtölur
about-the-matter	ummælum
above	ofan, ofar
a-bow	boga, bogann
a-boy	sveinn
abroad	utan
a-bull	griðungur
a-burn-out	örkola
accept	þiggja
accomplished	gervilegur
accomplishment	fær
accordingly	því
accumulated	græðir
accustomed	brugðist, venja
a-concern	varða
a-deal	kaup
advice	ráð
advise	ráðlegt
advised	ráða, ráðið
a-few	fá
affirmed	játuðu
after	aftur, eftir, síðan
against	við
a-good-deal	hóti
a-great-much	stórmjög
agreement	máldögum, stefna
ahead	fyrir
a-house	húsað
a-hundred	hundrað
a-kinsman	frændi
alf	álfs

English	Old Icelandic
all	á, alla, allan, allar, allir, allra, alls, allt, allur, öll, öllu, öllum
all-clear	allskörulega
all-good	allgott
all-little	alllítið, alllítil
all-many	allmargir
all-matters	almæltra
all-much	allmjög
allow	heimilt, láta, látum
allowed	láta
all-well	allvel
along	ein, með, undir
already	þegar
also	og
am	á, er
a-man	karl, maður, manna
among	í, milli
an-arrow	ör
and	á, eða, en, enda, og
an-even-man	jafnaðarmaður
angry	hermt
announcements	ummælum
another	aðra, annað, annar, öðru, önnur
answer	svara, svarar, svör
answered	svarað, svaraði, svarar, svöruðu
anti-sun-wise	andsælis
any	nokkuð, nokkura
anything	nokkuð, öðru
appeared	líst
appears	líst
appointed	ákveðnum, skipuðu
are	er, ert, erum, sért
areas	sveitir
are-repaid	launar
are-standing	stendur
are-you	ertu
Armannsfell (place)	Ármannsfelli
arms	hendi
Arngrim (name)	Arngrím, Arngrími, Arngríms, Arngrímur
a-roaming-man	reikanarmaður

Word List (English to Old Icelandic)

English	Old Icelandic
around	um
arrange	ráðast
article	greinir
as	á, að, er, í, sé, sem, vel
a-seat	seturúm
a-ship	skip
aside	hjá
ask	bið
asked	bað, biðja, biður, fréttu, spurði, spyr
ask-for	bið, biðja
as-might	máttu
a-solution	úrlausna
a-son	son
a-spear-point	odda
assembling-troops	liðsdrátt
Assembly-Headland (place)	Þingnes
assistance	ásjá, beina, greiða, lið, liðsinni
as-you-like	þvílíka
at	á, að, í
at-carried	atburðinn
a-tenant	landseti
a-tent	tjald
at-home	heima
a-thrall	þrælum
atone-for	bæta
autumn	haust, hausti, haustið
awake	vaka
away	braut, brott, brottu, snúið
a-week	viku
awhile	hríð, stund, stundir
a-wife	konu, konuna
awoke	vakna, vaknar
a-year	ærin

B, b

English	Old Icelandic
babble	fleiprir
back	bak
banned	bannir
banning	bönnum
bargain	fala
barren-ground	skermsl
battle	bardaga, berjast
be	gerast, sé, ver, vera, verða
be-able-to	mega
bear	berum, borið
beat	berja
became	gerðist, gerist, lagði, orðin, urðu, varð, verða, verði, verður
because	því
because-of	því
become	orðin, verða
bed	rekkju, sé
bed-clothing	föt
be-done	gera
been	verið
befalls	gerist
befell	ber
before	áður, fyrir, fyrr, fyrra, fyrri
befriended	vinsæll
began	hófst
be-given	gefast
be-helping	duga
behind	aftur
behold	líst
being	sé, vera
belligerance	þrjósku
bellowing	gelldi
bench	bekk
benefit	beini, kosti
benevolent	góðgjarnir
be-short-of	skorta
beside	hjá
best	best, besti
betrayed	svikið
betrothe	fastna, fastnir, föstnuð
betrothed	fastnaðir, fastnar
better	betra, betri, betur
between	með, milli
beyond	utan
bid	bað, bauð, bið, bíða, biðja, biður
bids	býður
big	mikill

Word List (English to Old Icelandic)

English	Old Icelandic
binding	strengi
birch-rafter	birkirafts
bite	hnígi
black	svarta
blame	lastaði
blocked	verja
blood	blóð
Blund (name)	Blund-, blunds
Blund-Ketill (name)	Blund-Katli, Blund-Ketill, Blund-Ketills
Blund-Ketill's (name)	Blund-Ketills
Blundsvatn (name)	Blundsvatn
bold	vasklegur
boldest	vaskasti
boldly	skörulega
bondage	höftum
bore	ala, bar, ber, borinn
Borgafjord (place)	Borgarfirði, Borgarfjarðar
Borgafjord (place)	Borgarfjörð
born-man	mannsbarn
both	báðum, bæði, beggja
bother	nenni
bought	kaupir, keypt, keypti
bound	binda, bundnar
bow	boga
brand	brandinn
brave-strong	garpur
breakfast	dagverðar
Breidabolstad (place)	Breiðabólstað
Breidafjord (place)	Breiðafirði
bridegroom	brúðguma
Broad-Beard (name)	breiðskeggs
broken	brugðið
brother	bróðir
brother-of	bróðir
brothers	bræðra
brought	færa, flytur, nær
brushwood	viðarköst
building	bólstað
built	bæinn
bulls	naut
Burg (place)	Borg
burn	brenna, brenni
burned	brenndur, brunnið, loguðu
burning	brenna
burnt	brunnið
but	en, enn
buy	kaupa
buying	kaup
by	hjá, í

C, c

English	Old Icelandic
call	kalla
called	kalla, kallaður, kallar
came	elur, kemur, kom, koma, komið, komnir, komu, komum
can	kann
can-get	nái
care	anntu
carried	bera, borið, flytja
carry	flytja
case-load	málahlut
cattle	fé, féið, fénað, fénu, fjár, fjárins, nautum
cattle-keeping	selför
caught	getur
caused	olli
celebrating	fagnað, fegnir
celebration	fagnaði
certain	víst
certainly	víst, vita
changed	breytt
chieftain	goði, höfðingjanna
chieftains	höfðingjar
child	barn
child-foster	barnfóstur
child-fostering	barnfóstri, barnfóstrinu
children	börn
child's-foster	barnfóstri
choice	kost, kostur
choose	kjósa, kost
clearing	rjóður
cliff-path	klifgötuna
climbed	stígur
cloak	skikkjunni
close	nær

Word List (English to Old Icelandic)

English	Old Icelandic	English	Old Icelandic
clothes	klæðin	debts	skuldir
cold	kaldur, kalt, köldu	decent	allsæmilegt
coldly	seint	decide	ráða
collected	safnaði	decision	ráð
come	gakk, kom, koma, komið, kominn, komir, komist, komna, komnir	deftly	þrífur
		departed	skiljast
		desperation	örvænti
		did	gera, gerðu, gerir
comes	kemur, komið	die	deyja
coming	komið, komnir, komu	dies	deyr
companions	félaga	difference	munur
company	lið, liði, liðs, líta, sveit	difficulty	óvingan, þungt, vandræði
conceal	leyna	direct	stefna
concern	varða	disappeared	hvarf
conclude	enda	discourage	letja
concluded	enda, lúka, málalyktir	discussed	ræðir
conclusions	málalyktir	discussing	mælir
consent	ráð	disliked	líkar, óþokkasælli
consider	hugsa, hyggja	dismount	stíga
considered	hyggja, þykjast	dismounted	stíga
cost	kost, kosti	disposition	skapsmunum
could	kunna, kunni, yrði	district	héraði, héraðsins
counsel	ráð, ráði, ráðum	district-administration	héraðsstjórn
countryside	sveitum	districts	héraða, héruð
cow	kú, kýr	do	ger, gera, gerðu, gerir
cower	kúgar	Dölum (place)	Dölum
crowd	fjölmennir	done	búið, gerr, gerst, gert
cunning	beittan	down	niður
custody	forsjá	dragged	draga
custom	vana, vanda	dragging	draga
		drawn	tefldir
		dread	uggir

D, d

English	Old Icelandic	English	Old Icelandic
danger	hætta	dreamed	dreymdi
daughter	dóttir, dóttur	drew	kippir
Daughter-of-Gunnar (name)	Gunnarsdóttir	dried	þornaði
		drive	rek, reka
Daughter-of-Tungu-Odd (name)	Tungu-Oddsdóttur	driven	reka, rekin
		drives	ekur
daughters	dætur	driving	rekur
day	dag, dags	drought	þorri
dead	dauður	drove	reka, rekur
dealings	viðskiptum	dwelled	búið
dealt	dælt	dwelling	bæ, bær
death	drepa	dwellings	bæinn, bæjarins
		dynamic-man	atgervismaður

Word List (English to Old Icelandic)

English	Old Icelandic

E, e

English	Old Icelandic
each	hver, hverjir, hverju, hverjum, hvern, hvert
each-side	hvorirtveggju
each-way	hvorratveggja
eager	ákafa
early	ár, snemma
earth	jarðir
Easterners (name)	Austmanns
eat	matast
eating	eta, etist, snæðings
Einar (name)	einar
either	heldur
either-side	hvorntveggja
either-way	annaðhvort
enclosure	túnið
end	enda, endið, lúkist
ended	lýkur
ends	lýkur
enemies	óvinir
enemy	mótstöðumaður
enjoy	njóta
enough	nóga, nógar
enquired	fréttist
entangle-with	vasast
enthralled	þjáður
envy	öfund
equal	jafnað, jafnaði, jafnan
equal-good	jafngott, jafnvel
equally	jafnan, jafnilla, jafnræði
equally-great	jafnmikinn
Erne (name)	Erni
errand	erindi
especially	einkum
estate	bænum
Esyuberg (place)	Esjubergi
even	jafnan
evening	kveld, kveldi, kveldið
everyone	hverjum
evil	illum
except	nema
exchanged	skipta, skipti
expect	væntir
expected	varði, von
experience	reyndi
expressed	tjá
eyes	augu
Eyjavaði (place)	Eyjavaði

F, f

English	Old Icelandic
fairly	heilli
fall	fallið
fallen	fallin
falls	falli
far	fjarri
fared	fara
far-from	fjarri
farm	búi, býr
farmhouse	bænum
farmyard	garða
fast	fast
father	faðir, föður
father-and-son	feðga, feðgar, mágar
feed	matar
feet	fótum
fell	féll, féllu, fellur
fellow	dreng, drengur
few	fátt
fewer	færra
few-men	fámennur
fields	velli
fiend-man	fjandmaður
find	fund, hitt
fire	eld, eldi, eldur
first	fyrst
Fitiar (place)	Fitjum
five	fimm
fixed	festar
fjord	firðinum
flaming	loganda
fodder	fóður, forkast
follow	fylgdu, fylgja
followed	fylgt
followers	félagar
following	fylgi
following-men	fjölmennari

Word List (English to Old Icelandic)

English	Old Icelandic
food	mat
fooled	gabbað
foot	fæti
for	á, er, fyrir, fyrr, í
forests	skógurinn
forty	fjóra
foster	fóstrar, fóstri
foster-child	barnfóstur
foster-father	fóstra, fóstri
fostering	fóstri
fought	berðist
found	fann, finna, fundið, hittast
four	fjögur, fjóra
free	frítt
friend	vin
friends	vina, vini, vinir, vinsæll, vinum
friendship	vináttu, vinfengi, vinsæll
from	á, að, af, frá, fram, fyrir, undan, undir, úr, við
from-home	heiman
from-now	fresti
from-said	frásögn
from-there	þaðan, þangað, þegar
from-the-south	sunnan
fulfilled	sáttum
fulfilment	efndir
full-of-food	mettir
fully	fullri
fully-outlawed	fullsektað
further	vora

G, g

English	Old Icelandic
gained	græddist
gather	safna
gathered	græddist, græðist, safna, safnaði, safnar
gathering	samandráttur
gave	fá, fagnar, gaf, gefur, veitti
Geir's (name)	Geirs
Geir's-Slope (place)	Geirshlíð
Gellir (name)	gelli, gellir, gellis
get	fá, fæ, fáið, getir, nái
get-spoiled	spillist
getting	fást, fengur
gifts	gjafar, gjafir
give	gef, gefa, gifta, veita
given	gaf, gefa, gefið, veitt, veittur
given-to	gefin
give-way	undan
gladly	gjarna
go	far, fara, ganga
goes	fari, fer, fór, gegnir
Gói (month, February)	Gói.
going	fara, farið, för, ganga, ganganda, gegna, gengi, gengur
going-away	farið
gone	farið
good	góð, góða, góðar, góðir, góðu, góðum, góður, gott
good-advice	heillaráða
good-doing	góðgjörnum
goods	fémunum, kaupskap, varningur, vöru
got	fá, fékk, föng, gátu, gekk, heimtir, nái
go-you	gakktu
grant	lag, leggja, veita
granted	leggja
grass	gras
grazing	útifé
great	afar, mikil, mikinn, mikla, miklu, stórmikið
great-big	mikill
greater	meiri
great-fee	stórfé
greatly	afar, drjúgastur, mikil, mikinn, stórilla
greeted	fagnar, heilsað, heilsar
greeting	kveðju
groups	flokkar
grown	vexti
guarded	verja
guest	gisti, gistingu

204

Word List (English to Old Icelandic)

English	Old Icelandic
guested	vistaðist
guesting	gistingu
Gunnar (name)	Gunnar, Gunnari
Gunnar's (name)	Gunnars
Gunnarsstadir (place)	Gunnarsstaði
Gunnvald (name)	Gunnvaldur

H, h

English	Old Icelandic
had	átt, átti, áttu, eiga, hafa, hafðar, hafði, hafðist, hafi, haft, hefði, hefðu, hefir, höfðu, lætur, lét
half-of	hálft
Halsa (place)	Hálsa
hand	handa, hendi, hendur, hönd, höndina
handmaidens	griðkonur
hands	hendur, höndum
handsome	vænn
hands-over	handsalar
hang-back	hinkur
happy-decision	happaráð
harbour	hafi
hard	harðla
hardly	varla
harm	meins
harm-like	hörmuleg
harsh-spoken	hastorður
has	hefir
have	átt, eiga, eigum, hæfir, hafa, hafi, hafið, hafir, haft, hefði, hefi, hefir, höfum, láta
have-right	leiðrétta
having	hafi
hay	hey, heyið, heyjum
hay-allowance	heyleigur
hay-crop	grasvöxtur
hay-feed	algjafta
hay-need	heyþroti
haystacks	heybjörg, heyin
hay-supply	heykost
he	hann, hans, henni, honum, sinn
head	höfuð
head-bearing	höfuðburður
hear	heyr, heyri
heard	frétti, heyra, heyrðu, heyrir, spyrjast
heaved	hefja
heavily	þröngva, þunglega
heavy	þyngra
heavy-load	hlass
heels	stökkur
held	hélst
Helgi (name)	Helga, Helgi, Helgu
Helgivatn (place)	Helgavatni
help	björg, hjálp, hjálpa
helping	duga
hens	hænsn
Hen-Thorir (name)	Hænsna-Þóri, Hænsna-Þórir, Hænsna-Þóris
her	hana, henni, hún
here	hér, hérna, hingað
hers	hana, hennar, síns
herself	sér
Herstein (name)	Hersteini, Hersteinn
hides	húðir
hiding	leyna
him	hann, hans, honum, sér, sig, sín
himself	sér, sig, sjálfum, sjálfur
his	hans, honum, sér, sig, sín, sína, sinn, sinna, sinni, síns, sínu, sínum, sitt
his-nose	nasirnar
Hlidarendi (place)	Hlíðarenda
hold	halda
holding	haldið
holds	haldi
home	heim, heima, heiman
homes	bæja
home-ways	heimleiðis
honour	sæmd, sóma
honourable	sómir
honoured	ágætur, sæmdur

Word List (English to Old Icelandic)

English	Old Icelandic	English	Old Icelandic
hope-abide	vonbiðlar	intends	ætlar
hopeful	vænlegt	into	í
horse	hest, hestinn, hestinum	invitation	bjóða, boðið
		invite	biðja, bjóða
horseback	baki	invited	bjóða, boðinn, býður
horses	hesta, hestar, hestum, hross, hrossa, hrossum	invited-people	boðsmenn, fyrirboðsmanna
		iron	járn
hospitable	beinn	is	er, sé
hospitality	vist	is-it	er
hostility	fjandskapar	is-that	er, það
house	húsi, húsin, húsum	it	að, hitt, það, það"
house-built	húsar		
house-choice	húsakost		
housed	húsað		
how	hve, hver, hverju, hversu, hví		

J, j

English	Old Icelandic
how-so	hverju, hversu
Hromund (name)	Hrómundi
hundred	hundruð, hundruðum
hundreds	hundruð
Hvamm (place)	Hvamm, Hvammi
Hvita (place)	Hvítá

English	Old Icelandic
Jofrid (name)	Jófríðar, Jófríði, Jófríður
Jorun (name)	Jórunn
Jorunn (name)	Jórunn
journey	ferð, ferðir, för
journeying	fara
journey-of-men	mannaferð
judged	dæmdust
judgement	dóma

I, i

K, k

English	Old Icelandic
I	eg, mér
ice-bound	íslög
idle-talk	gjálgrun
if	að, af, ef, hvort
ill	illa, ills, illt, illu
ill-harm	illbýli
in	á, að, en, enn, er, í, inn, inni
in-all	alls
increased	gæða
in-hand	höndum
injuries	áverkar
inlet	ósinn
inquired	frétti
inside	inn, inni
insist	heimta
instructions	ráðum
intend	ætla, ætlar, ætluð, ætlum
intended	ætla, ætlað, ætlar

English	Old Icelandic
keen-eyed	skyggnastur
keep	geyma
keeping	varnaði
Ketil (name)	Ketils
kill	drepa
killed	drepa, drepinn
kindled	kveiktu
kinds-of	kyns
kinsman	frænda, frændi
kinsmen	frændum
knew	kannast, veit, vissi, viti
knock	drepið
knocked	klappar
know	kann, veit, vita, vitum
knowing	kennist, víst, vita
known	kennt, víst, vitað

Word List (English to Old Icelandic)

English	*Old Icelandic*	*English*	*Old Icelandic*
knows	kann	look	sjá
know-you	veistu	looked	horfir, lítur
		looking	bragði
		lot	hluta, hlutur
		loudly	hátt
		low-deed	níðingsverk

L, l

		lower	neðra
lack-of-people	mannfátt	lucky-man	gæfumaður
laid	látið, leggst, lögðu	lying	liggur
land	land	lying-in	innarlega
lands	land		
lands-corners	landshorna		
last	síðasta		

M, m

late	seint, síð		
law-matter-standing	lögmálsstaðinn	made	gerð, gert
lay	lag, legg, leggst, leiðast	make	ger, gera
		make-known	kunnleika
laying	lá, lagi, lagið	make-use	neyta
lay-out	liggja	man	maður, mann, manna, manni, manns
lead	leiða		
leant	laut	manager	forráðsmaður
leaping	hleypur		
leapt	hlaupa, hleypur, stíga	manly	drengilegt, mannaða
		mantle	möttul
learned	spurði, spurt	many	fjöldi, fjórir, marga, margir, mart, mörgum
leave	legði		
led	leiddur		
left	létti	marriage	mægða
less	minnur	married	átti, gefin
less-dreary	ódauflegra	marry	gift
less-likely	óágengilegra	matter	mál, máls, málum
let	láta, látið, látir, láttu, látum, leita, lést, lét	matter-consideration	ásjámál
		matters	málum
let-up	létta	may	getur, má, mætti, máttu
let-us-go	förum		
let-us-sit	setjumst	me	mér, mig
lies	lýgur	meet	finnast, fund, fundar, hittast, móti
light	létt		
like	leikur, líkar	meeting	ákveðnum, mót, móti
liked	líkaði	meeting-going	mótgangi
likely	líkara, líklegra	men	mann, manna, manni, menn, mennina, mönnum
linen-breeches	línbrókum		
little	lítið, lítil, lítill, lítils, lítt		
lived	bjó, bjuggu	men-desiring	manngirnd
loaded	klyfjar	men-fallen	mannfall
locked	loku	men-travelling	mannferðin
long	langt, lengi, löngu	merchant	kaupdrengur
		merry	allkátir
longer	lengi	met	hitta, hitti, hittir, mætir

Word List (English to Old Icelandic)

English	Old Icelandic
might	gegndi, mátt, mátti, máttu, munt
milk	mjólka
milked	mjólkað
mind	hug, sinni, skapir
mine	mér, mín, mína, mínar, mínir, minn, míns, mínu, mínum, mitt
mis-advised	misráðið
misery	vesöld
mistrust	grunaði
money	fé, pening
mongrel	hundurinn
mood	skapi
more	fleira, fleiri, meir, meira, meiri, mér
more-helpful	nýtara
morning	morgun, morguninn
most	mest, mesta, mesti, mestu, mestur
most-angry	reiðasti
mostly	mestan
most-often	frekust
most-popular	vinsælasti
mother	móður
mountain-pasture	selinu
mounted	stíga
mouth	munni
move	flytjist
moving	flutningar
much	mikið, mikil, mikill, mikinn, mikla, miklu, mjög
must	hlýtur, munt
my	mér, mín, minna, míns, mínum
Myrar (place)	Mýrar
myself	sjálfa

N, n

English	Old Icelandic
named	heitir, hét, nefnir
near	ná, næst, náinn
nearby	hjá
nearest	næst
nearly	nær
necessary	ærið
necessities	nauðsynjum
need	þarf, þurfa
needed	krefur, þarf, þurfti, þyrfti
need-like	nauðsynlegra
need-much	nauðamikill
needs	þyrfti
neither	hvorgi
never	aldrei
new	nýlegar, nýst, nýtt
newer	nýlegar, nýlegra
news	frétt, fréttir, nýlundu, tíðinda, tíðindi, tíðindum
next	annan
night	nótt
nightfall	náttaði, náttar
night-quarters	náttstað
nine	níu
no	enga, engi, nei
noblest-women	kvenskörungur
noise	hark
none	enga, engan, engi, engu, engum
Norðura (place)	Norðurá
Norðurá (place)	Norðurá
Norduradal (place)	Norðurárdal
Norðurdæla (place)	Norðurdæla
north	norðan, norður
North-River (place)	Norðurá
North-River-Valley (place)	Norðurárdal
North-Tongue (place)	Norðurtungu
Norway (place)	Noregs
nose	nasir
not	eiga, eigi, ekki, engi, engu, né
nothing	einkis, einskis, engi, engu
now	nú

O, o

English	Old Icelandic
obeyed	hlýða

Word List (English to Old Icelandic)

English	Old Icelandic
obliged	skyldir
obstructed	ógreitt
Odd (name)	Odd, Oddi, Oddur
Odd's (name)	Odds
Oddson (name)	Oddsson
of	á, að, af, í, of, úr
of-all	allra
off	af, ofan
offer	bjóðast, boð, boðið, boðs
offered	bauð, bjóðist, boðið
of-few-words	fámálugur
of-little-milk	nytlétt
of-me	mitt
of-people	manna
often	oft, oftar
of-the-house	húsunum
of-your	þína
old-age	eldast
on	á, í
once	eitt
one	á, annar, einn, eins, einu, eitt, önnur
one-month	einmánuður
one's	eins
only	eina, einskis
open	opið
opposite	annan
or	eða, ýmist
ordered	skipar
Orn (name)	Erni, Örn
Ornolf (name)	Örnólf, Örnólfs, Örnólfur
Ornolfsdal (place)	Örnólfsdal
other	aðra, aðrir, annað, annar, annarra, öðrum, önnur
others	annarra, annars, öðrum
other-than	annar, önnur
other-things	annað
otherwise	ella
our	vor, voru, vorum
our-own	eigu
ours	okkar, vorri, vorum
ourselves	sjálfir
out	á, út, utan, úti
out-freed	útkvæmt
out-from	úr
out-house	útibúr, útibúrið
outlawed	sekir, sekur
outlawry	útlegðar
out-lying	utarlega
outnumbered	ofurliði
out-of	úr
outside	utan, úti
outstanding	afbragð
over	á, ofan, yfir
overpowered	aflvani
overwhelming	ofurefli
own	átt, eiga, eigin, eigum
owned	átt
ownership	eigur
owning	eignum

P, p

English	Old Icelandic
pack-loads	klyfjar, klyfjarnar
paid	goldið
pale-burnt	fölskaður
part	hlut, hluti
parted	skiljast, skilst
parts	hluta
passed	afliðnum, leið, líða, líður
passes	leið
pasture	haga, hagar
pay	fá
peace	kyrrt
penalty	sektir
people	manna, manni, manninn, mönnum
pierce	stungið
place	búið, leggir, stað
plan	ráðs
platform	pall
played	leikið
pledge	heit
pledged	heitið
point	tilgangur
poor	snauður

Word List (English to Old Icelandic)

English	Old Icelandic	English	Old Icelandic
popular	vinsæll	redeem	leysa
power	mátturinn, vald	Refur (name)	refur
powerful	ríkismunur	refuse	neita
praised	lofaði	regarded	þykja
preparation	viðbúnaður	release	leysa, leyst
prepare	búa	remained	léttir, liggja
prepared	búið, búnir	remember	minnast
prepartions	bú	reputation	metorð
presses	þröngt	reserved	gjaforði
proclaim	lýsa	residences	bústöðum
produce	landsnytjar	result-in	hlytist
profoundly	spaklega	retain	geyma
proposal	kost, tillag, tillög	return	skila
protection	umsjá	returned	aftur
provide	veitir	Reykjardal (place)	Reykjardal
provided-for	kost	rich	stórauðigur
provisions	vorri	ride	ríða
purchase	kaupa	rides	ríður
pushed	otar	riding	ríður
		riding-on	framreiðin
		right	heimilast, rétt, rétta, réttir, réttur, sannlegt

Q, q

English	Old Icelandic
quickly	fljótt, hratt, hvatlega, skjótt
quite	greiðlega

English	Old Icelandic
righted	réttir
rights	rétta, réttu
risk	ábyrgð
river	ána
robbed	rændi, rænt
robber-man	ránsmaður
robbery	rán, ráni, ránið
rode	reið, ríða, riðu, ríður
room	rúm
ropes	reip
rose	reis
rots	fúnar
roughly	hart
rule	ráða

R, r

English	Old Icelandic
raised	safna
raising	hefja
ran	hlaupa, hleypir, hleypur, hljóp
rarely	varla
rather	heldur, héldust, helst
reached	náðu, seilist
readily	reiðu
ready	búin
reason	sök
receive	þegið, þiggja
received	tekið
recompensed	iðgjöld
reconcile	sættast
reconciliation	bætur
red	rauður

S, s

English	Old Icelandic
safeguard	varðveita
saga	sögu

Word List (English to Old Icelandic)

English	Old Icelandic	English	Old Icelandic
said	er, kvað, kvaðst, kváðust, kveða, kveðst, mælt, mælti, sagði, sagðist, sagt, segði, segir, segist, segja, sögðu, talaði	shame	endemi, skömm
		share	miðla
		shared	deildum
		she	henni, hún
		sheep	sauðir
said-to	sagði	shepherd	hirði, sauðamaður
sailors	hásetar	shields	skildir
sake	sakir	shirt	skyrtu
same	einu, sama, samir	shoes	skó
sank	sígast	shortage	skortir
sat	sat, sátu, sest, sitja, situr	shot	skaut
		should	mun, mundi, mundu, muni, munt, muntu, munum, skulu, skuluð, skulum, skylda, skyldi, skyldu, skyldur, skylt
satisfied	unir		
saw	sá, sér, sjá		
saw-you	sástu		
say	seg, segja, tala		
saying	kvaðst, kveðst	should-you	muntu
Scotland (place)	Skotlandi	show	sýna
seat	sæti	sick	sjúk, sjúkur
seated	sæti	sickness	sótt, sóttarinnar
seats	sæti	side	síður
see	sé, séum, sjá, sjáir	silence	þegi
seemed	sýnt, þætti, þótti, þykir	silenced	þagnar
seems	hyggst, líst, sjá, sýnist, þætti, þykir, þykist	silent	þagði, þagnar
		silver	silfur
		similar	áþekkur
seen	reyndar, sá, sæst, sén, sénn	since	síðan
		sister-of	systur
see-you	séuð	sit	sitja, sitji, situr
self	sjálfur	sitting	setjast
self-judgement	sjálfdáðum, sjálfdæmi	six	sex
sell	selja, selji, sölu, sölur	Skaney-Fell (place)	Skáneyjarfjall
selling	seldi	Skeggja's-Sons (name)	Skeggjasonar
sent	fara, sendi		
separated	skildust	Skogarstrand (place)	Skógarströnd
servant-fees	þrælsgjöld	Skorradal (place)	Skorradal
servants	þræla	slanted	hallast
set	sett	slaughter	slátrað
settle	sætta, sættar, sitja	slaughtered	slátrað
settled	búið, byggðan, sætta, sáttir, setið, slitið	sleep	svefni
		sleep-thorn	svefnþorni
settlement	sætt	slump	hnígi
shall	mun, muni, munu, munuð, munum, skal, skalt, skulu, skulum	so	á, í, sá, slíkt, svo
		so-going	gegnir
shall-you	skaltu	sold	seldi, selur

Word List (English to Old Icelandic)

English	Old Icelandic	English	Old Icelandic
solution	úrlausna	Stafholt (place)	Stafholt
some	nokkuð, nokkur, nokkura, nokkurs, suma, sumum	Stafholtstungur (place)	Stafholtstungur
		stallions	stóðhross
some-of	nokkurar	stand	staðið, standa
someone	nokkura, nokkurs	standing	staddur, staðist
something	eitthvert, nokkuð	steal	ræni
somewhat	nokkuð, nokkuru, nokkurum	Steinsvað (place)	Steinsvað
		stepped	steig
son	son, syni	stepping	stigu
son-in-law	mági, mágur	still	kyrrt
son-of	son	stone	steinn
Son-of-Arngrim (name)	Arngrímsson	stood	standa, stóð
		straighten	rétta
Son-of-Blund-Ketill (name)	Blund-Ketillsson	straightened-up	réttist
Son-of-Egil (name)	Egilssyni	strange	kynlegt
Son-of-Helgi (name)	Helgason	strategy	brögðum
Son-of-Hlifar (name)	Hlífarson	stretch-out	rétta
Son-of-Hogni (name)	Högnasonar	Strider (name)	stígandi
Son-of-Ketil (name)	Ketilssonar	strong	sterkur
Son-of-Odd (name)	Oddsson, Oddssonar	struck	höggur, slá, slær, strykur
Son-of-Onund (name)	Önundarson	such	slík, slíka, slíkan, slíkt, slíku, slíkur
Son-of-Orlyg (name)	Örlygssonar		
Son-of-Rauda-Bjarni (name)	Rauða-Bjarnarson	suddenly	skyndilega
		sufficient	einhlítir, einhlítur
Son-of-Thori (name)	Þórissonar	sufficiently	duganda
Son-of-Ulf (name)	Úlfarssonar, Úlfssonar	suggestions	tillög
		suits	gegni
Son-of-Valbrand (name)	Valbrandsson	summer	sumar, sumarið, sumri
Son-of-Valthjof (name)	Valþjófssonar	summer-market	sumarkaup
		summer-pasture	sels
sons	son, sona, sonu	summoned	stefna, stefnir
soon	bráðlega, brátt, skjótar, snemma	suppose	ætla
		supposed	ætla
sought	sækja, sótt	surely	örvænt, sannast
sound	hljómur	suspect	gruna, grunar
south	suður	Svignaskard (place)	Svignaskarði
speak	mælir, tala	Svignaskardi (place)	Svignaskarði
spear-man	vígur	sword	sverð
spoke	kvað, kvaðst, kveðst, mælt, mælti, sagði	sword's-hilt	sverðshjöltin
spoken	mælt, talað		
spoken-of	látin		
sprang	sprettur, stökk		
spring	vorar		
stacks	stakkar		

Word List (English to Old Icelandic)

English	Old Icelandic	*English*	Old Icelandic
		the-company	liðinu, liðs
		the-cow	kúna
		the-day	dag, daginn
		the-district	héraði, héraðið, héraðinu

T, t

English	Old Icelandic
take	nem, tæki, taka, takir, tek, tekst
taken	fært, nema, taka, tekið
taken-away	affærði
take-you	taktu
talk	tölum
talked	talast, töluðu
talking	tal
tempted	freistað
ten	tigu
tenant-farms	leigulanda
tenants	landseta, landsetar
tens	tigi, tigir, tigu, tigum
tent	tjalda, tjaldið
test	reynið
than	að, en, síðan
thanes	þegna
thanked	þakkar
thanks	þökk
that	að, en, er, sem, það, þann, þenna, þetta
that-caused	olli
that-way	þannig
the	að, hið, hinn, hins, í, inn, sitt, það
the-asembly	þingheimurinn
the-assembly	alþingi, alþingis, þinghelgi, þingi, þingið, þinginu, þings, þingsins
the-assembly-sanctuary	þinghelginni
the-back	bak
the-barn	fjósi
the-best	best, hagastur
the-boy	piltinn, sveininum, sveinn, sveinninn
the-bride	brúðir
the-bridegroom	brúðgumi
the-burning	brennu, brennuna, brennunni
the-cattle	féið
the-chieftain	goða, goði

English	Old Icelandic
the-company	liðinu, liðs
the-cow	kúna
the-day	dag, daginn
the-district	héraði, héraðið, héraðinu
the-districts	héruðunum
the-door	durum, dyr, hurð
the-door-beam	hurðar, hurðina
the-door-ring	hurðarhringinn
the-doors	hurðar
the-earth	jörð
the-Easterners (name)	Austmenn
the-eastern-man	austmaður
the-Eastern-Men (name)	Austmanninum
the-enclosure	túnið
the-estate	bæinn, bæjarins, bænum
the-evening	kveldi
the-faring	farningar
the-farm	bænum, bærinn
the-farmer	bónda, bóndi, bóndinn
the-farmyard	garði
the-fence	garði
the-fire	eldurinn, logann
the-flock	flokki
the-floor	gólfið, gólfinu
the-ford	vaðið, vaðsins
the-front-door	hurðina, útihurðinni
the-harbour	höfn, höfnina
the-hay	heyið
The-Headland (place)	Nes
the-heath	heiði
the-hill	hól
the-hillside	hlíðinni
the-horses	hrossunum
the-house	bænum, hús, húsin, húsinu, húsum, húsunum
the-housekeeper	húskarl
the-houses	húsin
the-instigators	upphafsmaður
the-invitation	boð
their	sína, þeir, þeirra

213

Word List (English to Old Icelandic)

English	Old Icelandic	*English*	Old Icelandic
theirs	sín, sína, sinni, sínum, þeir, þeirra	*the-south*	sunnan
		The-Stamper (name)	hlammanda
the-land	land, landi	*the-steersman*	stýrimaður, stýrimann
the-lands	löndum	*the-stone*	steininn
the-load	klyfjar	*the-strand*	ströndinni
them	sér, þau, þeim	*the-string*	streng
the-main-room	stofu	*the-summer*	sumar
the-man	karl, maður, manninum	*the-table*	borð, borðum
the-matter	mál, mála, máli, málið, málinu, málum	*the-tables*	borð, borðið
		the-tenants	landsetum
the-morning	morgun	*the-tent*	tjaldið
the-most	flestra, mest, mestri	*The-Tongue (place)*	Tunguna
themselves	sér, sig	*the-towns*	bæjunum
then	en, enn, er, hið, hina, síðan, sinn, þá, þann, þau, þenna, þetta, þó, því	*the-trading-men*	kaupmönnum
		the-valleys	dalina
		the-way	háttað, leið, veg
		the-ways	leið
the-news	tíðinda, tíðindi	*the-wedding*	boðið, boðinu, boðs
the-night	nætur, nótt, nóttin	*the-western-men*	vestanmanna
the-north	norðan	*the-winter*	veturinn
the-older	fornum	*the-woman*	konu, konuna, konunnar
the-other	önnur		
the-pastures	haganum	*the-women*	konur
the-path	garði, götu, götuna, götunni, sneiðigata	*the-woods*	skógar, skóginn, skóginum
the-people	alþýðu	*the-worst*	verst
the-plot	tún	*they*	síðan, sinn, sinni, þær, þau, þeim, þeir, þeirra
the-port	höfninni		
the-price	verð		
the-purchase	kaupin	*the-yard*	tún
there	staðinn, þær, þangað, þar, þeir	*they-are*	eru
		they-were	eru, voru
there-are	eru	*thief*	þjófur
therefore	því	*think*	hyggja, þykjumst
the-robbery	ránið	*third*	þriðja
the-sake	sakirnar	*this*	í, þann, þenna, þess, þessa, þessi, þessu, þessum, þetta
the-same	sama		
these	þessa, þessi, þessir		
the-seat	pallinum	*this-case*	málinu
the-settlement	sættirnar	*this-exchange*	skipta
the-shield	skjöldur	*this-one*	þessa, þessi
the-ship	skip	*this-woman*	konuna
the-ship-arrival	skipkomuna	*Thorbjorn (name)*	Þorbjörn
the-situation	varið	*Thord (name)*	Þórð, Þórðar, Þórði, Þórður
the-slope	hlíðinni		
The-Slope (place)	Hlíðina	*Thorgeir (name)*	Þorgeirs
		Thori (name)	Þóri, Þóris

Word List (English to Old Icelandic)

English	Old Icelandic	English	Old Icelandic
Thorid (name)	Þuríðar	*to-me*	mér
Thorir (name)	Þóri, Þórir	*to-meet*	hitta, móti
Thori's (name)	Þóris	*to-mind*	hugnar
Thorkel (name)	Þorkatli, Þorkell, Þorkels	*took*	fagnar, nemur, taka, tekst, tekur, tók, tókst, víkur
Thorkel's (name)	Þorkels		
Thorodd (name)	Þórodd, Þóroddi, Þóroddur	*to-people*	manni
		to-reach	hittast
Thorolf (name)	Þórólfur	*to-rebuke*	ávíta
Thorstein (name)	Þorsteini	*Torfi (name)*	Torfi
Thorvald (name)	Þorvald, Þorvaldur	*torment*	raun
Thorvald's (name)	Þorvalds	*to-say*	segja
those	þeir	*to-see*	þykjast
though	þó	*to-sell*	selja
thought	hug, hugði, hugðist, þótt, þótti, þóttist, þykir, þykist	*to-stand*	staðar
		to-talk	tala
		to-travel	ferðin
thoughtful	hugsi	*towards*	mót
thoughts	hugur	*to-you*	þér, yður
threatening	heitan	*to-your*	þér
three	þrem, þremur, þrír, þrjá	*trading*	kaupum
		trading-men	kaupmenn
Thurid (name)	Þuríði, Þuríður	*trading-post*	kaupstefnur
tide-change	misgöngin	*traditions*	sið
tidings	tíðindi	*tragic*	hörmulegt
time	mund, tíma	*trampling*	spark
to	á, að, í, til	*travel*	fara, farir, ferð, ferðum
to-accept	þiggja		
to-be-oppressed	kúgast	*travelled*	fara, ferð, fór
to-buy	kaupa	*travelled-from*	ferð
to-come	koma, komast	*travelled-out*	utan
to-come-out	útgöngu	*travelling*	fara, farið, farinn, fer, ferð, ferðina
to-dress	klæðast		
to-get	hljótast, hljótist	*travelling-men*	farmönnum
together	saman, við	*Trefil (name)*	trefils
together-travelling	samfara	*Trefill (name)*	trefill
to-give	gefa	*trodden*	troðinn
to-go	fara, ganga	*trouble*	vandræði, vondum
to-have	hafa	*true*	
to-her	henni	*true-like*	sannlegra
to-him	honum, sig	*truly*	satt
to-kill	drepa	*trust*	traust, trausts
to-know	vissi	*Tungu-Odd (name)*	Tungu-Odd, Tungu-Oddi, Tungu-Odds, Tungu-Oddur
told	sagði, sagt, segir, sögðu, tala, töluð		
to-learn	spyrja	*Tungu-Odd's (name)*	Tungu-Odds

Word List (English to Old Icelandic)

English	Old Icelandic
turn-away	vísað, vísaðir
turned	hverfur, snúa, snúið, snýr, víkur
turned-back	hverfa, snýr
turned-out	reyndust
turn-out	reynast
twelve	tólf, tólfta
twice	tvisvar
two	tvær, tveir, tvo, tvö

Þ, þ

English	Old Icelandic
Þrælastraumur (place)	Þrælastraumur
Þverarhlíd (place)	Þverárhlíð
Þverarhlíð (place)	Þverárhlíð
Þverhlíðingar (place)	Þverhlíðingar

U, u

English	Old Icelandic
unburnt	óbrunnið
under	undir
understand	skilið
undertaken	undir
uneasy	ódælla
un-equally	ójafnað
unexpected	ófyrirsynju
un-friendship	óvináttu
unless	nema
unlike	ólíklegt
unpopularity	óvinsældin, óvinsældir
un-quiet	ókyrrt
un-spoken	ákveðið
un-stocked	óbirgur
until	til
unworthy	óvirt
up	upp
us	okkur, oss
used-to	vanur
useful	gagni

V, v

English	Old Icelandic
valuables	fémætt
value	virðir
Vatn (Water) (place)	Vatni
very-few	allfáir
Vidfari (name)	Víðfari
Vidimyr (place)	Víðimýri
voice	rödd
vouch	vörslu
voyage	ferð

W, w

English	Old Icelandic
wailing	veinan
walking	ganganda
wandered	reikar
wanders	reikar
wares	varnaði, varning, voru
was	er, gerist, væri, var, varð, voru
was-awake	vekti
was-named	heitir
way	veg
we	oss, vér, við
wealth	fé, féið
wealth-with-betokened	fjárviðtökunni
wealthy	auðga, auðgastur
wealthy-man	auðigur, auðmaður
weapons	vopn
we-are	erum, vér
weather	veðri
wedding-feast	boði
week	viku, víkur
welcome	komnir
well	er, góðrar, sekt, vel
went	færi, fara, farið, fer, fór, fóru, ganga, gekk, gengi, gengið, gengur, gera
were	er, væri, væru, var, voru, vorum
west	vestan, vestur
we-think	þykjumst

Word List (English to Old Icelandic)

English	Old Icelandic
what	að, er, hvað, hver
when	er, sem
where	er, hvar, sem, voru
whether	hvort
which	en, er, hvert, hvort, sem
while	en
whip	sviga
whipped	keyrir
whistled	blístrar
who	er, hver, hverjir, sem
why	hví
wife	kona
wildly	óðlega
will	gjarna, mun, munu, vil, vilji, viljum, vill, vilt
willed	vildi, vilja, vill
willingly	gjarna
will-you	viltu
win	uni, unnið
wind	vindur
window	gluggur
winter	vetri, vetur, veturinn
winter-house	veturhúsa
winter-need	vetrarnauð
winters	vetur
wise	vitran, vitur
wish	vil, vildi, vilja, vilt
wished	vildi, vildu, vilja, vill
wishes	vill
wish-to	viljum
wit	viti
with	í, með, við, víða
with-goings-on	meðferðina
with-laid	viðbúningur
without	án
withstand	standa
witnesses	votta, vottar
woeful	válegra
wolves	úlfs
woman	kona
women	konur
wonder	kynlegt
wood	við
woods-outskirts	skógarnef
word	orð
words	orð, orða, orðið
word-sickened	orðsjúkur
work	verki
work-men	verkmanna
workshop	smiðju
worse	verr, verra, verri
worst	versta
worth	verð, verður, vert, virt
worthiness	virðing
worthy	verða, verður, virðing, virðulegur
would	mun, mundi, mundu, muni, munir, munt, munu, skyldu, vildu
would-be	væri
wounded	særum, sár
wrong	rangt, röngu

Y, y

English	Old Icelandic
yard	garði
yes	já
you	í, þér, þig, þinn, þinni, þú, yður
your	þína, þinn, þinna, þinni, þitt, yðrum, yður, yðvar, ykkarn
yours	sinn, sinni, þín, þína, þinn, þinnar, þinni, þíns, þínu, þínum, þitt, yður
yule	jól

A Word Comparison of Old Norse and Old Icelandic Words

Old Norse	Old Icelandic	English
á	í	to
áðr	áður	before
æfar	afar	great
ærit	ærið	necessary
ætlak	ætla	suppose
ætlat	ætlað	intended
ætlat	ætluð	intend
aftr	aftur	after
aftr	aftur	behind
aftr	aftur	returned
ágætr	ágætur	honoured
aldri	aldrei	never
alllítit	alllítið	all-little
allmjök	allmjög	all-much
allr	allur	all
allsæmiligt	allsæmilegt	decent
allsköruliga	allskörulega	all-clear
áminnast	minnast	remember
annarr	annar	another
Annarr	annar	one
annarr	annar	other
annarr	annar	other-than
annarrra	annarra	other
annarrra	annarra	others
annat	annað	another
Annat	annað	other
annat	annað	other-things
annathvárt	annaðhvort	either-way
Arngrímr	Arngrímur	Arngrim (name)
at	að	as
at	að	at
at	að	if
at	að	in
at	að	it
at	að	of
at	að	than
at	að	that
at	að	the
at	að	to
at	í	to
at	og	and
atgervismaðr	atgervismaður	dynamic-man
ápekkr	ápekkur	similar
átta	átti	had
auðgastr	auðgastur	wealthy
auðigr	auðigur	wealthy-man
auðmaðr	auðmaður	wealthy-man
austmaðr	austmaður	the-eastern-man
Bærr	bær	dwelling
bætr	bætur	reconciliation
barnfóstr	barnfóstur	child-foster
barnfóstr	barnfóstur	foster-child
berr	ber	befell
berr	ber	bore
Betr	betur	better
bezt	best	best
bezt	best	the-best
bezti	besti	best
biðr	biður	asked
biðr	biður	bid
boðit	boðið	invitation
boðit	boðið	offer
boðit	boðið	offered
boðit	boðið	the-wedding
borðit	borðið	the-tables
borit	borið	bear
borit	borið	carried
bráðliga	bráðlega	soon
brenndr	brenndur	burned
brugðit	brugðið	broken
brugðizt	brugðist	accustomed
brunnit	brunnið	burned
brunnit	brunnið	burnt
búit	búið	done
búit	búið	dwelled

A Word Comparison of Old Norse and Old Icelandic

Old Norse	Old Icelandic	English	Old Norse	Old Icelandic	English
búit	búið	place	*fekk*	fékk	got
búit	búið	prepared	*fell*	féll	fell
búit	búið	settled	*Fellr*	fellur	fell
burt	brott	away	*Fellu*	féllu	fell
býðr	býður	bids	*fengr*	fengur	getting
býðr	býður	invited	*ferð*	ferðin	to-travel
dæmðust	dæmdust	judged	*ferr*	fer	goes
dætr	dætur	daughters	*ferr*	fer	travelling
dauðr	dauður	dead	*Ferr*	fer	went
drengiligt	drengilegt	manly	*fjandmaðr*	fjandmaður	fiend-man
drengr	drengur	fellow	*fjölði*	fjöldi	many
drepit	drepið	knock	*flytizt*	flytjist	move
dreymði	dreymdi	dreamed	*flytr*	flytur	brought
drjúgastr	drjúgastur	greatly	*fóðr*	fóður	fodder
dyrr	dyr	the-door	*fölskaðr*	fölskaður	pale-burnt
einhlítr	einhlítur	sufficient	*forráðsmaðr*	forráðsmaður	manager
einmánuðr	einmánuður	one-month	*freistat*	freistað	tempted
ek	eg	I	*fullsekðat*	fullsektað	fully-outlawed
ekki	eigi	not	*fundit*	fundið	found
ekr	ekur	drives	*Fylgðu*	fylgdu	follow
eldr	eldur	fire	*gabbat*	gabbað	fooled
eldrinn	eldurinn	the-fire	*gæfumaðr*	gæfumaður	lucky-man
elr	elur	came	*garpr*	garpur	brave-strong
em	er	am	*gefit*	gefið	given
er	vel	as	*gefr*	gefur	gave
erendi	erindi	errand	*gengit*	gengið	went
etizt	etist	eating	*gengr*	gengur	went
Eyjavati	Eyjavaði	Eyjavaði (place)	*gerði*	gekk	went
fagnat	fagnað	celebrating	*gerr*	ger	do
fáir	getir	get	*gerviligr*	gervilegur	accomplished
fallit	fallið	fall	*gerzt*	gerst	done
fámáligr	fámálugur	of-few-words	*getr*	getur	caught
fámennr	fámennur	few-men	*getr*	getur	may
farit	farið	going	*gjafar*	gjafir	gifts
farit	farið	going-away	*gluggr*	gluggur	window
farit	farið	gone	*góðr*	góður	good
farit	farið	travelling	*goldit*	goldið	paid
farit	farið	went	*gólfit*	gólfið	the-floor
feðr	föður	father	*grasvöxtr*	grasvöxtur	hay-crop
féit	féið	cattle	*greiðliga*	greiðlega	quite
féit	féið	the-cattle	*griðungr*	griðungur	a-bull
féit	féið	wealth	*Gunnarr*	Gunnar	Gunnar (name)

A Word Comparison of Old Norse and Old Icelandic

Old Norse	Old Icelandic	English
Gunnvaldr	Gunnvaldur	Gunnvald (name)
hæns	hænsn	hens
Hænsa-Þóri	Hænsna-Þóri	Hen-Thorir (name)
Hænsa-Þórir	Hænsna-Þórir	Hen-Thorir (name)
Hænsa-Þóris	Hænsna-Þóris	Hen-Thorir (name)
hafim	höfum	have
hagastr	hagastur	the-best
hallazt	hallast	slanted
hastorðr	hastorður	harsh-spoken
háttat	háttað	the-way
haustit	haustið	autumn
hefða	hefði	had
hefða	hefði	have
heilsat	heilsað	greeted
heitit	heitið	pledged
heldr	heldur	either
heldr	heldur	rather
heldust	héldust	rather
helzt	helst	rather
Helzt	hélst	held
hendr	hendur	hand
hendr	hendur	hands
heraða	héraða	districts
heraði	héraði	district
heraði	héraði	the-district
heraðinu	héraðinu	the-district
heraðit	héraðið	the-district
heraðsins	héraðsins	district
heraðsstjórn	héraðsstjórn	district-administration
heruð	héruð	districts
heruðunum	héruðunum	the-districts
heyit	heyið	hay
heyit	heyið	the-hay
hingat	hingað	here
hinkr	hinkur	hang-back
hleypr	hleypur	leaping
hleypr	hleypur	leapt
hleypr	hleypur	ran
hljómr	hljómur	sound
hlutr	hlutur	lot
hlýtr	hlýtur	must
hníga	hnígi	bite
hníga	hnígi	slump
höfuðburðr	höfuðburður	head-bearing
Höggr	höggur	struck
hon	hún	her
Hon	hún	she
hörmulig	hörmuleg	harm-like
hörmuligt	hörmulegt	tragic
hugða	hugði	thought
hugr	hugur	thoughts
hundrinn	hundurinn	mongrel
hundruð	hundruðum	hundred
húsat	húsað	a-house
húsat	húsað	housed
hvárirtveggju	hvorirtveggju	each-side
hvárntveggja	hvorntveggja	either-side
hvárratveggja	hvorratveggja	each-way
hvárrgi	hvorgi	neither
hvárt	hvort	if
hvárt	hvort	whether
Hvárt	hvort	which
hvat	hvað	what
hvatliga	hvatlega	quickly
hvé	hve	how
hverfr	hverfur	turned
hverir	hverjir	each
hverir	hverjir	who
hverr	hver	each
hverr	hver	how
Hverr	hver	who
inn	hinn	the
innarliga	innarlega	lying-in
ins	hins	the
it	hið	the
it	hið	then
jafnaðarmaðr	jafnaðarmaður	an-even-man
jafnat	jafnað	equal
játtuðu	játuðu	affirmed
Jófríðr	Jófríður	Jofrid (name)
kaldr	kaldur	cold

A Word Comparison of Old Norse and Old Icelandic

Old Norse	Old Icelandic	English	Old Norse	Old Icelandic	English
kallaðr	kallaður	called	*lýkr*	lýkur	ends
kappsamr	kappsamur	zealous	*maðr*	maður	a-man
kaupdrengr	kaupdrengur	merchant	*maðr*	maður	man
kemr	kemur	came	*maðr*	maður	the-man
kemr	kemur	comes	*mágr*	mágur	son-in-law
kennumst	kennist	knowing	*málalykðir*	málalyktir	concluded
komit	komið	came	*málalykðir*	málalyktir	conclusions
komit	komið	come	*málit*	málið	the-matter
komit	komið	comes	*manngirnð*	manngirnd	men-desiring
komit	komið	coming	*margt*	mart	many
komizt	komist	come	*máttrinn*	mátturinn	power
Kómu	komu	came	*mestr*	mestur	most
kómum	komum	came	*mik*	mig	me
kostr	kostur	choice	*mikit*	mikið	much
krefr	krefur	needed	*minnr*	minnur	less
kvaðst	kveðst	said	*misráðit*	misráðið	mis-advised
kvaðst	kveðst	spoke	*mjök*	mjög	much
Kvámu	komu	coming	*mjólkat*	mjólkað	milked
kveikti	kveiktu	kindled	*morgin*	morgun	morning
kveldit	kveldið	evening	*morgin*	morgun	the-morning
kvenskörungr	kvenskörungur	noblest-women	*morgininn*	morguninn	morning
			móti	við	with
kynligt	kynlegt	strange	*mótstöðumaðr*	mótstöðumaður	enemy
Kynligt	kynlegt	wonder			
lætr	lætur	had	*munr*	munur	difference
lagit	lagið	laying	*Mynda*	mundi	should
látim	látum	let	*myndi*	mundi	should
leiddr	leiddur	led	*myndi*	mundi	would
leikit	leikið	played	*myndi*	mundu	would
leikr	leikur	like	*nætr*	nætur	the-night
lek	legg	lay	*náir*	nær	brought
lézt	lést	let	*nasarnar*	nasirnar	his-nose
líðr	líður	passed	*nátt*	nótt	the-night
Liggr	liggur	lying	*nauðsynligra*	nauðsynlegra	need-like
líkligra	líklegra	likely	*nemr*	nemur	took
lítit	lítið	little	*niðr*	niður	down
lítr	lítur	looked	*nökkur*	nokkur	some
lízt	líst	appeared	*nökkura*	nokkura	any
lízt	líst	appears	*nökkura*	nokkura	some
lízt	líst	behold	*nökkura*	nokkura	someone
lízt	líst	seems	*nökkurar*	nokkurar	some-of
Lýgr	lýgur	lies	*nökkurs*	nokkurs	some
Lýkr	lýkur	ended	*nökkurs*	nokkurs	someone

A Word Comparison of Old Norse and Old Icelandic

Old Norse	Old Icelandic	English
nökkuru	nokkuru	somewhat
nökkurum	nokkurum	somewhat
nökkut	nokkuð	any
nökkut	nokkuð	anything
nökkut	nokkuð	some
nökkut	nokkuð	something
nökkut	nokkuð	somewhat
norðr	norður	north
Norðrá	Norðurá	Norðura (place)
Norðrá	Norðurá	Norðurá (place)
Norðrá	Norðurá	North-River (place)
Norðrárdal	Norðurárdal	Norduradal (place)
Norðrárdal	Norðurárdal	North-River-Valley (place)
Norðrdæla	Norðurdæla	Norðurdæla (place)
Norðrtungu	Norðurtungu	North-Tongue (place)
Nóregs	Noregs	Norway (place)
nú	þá	then
nýligar	nýlegar	new
nýligar	nýlegar	newer
nýligra	nýlegra	newer
nýtra	nýtara	more-helpful
nýtzt	nýst	new
óágengiligra	óágengilegra	less-likely
óbirgr	óbirgur	un-stocked
óbrunnit	óbrunnið	unburnt
ódaufligra	ódauflegra	less-dreary
Oddr	Oddur	Odd (name)
óðliga	óðlega	wildly
ofrefli	ofurefli	overwhelming
ofrliði	ofurliði	outnumbered
ok	og	also
ok	og	and
okkarr	okkar	ours
okkr	okkur	us
ólíkligt	ólíklegt	unlike
opit	opið	open
ór	úr	about
ór	úr	from
ór	úr	of
ór	úr	out-from
ór	úr	out-of
orðit	orðið	words
orðsjúkr	orðsjúkur	word-sickened
órlausna	úrlausna	solution
órlausnar	úrlausna	a-solution
Örnólfr	Örnólfur	Ornolf (name)
ráðit	ráðið	advised
ráðligt	ráðlegt	advise
ræna	ræni	steal
rænti	rændi	robbed
ránit	ránið	robbery
ránit	ránið	the-robbery
ránsmaðr	ránsmaður	robber-man
rauðr	rauður	red
refr	refur	Refur (name)
reikunarmaðr	reikanarmaður	a-roaming-man
rekr	rekur	driving
rekr	rekur	drove
réttr	réttur	right
reynda	reyndi	experience
reyndist	reyndust	turned-out
ríðr	ríður	rides
ríðr	ríður	rode
ríkismunr	ríkismunur	powerful
rjóðr	rjóður	clearing
sæmð	sæmd	honour
sæmðr	sæmdur	honoured
sætzt	sæst	seen
sakar	sakir	sake
samandráttr	samandráttur	gathering
sannligra	sannlegra	true-like
sannligt	sannlegt	right
sárr	sár	wounded
Sauðamaðr	sauðamaður	shepherd
séð	séuð	see-you
segir	sagði	said
sekð	sekt	well
sekðir	sektir	penalty

A Word Comparison of Old Norse and Old Icelandic

Old Norse	Old Icelandic	English	Old Norse	Old Icelandic	English
sekr	sekur	outlawed	spakliga	spaklega	profoundly
seli	selji	sell	sprettr	sprettur	sprang
Selr	selur	sold	spyrr	spyr	asked
sém	séum	see	staddr	staddur	standing
sér	sért	are	staðit	staðið	stand
setzt	sest	sat	staðizt	staðist	standing
sezt	sest	sat	stendr	stendur	are-standing
síðr	síður	side	sterkr	sterkur	strong
sik	sig	him	stígr	stígur	climbed
sik	sig	himself	stökkr	stökkur	heels
sik	sig	his	stórauðigr	stórauðigur	rich
sik	sig	themselves	stórmikit	stórmikið	great
sik	sig	to-him	stórmjök	stórmjög	a-great-much
silfr	silfur	silver	strykr	strykur	struck
sinna	sína	his	stungit	stungið	pierce
siti	sitji	sit	stýrimaðr	stýrimaður	the-steersman
sitr	situr	sat	suðr	suður	south
sitr	situr	sit	sumarit	sumarið	summer
sjá	sjáir	see	svá	svo	so
sjálfr	sjálfur	himself	svara	svöruðu	answered
Sjálfr	sjálfur	self	svarat	svarað	answered
sjúkr	sjúkur	sick	svikit	svikið	betrayed
skilðust	skildust	separated	talat	talað	spoken
skilit	skilið	understand	talim	tölum	talk
skipkvámuna	skipkomuna	the-ship-arrival	tekit	tekið	received
skjöldr	skjöldur	the-shield	tekit	tekið	taken
skógrinn	skógurinn	forests	tekr	tekur	took
sköruliga	skörulega	boldly	þangat	þangað	from-there
skyggnstr	skyggnastur	keen-eyed	þangat	þangað	there
skylda	skyldi	should	Þat	það	it
skyldr	skyldur	should	Þat	það	that
skyndiliga	skyndilega	suddenly	þat	það	the
slátrat	slátrað	slaughter	þat	það"	it
slátrat	slátrað	slaughtered	þat	þetta	that
slíkr	slíkur	such	þegit	þegið	receive
slitit	slitið	settled	þeira	þeirra	their
snauðr	snauður	poor	þeira	þeirra	theirs
snúit	snúið	away	þeira	þeirra	they
snúit	snúið	turned	þik	þig	you
sonr	son	son	þingheimrinn	þingheimurinn	the-asembly
sonr	son	son-of	þingit	þingið	the-assembly
sonr	son	sons			

A Word Comparison of Old Norse and Old Icelandic

Old Norse	Old Icelandic	English	Old Norse	Old Icelandic	English
þjáðr	þjáður	enthralled	tvau	tvö	two
þjófr	þjófur	thief	tysvar	tvisvar	twice
Þórðr	Þórður	Thord (name)	unnit	unnið	win
Þóroddr	Þóroddur	Thorodd (name)	upphafsmaðr	upphafsmaður	the-instigators
Þórólfr	Þórólfur	Thorolf (name)	útan	utan	abroad
þorrnaði	þornaði	dried	útan	utan	beyond
Þorvaldr	Þorvaldur	Thorvald (name)	útan	utan	out
þóttumst	þóttist	thought	útan	utan	outside
þraut	braut	away	útan	utan	travelled-out
þrífr	þrífur	deftly	útarliga	utarlega	out-lying
þrjózku	þrjósku	belligerance	vaðit	vaðið	the-ford
þrjú	þremur	three	vænligt	vænlegt	hopeful
þungliga	þunglega	heavily	væri	væru	were
Þuríðr	Þuríður	Thurid (name)	váligra	válegra	woeful
þykkir	þykir	seemed	ván	von	expected
Þykkir	þykir	seems	vánbiðlar	vonbiðlar	hope-abide
þykkir	þykir	thought	vanða	vanda	custom
Þykkist	þykist	thought	vándum	vondum	trouble
þykkizt	þykist	seems	vanr	vanur	used-to
þykkja	þykja	regarded	vápn	vopn	weapons
þykkjast	þykjast	considered	var	er	was
þykkjast	þykjast	to-see	vára	vora	further
þykkjumst	þykjumst	think	várar	vorar	spring
þykkjumst	þykjumst	we-think	varit	varið	the-situation
þyrfta	þyrfti	needed	varningr	varningur	goods
tíðenda	tíðinda	news	várr	vor	our
tíðenda	tíðinda	the-news	várri	vorri	ours
tíðendi	tíðindi	news	várri	vorri	provisions
tíðendi	tíðindi	the-news	váru	eru	they-are
tíðendi	tíðindi	tidings	váru	voru	our
tíðendum	tíðindum	news	váru	voru	wares
tilgangr	tilgangur	point	váru	voru	was
tjaldit	tjaldið	tent	váru	voru	were
tjaldit	tjaldið	the-tent	Váru	voru	where
tókt	tókst	took	várum	vorum	our
Tungu-Oddr	Tungu-Oddur	Tungu-Odd (name)	várum	vorum	ours
túnit	túnið	enclosure	várum	vorum	were
túnit	túnið	the-enclosure	vaskligr	vasklegur	bold
tvá	tvo	two	vátta	votta	witnesses
			váttar	vottar	witnesses
			veittr	veittur	given
			veiztu	veistu	know-you

A Word Comparison of Old Norse and Old Icelandic

Old Norse	Old Icelandic	English
vekði	vekti	was-awake
vel	er	well
verðr	verður	became
verðr	verður	worth
verðr	verður	worthy
verit	verið	been
vesölð	vesöld	misery
vestr	vestur	west
vetr	vetur	winter
vetr	vetur	winters
vetrhúsa	veturhúsa	winter-house
vetrinn	veturinn	the-winter
Vetrinn	veturinn	winter
viðbúnaðr	viðbúnaður	preparation
viðrbúningr	viðbúningur	with-laid
vígr	vígur	spear-man
víkr	víkur	took
víkr	víkur	turned
víkr	víkur	week
Vilda	vildi	wish
vili	vilji	will
vill	vilt	will
vill	vilt	wish
Vindr	vindur	wind
virðuligr	virðulegur	worthy
vísat	vísað	turn-away
vissa	vissi	knew
vit	við	with
vitat	vitað	known
vitr	vitur	wise
vitu	vita	know
vörzlu	vörslu	vouch
yðar	yðvar	your
yðr	yður	to-you
yðr	yður	you
yðr	yður	your
yðr	yður	yours
Ýmisst	ýmist	or

www.ingramcontent.com/pod-product-compliance
Lightning Source LLC
Chambersburg PA
CBHW051404070526
44584CB00023B/3284